Christopher Hi Roadmaker

Marguerite Bryant

Alpha Editions

This edition published in 2024

ISBN : 9789367240199

Design and Setting By
Alpha Editions
www.alphaedis.com
Email - info@alphaedis.com

As per information held with us this book is in Public Domain.
This book is a reproduction of an important historical work. Alpha Editions uses the best technology to reproduce historical work in the same manner it was first published to preserve its original nature. Any marks or number seen are left intentionally to preserve its true form.

Contents

CHAPTER I ....- 1 -
CHAPTER II ....- 10 -
CHAPTER III ....- 20 -
CHAPTER IV ....- 31 -
CHAPTER V ....- 41 -
CHAPTER VI ....- 51 -
CHAPTER VII ....- 63 -
CHAPTER VIII ....- 74 -
CHAPTER IX ....- 82 -
CHAPTER X ....- 89 -
PART II ....- 95 -
CHAPTER XI ....- 97 -
CHAPTER XII ....- 103 -
CHAPTER XIII ....- 114 -
CHAPTER XIV ....- 124 -
CHAPTER XV ....- 132 -
CHAPTER XVI ....- 137 -
CHAPTER XVII ....- 145 -
CHAPTER XVIII ....- 150 -
CHAPTER XIX ....- 158 -
CHAPTER XX ....- 165 -
CHAPTER XXI ....- 175 -
CHAPTER XXII ....- 182 -
CHAPTER XXIII ....- 188 -
CHAPTER XXIV ....- 196 -
CHAPTER XXV ....- 204 -

- CHAPTER XXVI .... - 210 -
- CHAPTER XXVII .... - 218 -
- CHAPTER XXVIII .... - 226 -
- CHAPTER XXIX .... - 235 -
- CHAPTER XXX .... - 241 -
- CHAPTER XXXI .... - 245 -
- CHAPTER XXXII .... - 251 -
- CHAPTER XXXIII .... - 257 -
- CHAPTER XXXIV .... - 260 -
- CHAPTER XXXV .... - 265 -
- CHAPTER XXXVI .... - 269 -
- CHAPTER XXXVII .... - 278 -

CHAPTER I

It was a hot July day, set in a sky of unruffled blue, with sharp shadows across road and field, and a wind that had little coolness in it playing languidly over the downland. The long white dusty road kept its undeviating course eastward over hill and dale, through hamlet and town, till it was swallowed up in the mesh-work of ways round London, sixty-three miles away according to the mile-stone by which a certain small boy clad in workhouse garb was loitering. He had read the inscription many times and parcelled out the sixty-three miles into various days' journeys, but never succeeded in bringing it within divisionable distance of the few pennies which found their way into his pockets. His precocious little head carried within it too bitter memories of hungry days, and too many impressions of the shifts and contrivances by which fortune's votaries bamboozle from that fickle Goddess a meagre living, to adventure on the journey unprepared. Moreover, Mr. and Mrs. Moss of the Whitmansworth Union were not unkind, and meals were regular, so he did not run away from the house that had opened its doors to him and an exhausted mother six months ago. But he still dreamt of London as the desideratum of his fondest hopes, and that, in spite of a black terror crouching there and carefully nurtured by the poor mother in the days of their wanderings. He saw it all through a haze of people and experiences, of friends and foes, and it was the Place of Liberty.

Therefore, when escape was possible from the somewhat easy rule of the Union, he hurried away to the mile-stone on the "Great Road," as it was called about here. The stone with its clear distinct black lettering, seemed to bring him nearer London, and he would spend his time contentedly flinging pebbles into the river of dust at his feet, or planning out in his active little mind what he would do when old Granny Jane's prophecy came true.

There was a wide strip of turf on each side of the road bejewelled with poppies and daisies, matted with yellow and white bedstraws, carpeted with clovers, and over all lay a coating of fine chalky dust, legacy of passing cart and carriage.

The boy was very hot and very dusty, and a little sleepy. He lay on his back drumming his heels on the turf and watching an exuberant lark tower up into the sky above him. He was not unmindful of the lark's song, but he vaguely wondered if a well-thrown stone could travel as far as the dark mounting speck.

"It's a year ago I am sure since that old woman told me my fortune," he said, suddenly sitting up. "I wonder if it will come true. Mother said it was nonsense."

It was a lonely stretch of road. The mile-stone was on the summit of a rise and the ground sloped away on his right to a reach of green water-meadow through which a chalky trout-stream wandered, and the red roof of an old mill showed through a group of silvery poplars and willows. On the other side of the road were undulating fields that dwindled from sparse cultivation to bare down-land. There was no sign of any house except the distant mill, but directly over the summit of the hill, happily hidden, an ugly little red-brick mushroom of a town asserted itself, overgrowing in its unbeautiful growth the older picturesque village of Whitmansworth.

The faint sharp click of horses' hoofs stepping swiftly and regularly swept up the road towards the boy. He stood up the better to see the approaching vehicle which was coming from out of the east towards him. Two horses, he judged, listening intently. Presently a distant dark spot on the road evolved itself into a carriage—a phaeton and a pair of iron grey horses. It was long before the days of motors, when fine horses and good drivers were common enough in England, but even the small boy recognised that these animals were exceptional and were stepping out at a pace that spoke of good blood, good training and good hands on the reins.

He watched them trot full pace down the opposite hill and breast the steep rise after without a break in the easy rhythm of their movements. It was a matter of their driver's will rather than their pleasure that made them slacken pace as they neared the mile-stone.

The lonely little figure standing there was clearly visible to the travellers in the phaeton. The man who was driving looked at him casually, looked again with sudden sharp scrutiny, and abruptly pulled up his horses. He thrust the reins into his companion's hands, and was off the box before the groom from behind could reach the horses' heads.

The owner of the phaeton came straight towards the small boy who was watching the horses with interest, pleased at the halt and oblivious of his own connection with it. The traveller was a man who looked forty-eight despite his frosted hair, and was in reality ten years older. He was tall, well beyond average height, thin, well-fashioned, with a keen kindly face, clean shaven. His mouth was humorous, and there was a certain serenity of expression and bearing that invited confidence. The boy, casting a hasty glance at him as he approached, thought him a very fine gentleman indeed: as in fact he was, in every possible meaning of the word.

"Is this Whitmansworth?" demanded the owner of the phaeton. His tone was not aggressive. The boy gave him as straight a look of judgment as he himself received.

"Down there it is," with a nod of his head in the direction of the distant townlet.

"And not up here?"

"Dunno, they calls it the Great Road."

The stranger still stood looking down at him fixedly.

"Is your name James Christopher Hibbault?"

Without warning, without time for the canny little morsel of humanity to weigh the wisdom of an answer, the question was shot at him and he was left gasping and speechless after an incriminating "Yes," forced from him by the suddenness of the onslaught, and the truth-compelling power of those keen eyes. "Least it's Hibbault," he added unwillingly. "Jim, they calls me."

"I think it is Christopher as well, and I prefer Christopher. And what are you doing on the Great Road at this hour in the afternoon, Christopher?"

And Jim—or Christopher,—trained and renowned for a useful evasiveness of retort in those far-off London days, answered mechanically: "Waiting for the fortune to come true."

Then the hot blood rushed to his face from sheer shame at his own betrayal of the darling secret of his small existence.

"Your fortune?" echoed the other slowly. "Fortunes do not come for waiting. What do you mean?"

"It was the old woman said so—mother didn't believe it. She said as how my fortune would come to me on the Great Road. There wer'n't no Great Road there, so when I heard as how they called this the Great Road, I just stuck to it."

It was a long speech. The boy had none of the half-stupid stolidity of the country-bred, and yet lacked something of the garrulity of the cute street lad. His voice too was a surprise. The broad vowels seemed acquired and uncertain and jarred on the hearer with a sense of misfit.

"Do you live at Whitmansworth Union?"

There was a faint tinge of resentment in the short "Yes."

How did the gentleman know it, and, anyhow, why should he tell him? Jim felt irritated.

The owner of the phaeton stood still a moment with one hand on the dusty little shoulder, and then looked round at the water-meadows, the distant copses, the more distant shimmering downs. Then he laughed, saying something the boy did not understand, and looked down at the sharp inquiring little face again.

"Which means, Christopher, hide-and-seek is an easy game when it's over," he explained. "Come and show me where you live."

They walked back towards the carriage together. The elderly gentleman holding the reins was looking back at them; so was the groom. The elderly gentleman cast a puzzled, inquiring glance from the boy to his companion as they came near.

"Fortune meets us on the road-side, Stapleton," said the owner of the phaeton. "Let me introduce you to Christopher Hibbault. Get up, child."

Get up? Mount that quietly magnificent carriage, ride behind those beautiful animals with their pawing feet and arched necks? The small boy stood still a moment to appreciate the greatness of the event.

"Are you afraid, Christopher?"

Resentment sprang to life. Yet it was almost well so transcendent a moment should have its pin prick of annoyance. With a "No" of ineffable scorn, Jim—or Christopher—the name was immaterial to him—clambered up into the high carriage and wedged himself between the elderly gentleman and the inquisitive driver, who had regained his seat and the reins.

Christopher's experiences of driving were of a very limited nature, and certainly they did not embrace anything like this. He had no recollection of ever having travelled by train, and it was the question of pace that fascinated him, the rapid, easy swinging movement through the air, the fresh breeze rushing by, the distancing of humbler wayfarers, all gave him a strange sense of exhilaration. Years afterward, when flesh and blood were all too slow for him and he was one of the best motorists in England, if not in Europe, he used to recall the rapturous pleasure of that first drive of his, that first introduction to the mad, tense joy of speed that ever after held him in thrall.

The owner of the phaeton and the elderly gentleman whom he had called Stapleton exchanged no remarks, but they both cast curious, thoughtful glances at their small companion from time to time. They had to rouse him from his rhapsody to ask the way at last. He answered concisely and shortly with no touch of the local burr.

"How came you to be so far away?" demanded Jim's fine gentleman as they were passing through the market-place.

Jim was engaged in superciliously ignoring the amazed stares of the town boys who were apt to look down on the "workhouse kid," though he attended the Whitmansworth school. Once past them he answered the question vaguely.

"The master was out: I hadn't to do anything."

"And you had permission to wander where you liked?"

To this Jim did not reply. He had *not* permission, but he counted on the good nature of Mrs. Moss, with whom he was a favourite, to plead his cause with her husband.

"Had you permission?" demanded his questioner again, bending down suddenly to look in the boy's face with his disconcerting eyes.

It would have seemed to Jim on reflection a great deal more prudent and quite as easy to have said "yes" as "no," but the "no" slipped out, and the questioner smiled, not ill-pleased.

At last they came to a standstill before the door of the Whitmansworth Union. Jim, with a prodigious sigh, prepared to descend. The glorious adventure was over. Also he prepared to slip away to a more lowly entrance, but was stopped by a retaining hand.

The porter, no friend of Jim's, stared with dull amazement at the apparition of the fine turn-out, and the still finer gentleman waiting on the doorstep with that little "varmint" of a Hibbault. He signed to the boy angrily to begone, as he ushered the visitor in.

"The boy will stay with me," said the owner of the phaeton quietly, and they were accordingly shown into that solemn sanctum, the Board Room. It was a cheerful room with flowers in the window and a long green-covered table with comfortable chairs on each side, but it struck a cold note of discomfort in Jim's heart. The first time he had entered it, about six months ago, the chairs had been occupied by ten more or less portly gentlemen who informed him that his mother, now being dead (she had died two days previously), they had decided to give him a home for the present, and would educate him and teach him a trade, and that he should be very grateful and must be a good boy.

Jim had said tearfully he would rather go back to London and Mrs. Sartin, which appeared to surprise them very much, and they were at some pains to point out the advantages of a country life, which did not appeal to him at all. Then one of them, who had not spoken before, said abruptly, "his mother had wished him to stay there, and there was an end of it."

That was six months ago. Jim remembered it all very distinctly as he waited with his companion in the Board Room.

Mr. Moss bustled in: he was a stout, cheerful man of hasty temper, but withal a man one could deal with—through his wife—in Jim's estimation.

He held the card the visitor had sent in between his fingers and looked flurried and surprised. Jim noticed he bowed to the stranger, but did not offer to shake hands as he did with the doctor and parson and the few rare visitors the boy had observed. So Jim concluded *his* gentleman was a very great gentleman indeed, as he had all along suspected.

"My name is Aston—Charles Aston"—said the owner of the phaeton in his pleasant voice. "I have driven down from London to make inquiries about a small boy I have reason to believe came under your care about seven months ago: Hibbault by name."

"Yes, sir,—Mr. Aston," said Mr. Moss, assuming an air of importance, "and that is the boy himself."

"A good boy, I hope?" He bestowed on him one of those keen, sharp glances Jim was beginning not to resent.

"Not bad as boys go," Mr. Moss answered dubiously, scratching his chin, "but his bringing up has been against him. London, sir,—and then tramping about the country for a year."

Jim regarded Mr. Aston anxiously to see how this somewhat negative character struck him, but he was still looking at Jim and seemed to pay small heed to Mr. Moss's words.

"We passed him on the road," he said; "I was struck by the likeness to someone I knew, and I thought there could not be two boys so like in Whitmansworth. You were master here when he was admitted?"

"Oh, yes, Mr. Aston. It was in November last, on a Thursday night, I remember, because service was on. The mother was clean exhausted, and was taken to the infirmary at once and—"

Mr. Aston interposed.

"Christopher, go out and stay by the carriage till I call you, and ask the gentleman—Mr. Stapleton—to come in here."

And James Christopher Hibbault obeyed without so much as a glance for permission at Mr. Moss.

He delivered his message and then interviewed the groom, who seemed used to waiting. The tea bell rang, but Jim, though hungry, never thought of disobeying his orders. The hall porter came out and went off on his bicycle and presently returned with Mr. Page, one of the Board gentlemen.

The groom eventually grew communicative and told Jim the horses' names were Castor and Pollux, and there wasn't their match in the country, no more in all London, though to be sure Mr. Aston had some fine horses at Marden Court.

"Is that where he lives?" inquired Jim.

It appeared he lived there sometimes, but Mr. Nevil,—Jim did not know who that was—lived there mostly. Mr. Aston spent most of his time in London with Mr. Aymer. They had left London the previous day, Jim learnt, and had been driving to queer out-of-the-way places, always stopping at Unions.

At which point the door opened and Mr. Aston came out, and with him Mr. Page and Mr. and Mrs. Moss and Mr. Stapleton with a bundle of papers in his hand, and all these people looked at Jim in a perplexed way, except Mr. Aston, who appeared quite happy and unconcerned.

"Say good-bye to Mrs. Moss, Christopher," he said authoritatively. "You are coming with me."

"Where to?" demanded the boy with a sudden access of caution.

"To London."

Christopher began to scramble up into the carriage and was unceremoniously hauled down.

"Manners, Christopher. Mrs. Moss is waiting to say good-bye."

Now, Mrs. Moss had been very kind to the little waif and taken him to her motherly childless heart, and in spite of her excitement over this wonderful event, or because of it, she could not refrain from a few tears. Jim was not indifferent to the fact—any more than he had been to the lark's song, but he secretly thought it very inconsiderate of her to cloud this extraordinary adventure with anything so depressing as tears. He was the more aggrieved as against his will, against all reason and all tradition of manliness, he found objectionable salt drops brimming up in his own eyes. A culminating point was reached, however, when Mrs. Moss fairly embraced him. It should be stated that on occasions and in private Jim had no sort of objection to being cuddled by Mrs. Moss, who was a comfortable, pillowy sort of person.

The ordeal was over at last and he was clambering up into the carriage when Mrs. Moss bethought her he had had no tea.

Mr. Aston protested they were going to stop at Basingstoke, but the good woman insisted on provisioning the boy with a wedge of cake and tucking a clean handkerchief of her own into his pocket.

"We shall sleep at Basingstoke, and I'll send back his clothes by post," said Mr. Aston. "No doubt we can get him some sort of temporary outfit there."

Jim, who had been secretly afraid he would be relegated to the back seat with the groom, breathed a sigh of relief as Mr. Aston mounted to his place. That gentleman apparently understood the innermost soul of the boy, for he gravely asked Mr. Stapleton to find room for a companion, and then with a toss of their proud heads Castor and Pollux moved off. Mr. Aston raised his hat courteously to Mrs. Moss, and Jim, observing, made an attempt to remove his own dingy little cap, a performance everyone took as a matter of course untill he had gone, when Mrs. Moss remembered it and exclaimed to her husband: "Didn't I always say, Joseph, he wasn't like the rest of them?"

But Joseph only said "Umph," and went in doors.

"We will telegraph to Aymer from Basingstoke," said Mr. Aston as they started, and after that there was silence.

The monotonous click-clack of the horses' feet lulled the tired child into blissful drowsiness. He had had too many ups and downs in his eleven years of life to be alarmed at this unexpected turn of fortune, and he was still too young to grasp how great a change had been wrought in that life since the hot hour he had spent lying by the mile-stone on the Great Road.

As they clattered through the narrow streets of the country town in the light of the long July evening Christopher sat up and rubbed his eyes.

"I've been here before," he volunteered.

Mr. Aston effected a skilful pass between a donkey cart and two perambulators.

"Yes, quite right, you have. What do you remember about it, Christopher?"

The boy looked dubious and a little distressed, but just then they passed a chemist's shop.

"We went there," he cried. "Mother got something for her cough, so she couldn't have any supper. We stayed at a horrid old woman's, a nasty, cross thing."

"You did not go to the Union, then?"

"No, we had some money, a whole shilling and some pennies."

Mr. Aston said something under his breath and Mr. Stapleton murmured "tut-tut-tut."

"That's how we first missed the trail, Stapleton," he said, and then as they walked up a steep hill he spoke to the boy.

"Christopher, I want you to tell me anything you remember about your mother and the old days if you wish it, but you must not talk about that to Aymer. It would make him unhappy."

"Who is Aymer?" asked Christopher, not unreasonably.

"Aymer is my son, my eldest son. You are going to live with him."

"Is he a boy like me?"

"No, he is quite big, grown up, but he can't get about as you can, he is—a cripple."

He said the words with a sort of forced jerk and half under his breath, but Christopher heard them and shivered.

"Do you live there, too?" he asked, pressing a little nearer the man who was no longer a stranger.

"Live where?"

"With the—your son."

"Yes, I live there too. My boy couldn't get on without me—and here's the White Elephant, which means supper and bed for a tired young man. Jump down, Christopher."

CHAPTER II

The spirit of waning July hung heavily over London. In mean streets and alleys it was inexpressibly dreary: the fagged inhabitants lacked even energy to quarrel.

But on the high ground westward of the Park, where big houses demand elbow-room and breathing space and even occasionally exclusive gardens, a little breeze sprang up at sundown and lingered on till dusk.

In this region lies one of the most beautiful houses in London, the country seat of some fine gentleman in Queen Anne's day. It hid its beauties, however, from the public gaze, lying modestly back in a garden whose size had no claim to modesty at all. All one could see from the road, through the iron gates, was a glimpse of a wide portico, and a long row of windows. It stood high and in its ample garden the breeze ran riot, shaking the scent from orange and myrtle trees, from jasmine and roses, and wafting it in at the wide open windows of a room which, projecting from the house, seemed to take command of the garden.

It was a large room and the windows went from ceiling to floor. It was also a very beautiful room. In the gathering dusk the restful harmonies of its colours melted into soft, hazy blue, making it appear vaster than it really was. Also, it was unencumbered by much furniture and what there was so essentially fitted its place that it was unobtrusive. Three big canvases occupied the walls, indiscernible in the dim light, but masterpieces of world fame, heirlooms known all over Europe. There was a curious dearth of small objects and unessentials, nothing in all the great space that could fatigue the eye or perplex the brain of the occupant.

The owner of the room was lying on a big sofa near one of the open windows. Within reach was a low bookcase, a table with an electric reading lamp, and a little row of electric bells, some scattered papers and an open telegram.

The man on the sofa lay quite still looking into the garden as it sunk from sight under the slowly falling veil of purple night.

He was evidently a tall man, with the head and shoulders of an athlete, and a face of such precise and unusual beauty that one's instinct called out, "Here, then, God has planned a man."

Aymer Aston, indeed, was not unlike his father, but far more regular in feature, more carefully hewn, and the serenity of the older face was lacking. Here was the face of a fighter, alive with the strong passions held in by a stronger will. There was almost riotous vitality expressed in his colouring, coppery-coloured hair and dark brows, eyes of surprising blueness and a tanned skin, for he spent hours lying in the sun, hatless and unshaded, with the avowed intention of "browning"; and he "browned" well except for a queer white triangled scar almost in the centre of his forehead, an ugly mark that showed up with fresh distinctness when any emotion brought the quick blood to his face. There was indeed nothing in his appearance to suggest a cripple or an invalid.

Nevertheless, Aymer Aston, aged thirty-five, the best polo-player, the best fencer, the best athlete of his day at College, possessing more than his share of the vigour of youth and glory of life, had, for over ten years, never moved without help from the sofa on which he lay, and the strange scar and a certain weakness in the left hand and arm were the only visible signs of the catastrophe that had broken his life.

A thin, angular man entered, and crossed the room with an apologetic cough.

"Is that you, Vespasian?" demanded his master without moving. "Have they come?"

"No, sir, but there is a message from the House. I believe Mr. Aston is wanted particularly."

"What a nuisance. Why can't they let him alone? He might as well be in office."

The man, without asking permission, rearranged his master's cushions with a practised hand.

"The young gentleman had better have some supper upstairs, sir, as it's so late," he suggested. "I'll see to it myself."

"Send him in to me directly they come, Vespasian."

"Yes, sir."

He withdrew as quietly as he had entered and Aymer continued to look out at the dark, and think over the change he, of his own will, was about to make in his monotonous existence. He was so lost in thought he did not hear the door open again or realise the "change" was actually an accomplished fact till a half-frightened gasp of "Oh!" caught his ear. He turned as well as he could, unaided.

"Is that you, Christopher?"

The voice was so singularly like Mr. Aston's that Christopher felt reassured. The dim vastness of the room had frightened him, also he had thought it empty.

"Come over here to me," said Aymer, holding out his hand, "I can't come to you."

Christopher nervously advanced. The brightness of the corridor outside left his eyes confused in this dim light. Aymer suddenly remembered this and turned on a switch. The vague shadowy space was flooded with soft radiance. It was like magic to the small boy.

He was first aware of a gorgeous glint of colouring in a rug flung across the sofa, and then of a man lying on a pile of dull-tinted pillows, a man with red hair and blue eyes, watching him eagerly.

Children as a rule are not susceptible to physical beauty, turning with undeviating instinct to the inner soul of things, with a fine disregard for externals, but Christopher, in this, was rather abnormal. He was very actively alive to outward form.

Since Mr. Aston had told him Aymer was a cripple Christopher had been consumed with unspeakable dread. His idea of a cripple was derived from a distorted, evil-faced old man who had lived in the same house that had once sheltered his mother and him. The mere thought of it made him sick with horror. And when the tall gentleman in black, who had met them in the entrance hall and escorted him here, had opened the door and put him inside, he had much ado not to rush out again. He conquered his fear with unrecognised heroism, and this was his reward.

He stood staring, with all his worshipful admiration writ large on his little tired white face. Aymer Aston saw it and laughed. He was quite aware of his own good looks and perfectly unaffected thereby, though he took some pains to preserve them. But his vanity had centred itself on one thing in his earlier life, and that, his great strength, and it died when that was no more.

"Little Christopher," he said, "come and sit down by me: you must be tired to death."

"Are you Mr. Aymer?" demanded Christopher, still staring.

"Yes, only you mustn't call me that, I think. I wonder what you will call me?"

Christopher offered no solution to the problem.

"Would you like to live here with me?"

He looked round. A dim sense of alarm crept back. The room looked so empty and unreal, so "alone." Without knowing why, Christopher, who had never had a real home to pine for, felt miserably homesick.

Aymer watched him closely and did not press the question. Instead, he asked him in a matter-of-fact way to shut the window for him.

The boy did so without blundering. The window-fastening was new to him, and Aymer noticed he looked at it curiously and shut it twice to see how it went. Then he sat down again and continued to gaze at Aymer.

"I forgot, I was to tell you something," he said suddenly, his face wrinkling with distress. "The other one—the gentleman who brought me—"

"My father?"

Christopher nodded. "I oughtn't to have forgotten. He said he had to go to the House, but he'd be back quite soon, he hoped."

"He's had no dinner, I suppose," grumbled Aymer.

"Yes, we had dinner at—I forget the name of the place—and tea. And yesterday we had dinner too."

"That was wise," said Aymer gravely. "Where's Mr. Stapleton?"

"He went home by train this morning. I sat in his place all the time, not at the back."

He paused thoughtfully. An idea that had been dimly forming in his brain, took alarming shape. A small companion at the Union had lately been sent out as a page to a kindly family. Christopher wondered if that was the meaning of all these strange adventures for him. At the same time he was conscious of so vast a sense of disappointment that he was compelled to put his Fate to the test at once. He jerked out the inquiry with breathless abruptness.

"Am I going to be your page?"

"Page?" Aymer Aston echoed the words with consternation; then held out his hand to the child.

"Didn't my father tell you?" he asked.

A kind of nervous exasperation seized on Christopher. He was tired, overwrought, puzzled and baffled.

"No one tells me anything," he said petulantly, blinking hard to keep back the tears; "they just took me."

"Do you want to be a page boy?"

"No." It was emphatic to the point of rudeness.

Aymer put his arm round him and drew him near, laughing.

"You are not going to be a page," he said, "you are going to be"—he hesitated—"to be my own boy—just as if you were my son. I've adopted you."

"Why?"

Christopher's dark eyes were fixed on the blue ones and then he saw the scar for the first time. It interested him so much he hardly heard Aymer's slow answer when it came.

"I have a great deal of time on my hands, and I should have liked a son of my own. As I can't have that I've adopted you. Don't you think you can like me?"

Christopher looked round the room and back at the sofa. The voice was kind and the arm that was round him gripped him firmly; also, Mr. Aston had said he lived here too. That was reassuring. He was not quite certain how he felt towards this strangely fascinating man, but he was quite sure of his sentiments towards Mr. Aston.

"Mr. Aston lives here, doesn't he?"

"Yes; do you like him best?"

"I like him very much," said Christopher truthfully, and added considerately, "You see, I've known him longer, haven't I?"

"You must like me too."

Christopher was too young to read the passionate hunger in the voice and the look. It was gone in a moment.

Aymer released him, laughing.

"Is there anyone else?" asked the boy, looking vaguely round.

"Anyone else living here? Only the servants."

"I don't mean that." A puzzled look came into his face. "I mean—there was Mrs. Moss and Grannie Jane, and Mrs. Sartin and Jessy and mother." Then he recollected Mr. Aston's prohibition and got red and embarrassed.

"You mean—a woman," said Aymer in a strangely quiet voice.

Christopher noticed the scar again, clear and distinct. Aymer took out a cigarette and lit it carefully. Christopher watched dumbly. He wanted to cry: for no reason that he could discover. Presently Aymer turned to him as he sat on a low chair by the side of the wide sofa and put his arm round him again.

"I'm sorry, little Christopher," he said rather huskily, perhaps because he was smoking, "but I'm afraid I can't give you that, old chap. We only—remember them here."

The tired child yielded to the slight pressure of the arm—his head dropped against his new friend—the room was very quiet—only Mr. Aymer must have been mistaken. It seemed to Christopher a thin black-clad woman was in the room—somewhere—she was looking at Aymer and would not see him at first—then she turned her head—he called "Mother," and opened his eyes to find Mr. Aymer bending over him.

When Mr. Aston had returned and found Aymer smoking composedly with one arm round the sleeping boy, he had pointed out with great care the enormity of a small child being out of bed at eleven o'clock.

Aymer put down his cigarette and looked at his charge.

"Vespasian did come for him," he confessed; "I thought it a pity to wake him till you came. It's just as I feared," he added with assumed pathos, "you have had first innings and I shall have to take a second place."

"It's only just that he got used to me: I hardly talked to him at all," pleaded Mr. Aston humbly, and Aymer laughed. Whereupon Christopher woke up, rubbing his eyes, and smiled sleepily at Mr. Aston.

"I gave him the message, not just at once, but almost."

His first friend sat down and drew him to his knee.

"Well, what do you think of my big boy?" asked Mr. Aston. "I've been scolding him for not sending you to bed."

Christopher looked from one to the other with solemn eyes, blinking in the light.

"Scolding him? Isn't he too big to be scolded?"

The men laughed and involuntarily glanced at each other in a curiously conscious manner.

"He does not think anyone too big to scold," sighed Aymer resignedly. "Father, about the name: I'd rather tell him to-night." His voice was a little hurried. Mr. Aston glanced at him questioningly.

"As you like, Aymer—if he's not too sleepy to listen. Are you, Christopher?"

"I'm not tired," answered Christopher, valiantly blinking sleep out of his eyes.

It was Aymer who spoke, slowly and directly. Mr. Aston kept his eyes on the boy and tried not to see his son.

"What is your real name, Christopher, do you know?"

"James Christopher Hibbault, but they calls me Jim, except him."

In his sleepiness and agitation the boy had dropped back into country dialect. Aymer winced.

"That is the only name you know? Well, Christopher, it's a good name, but all the same I want you to forget it at present. I want you to call yourself always, Christopher Aston. Do you think you can remember?"

The newly-named one stood silent, puzzling out something in his mind.

"Will it make me not belong to mother?" he said at last.

There was a faint movement on the sofa. It was Mr. Aston who answered, putting his hand gently on the boy's head.

"No, little Christopher, nothing will make you cease to belong to her; we do not wish that. But it will be more easy for you to have our name. We want Christopher Aston to have a better time than poor little Jim Hibbault. Only, Christopher, remember Aston is my name, and I am only lending it to you, and you must take very great care of it."

"Isn't it his name too?" The child edged a little nearer his friend, and looked at Aymer.

"Yes, it's Aymer's name too. And, Christopher, if we were both to give you everything we possess we could not give you anything we value more than the name we lend you, so you must be very good to it. Now, Aymer, I insist on your ringing for Vespasian: the child should have been in bed hours ago. I must really buy you a book of nursery rules."

Vespasian was apparently of the same mind as Mr. Aston. Disapproval was plainly expressed on his usually impassive face when he entered.

"Is that Vespasian?" demanded Christopher.

"Yes, and you will have to do just what he tells you, Christopher, just as I have to," said Aymer severely.

Christopher regarded him doubtfully: he was not quite sure if he were serious or not. He did not look as if people would tell him to do things, yet the grave man in black did not smile.

"It's a funny name," he said at last, not meaning to be rude.

"Vespasian was a great general," remarked Aymer, and then added hastily, seeing the boy's bewilderment increased, "Not this one, the General's dead, but this is a good second."

"Aymer, you are incorrigible," expostulated Mr. Aston. "Good-night, little Christopher."

He kissed him and Christopher's eyes grew large with wonder. He did not know men did kiss little boys, and he ventured slyly to rub his cheek against the black sleeve.

"Good-night, Christopher." Aymer held out his hand, and then suddenly, half shyly, and half ashamed, kissed him also, and Vespasian bore him off to bed.

The two men sat silently smoking, avoiding for the moment the subject nearest their hearts, Aymer, because he was fighting hard to get some mastering emotion under control, and he loathed showing his feelings even to his father; Mr. Aston, because he was aware of this and wanted Aymer to have time.

All that day he had been secretly dreading to-night, shrinking like a coward from a situation which must arouse in his son memories better forgotten. He was not a man given to shirking unpleasing experiences to save his own heart a pang, but he was a veritable child in the way that he studied to preserve his eldest son from the like.

It was Aymer who first spoke in his usual matter-of-fact tone.

"Had you any difficulties?"

"None whatever," answered his father, crossing his legs and preparing to be communicative. "Stapleton had been all over the ground before and knew every point. We went first to Surbiton Workhouse, since she told Felton she stayed there. They found the entry for us. Then we went on to Hartley, which is quite a small village and off the main road. We stayed the night there, and went to the cottage where Felton had seen her. It was quite true, all he said. The old woman remembered distinctly a tramp-looking man stopping and calling to her over the gate. They sat in the garden and talked together for some time. She and the boy had been there a month, but they went the day after Felton's visit—seemed frightened, the old lady said. Apparently they meant to go to Southampton, for she had asked the way there. Basingstoke must have been the next stop, but we did not know where until the boy told us. They were in funds, so did not go to the House. We got to Whitmansworth the next afternoon. Then a strange thing happened, one of those chance coincidences that put to rout all our schemes. There is a hill going into Whitmansworth with a milestone on the top. I drove slowly, as I wanted to see if it really were the place, and by the stone was a small boy. The likeness was so absurd that it might have been …" he stopped abruptly and examined his cigar, "had I not been seeking him I should have seen it. I found out his name, and that I was right, and took him up and drove to the Union. They raised no objections—it was only a matter of form. The master and his wife seem to be good people, and to have been kind to the boy."

He came to a pause again. Aymer still waited. Mr. Aston walked to the window and looked out at the night, and then went on without turning:

"She had never left the slightest clue or given any hint whatever as to her identity. She was going to Southampton, she said. But she was dying of exhaustion then. They could do nothing for her. She asked them to keep the boy. The Mosses took a fancy to him, and it was managed. She would not say where she came from."

Aymer lay very still, his face set and immovable.

"The strength of her purpose: think of it, in a woman!" said Mr. Aston a little unsteadily; "the boy should have grit in him, Aymer."

"What did they say of the boy?"

"Ah." Mr. Aston resumed his seat with a sigh.

"Well, what's your own impression, Aymer?"

"I am satisfied."

Mr. Aston leant forward with a wealth of affection in his kind eyes, and straightened the edge of the gorgeous sofa cover. "Aymer, old chap, you are too sensible, I know, to imagine it is going to run easily and smoothly from the first. The boy will come out all right: he is young enough to shape, and worth shaping. But he has had everything against him except one thing. It means many troubles and disappointments for you, but I believe it will have its compensations. It will help fill your life, at least."

"I understand," said Aymer, steadily. "I should like to tell you just how I feel about it, father. Putting aside entirely the question of it being—Christopher—. That was a stroke of Providence, shall we say? I had you and Nevil, and the children. Life was not altogether empty, sir. But I felt I had learnt something from life,—from myself,—mostly from you,—that might be useful to a man. Not to pass this on," the steady voice lost its main quality for a moment, "seemed a waste. I told you all this when I first spoke of adopting someone; and at that precise moment the clue which led us to Christopher was put into our hands. There was no choice then. I say this again because I want you to remember that the idea that first started my plan is still the main one. Christopher, being Christopher, does not alter it. There is only this thing certain," he raised himself a very little on his right arm and laid down his cigarette deliberately, "I've taken the boy and I mean to do my best by him, but he is mine now. If the fate that—she died to save him from—comes to him, it must come. I will not stand in his way, but I will have no hand in bringing it to pass, I will raise no finger to summon it, nor will I call him from it, if it come. Until, and unless it comes, he is mine. I think even she would let me have him on those conditions." He lay back again, his flushed face still witnessing to the force of his feeling.

"On any conditions," said his father, "if she knew you now. Only you must bear the chance in mind in dealing with him. And it's only fair to tell you the Union Master's report on him."

"Let's have it."

"Fairly docile, but inclined to argue the point. Truthful,—I discovered that myself—but either through lack of training or—according to the Master—through bad training in London, he is—" Mr. Aston stumbled over a word, half laughed, and then said, "well, he has a habit of acquisitiveness, shall we call it? When you think of her history it seems at once natural and strange. They had not known him to actually take things—money, that is,—but if he found any—and he appears to have luck in finding things—he was not particular to discover the real owner. It may be a difficulty, Aymer."

"Hereditary instinct," said Aymer a little shortly.

"Well, my own theory is that acquisitiveness is generosity inverted," concluded Mr. Aston thoughtfully, "and that heredity is merely a danger signal, though it may mean fighting. I believe you can do it, my dear boy, but it is a big job."

"I hope so, I was a born fighter, you know."

"You have not done badly that way, son Aymer," returned his father quietly.

"You mean you have not. You are very gracious to a vanquished man, sir."

It was one of his rare confessions of his indebtedness to his father, and perhaps Mr. Aston was more embarrassed at receiving it than Aymer in confessing it. For the indebtedness was undeniable. The Aymer Aston of the present day was not the Aymer Aston of the first bitter years of his imprisonment. The fight had been a long one: but whether the love, the patience, the forbearance of the elder man had regenerated the fierce nature, or whether he had only assisted the true Aymer to work out his own salvation was an open question. Certainly those dark years had left their mark on Mr. Aston, but, for a certainty they were honourable scars, and he, the richer for his spent strength. He had sacrificed much for him, but the reward reaped for his devotion was the knowledge that of their friendship was woven a curtain of infinite beauty that helped to shut away the tragedy of Aymer's life.

CHAPTER III

The question that chiefly occupied Mr. Aston's mind during the first days of Christopher's advent was whether Aymer had gathered in those ten long years of captivity sufficient strength of purpose to set aside once and for all the sharp emotions and memories the boy's presence must inevitably awake.

When Aymer had first approached him on the subject of adopting a boy he had consented willingly enough, but when, coincident with this, Fate—or Providence—had pointed out to them the person of Christopher Hibbault, he, Mr. Aston, though he agreed it was impossible to disregard the amazing chance, had sighed to himself and trembled lest the carefully erected edifice of control and endurance that hedged in his son should be unequal to the strain.

But after the first evening Aymer Aston betrayed by no sign whatever that the past had any power to harm him through the medium of little Christopher, and his father grew daily more satisfied and content over the wisdom of their joint action. They stayed in town all that summer. Mr. Aston was acting as Secretary to a rather important Commission and even when it was not sitting he was employed in gathering in information which could only be obtained in London. Nothing would induce Aymer to go away without his father. He hated the publicity of a railway journey even after ten years of helplessness, and the long drive to Marden Court could not be undertaken lightly. So they stayed where they were, a proceeding which seemed less strange to Christopher than to such part of the outside world who chose to interest itself in Mr. Aston's doings.

The August sun dealt gently with the beautiful garden, and not a few hardworking men, tied, like Mr. Aston, to town, congratulated themselves on his presence, when they shared its restful beauty in the hot summer evenings.

Christopher meanwhile adapted himself to his new life with amazing ease. He accepted his surroundings without question, but with quiet appreciation, and if certain customs, such as a perpetual changing of clothes and washing of hands were irksome, he took the good with the bad, and accommodated himself to the ways of his new friends resignedly. But he was haunted with the idea that the present state of things would not and could not last, and it was hardly worth while to do more than superficially conform to the regulations of the somewhat monotonous existence.

Most of the ten years of his life had been spent under the dominant influence of a devoted woman. All that he had learnt from mankind had been a cunning dishonesty that had nearly ruined his own small existence and indirectly caused his mother's death. Women, indeed, had always been near him, and there were times when he thought regretfully of Mrs. Moss. There were none but menservants at Aston house, and the only glimpse of femininity was afforded by the flying visits of Constantia, Mr. Aston's married daughter. She would at times invade Aymer's room, a vision of delicate colourings and marvellous gowns. She was a tall, dark, lovely woman who carried on the traditional family beauty with no poverty of detail. She seemed to Christopher to be ever going on somewhere or returning from somewhere. He liked to sit and watch her when she flashed into the quiet room, and spent perhaps half an hour making her brother laugh with her witty accounts of people and matters strange to Christopher. She was kind to the boy, when she remembered him, lavish with her smiles and nonsense and presents, but it was like entertaining a rainbow, an elusive, shadowy thing of beauty. She could not be said to denote the Woman in the House. Christopher, as he wandered about the big silent rooms and long corridors, was perforce obliged to take with him for company a more shadowy presence, an imaginary vision of another woman, also tall and dark, but without Constantia Wyatt's irresponsible gaiety and dazzling smile. He would escort this phantom Woman through his favourite rooms, pointing out the treasures to her. He even apportioned her a room for herself, behind a closed door at the end of the wing opposite to which Aymer Aston lived. For it was here he had first discovered with what ease the image of his dead mother fitted into the surroundings he had never shared with her. It was rather an uncanny, eerie idea, and had Christopher been at all morbid or of a dreamy disposition it might have been a very injudicious fancy: but he was the personification of good health and robust spirits. His vivid imagination flitted as naturally and easily round the memory of his dead mother as it rejoiced in the adventures of the Robinson family, or thrilled over the history of John Silver. It was just a deliberate fancy that he indulged in at will, and the only really fantastical thing about it was that he invariably started his tour with the imaginary Woman from the door of the closed room. At the end of October, when he had fairly settled into the regular routine of Aston House, a tutor was procured for him. School, for more reasons than one, was out of the question. Christopher's previous existence would hardly have stood the inquisition of the playground, and Aymer, moreover, wanted to keep him under his own eye. The boy's education had been of a somewhat desultory nature. He could read and write, and possessed a curious store of out-of-the-way knowledge that would upset the most carefully prepared plan of his puzzled tutor. That poor gentleman was alternately scandalised by the boy's ignorance and amazed at his appetite for knowledge. He showed an astonishing aptitude for figures while he evinced a shameful contempt for history and languages. Indeed, he could only be made to struggle with Latin Grammar by Aymer's stories of Roman heroes in the evening and the ultimate reward of reading them for himself some day.

The year wore on, ran out, with the glories of pantomime and various holiday joys with Mr. Aston. Christopher by this time had accepted his surroundings as permanent, with regard to Mr. Aston and Aymer, though he still, in his heart of hearts, had no belief that so far as he was concerned they might not any day vanish away and leave him again prey to a world of privations, wants and disagreeables generally.

He was forever trying to make provision against that possible day, and laid up a secret hoard of treasure he deemed might be useful on emergency. With the same idea he made really valiant attempts to put aside a portion of his ample pocket-money for the same purpose, but it generally dwindled to an inconsiderable sum by Saturday. Aymer kept him well supplied and encouraged him to spend freely. He was told again and again the money was given him to spend and not to keep, and that the day of need would not come to him. He would listen half convinced, until the vision of some street arabs racing for pennies would remind him of positive facts that had been and therefore might be again, and cold prudence had her say. But this trait was the result of experience and not of nature, for he was generous enough. Not infrequently the whole treasury went to the relief of already existing needs outside the garden railings, and he could be wildly extravagant. Aymer never questioned him. He sometimes laughed at him when he had wasted a whole week's money on some childish folly, and told him he was a silly baby, which Christopher did not like. However, he found he had to buy his own experiences, and he soon learnt that no folly however childish annoyed "Cæsar" so much as accumulated wealth for no particular object but a possible future need.

Christopher had christened Aymer "Cæsar" shortly after his introduction to the literary remains of one, Julius, from some fanciful resemblance, and the name stuck and solved a difficulty.

In the same manner he bestowed the distinctive title of St. Michael on Mr. Aston, from his likeness to a famous picture of that great saint in a stained glass window he had seen, and it also was generally adopted.

No one made any further attempt to explain his introduction into the family, or the general history of that family. He was just "grafted in," and left to discover what he could for himself, and he certainly gathered some fragmentary disconnected facts together.

"What is a Secletary?" demanded Christopher one day from the hearth-rug, where he lay turning over old volumes of the *Illustrated London News*.

"A Secretary, I suppose you mean. A Secretary is a man who writes letters for someone else."

"Who does St. Michael write letters for?"

"He used to write letters for the Queen, or rather on the Queen's business. What book have you got there?"

Christopher explained.

"There is a picture of him. Only he hasn't got grey hair: and underneath Perma n-e-n-t, Permanent Undersecretary of State for Foreign Affairs. What does it mean, Cæsar?"

Cæsar, otherwise Aymer, considered a moment.

"Permanent means lasting, going on. You ought to know that, Christopher."

"But he isn't going on."

"He could have done so."

"Why didn't he? Didn't he like it?"

"Yes, very much. He was trained for that kind of thing."

"Did he get tired of writing letters, then?"

"No."

Aymer was apt to become monosyllabic when a certain train of thought was forced on him. Also a short deep line of frown appeared under the white scar: but Christopher had not yet learnt to pay full heed to these signs: also he had a predilection for getting at the root of any matter he had once begun to investigate, so he began again:

"Why didn't he go on being permanent, then?"

"He thought he had something else he ought to do."

"Was the Queen angry?"

"I don't know."

"What was it?"

Aymer cut the leaves of the book he was trying to read rather viciously.

"Taking care of me," he said shortly.

Christopher got up on his knees and stared.

"Hadn't you got Vespasian then?"

"Good heavens, Christopher, are you a walking inquisition? My father gave up his appointment—if you must know, because of my—" he stopped, and went on doggedly, "of my accident. I wasn't particularly happy when I found I had to stay on a sofa all the rest of my life, and he had to teach me not to make an idiot of myself. Now you know all about it and need not bother anyone else with questions."

Christopher thought he knew very little about it, but he had learnt what he set out to know and was moreover now aware that the subject was distasteful to Aymer, so he politely changed it. "Robert's brother has got some very nice guinea-pigs," he said thoughtfully.

"Who is Robert?"

"Robert is the under footman. I forgot you don't know him."

Christopher recollected with momentary embarrassment Aymer's inaccessibility to the general domestic staff.

"He wants to find a home for them," he added hastily; "he doesn't mind where, so long as it's a happy home."

Aymer guarded a smile. Christopher was already notorious for ingenious methods of getting what he wanted.

"It would be a pity for them to be ill-treated, of course," he agreed gravely.

Christopher shuffled across the floor to the side of the big sofa.

"It's rather a happy home here, you know," he remarked suggestively, touching Aymer's arm tentatively with one finger.

"I am glad you think so. Do you consider the atmosphere equally suitable for guinea-pigs?"

"I should like them." He rubbed his cheek caressingly on Aymer's hand. "May I, Cæsar?"

"Not to keep in your bedroom as you did the bantam."

"But in the garden—or yard. *Please*, dear Cæsar."

"You ridiculous baby, yes. If you make a house for them yourself."

Christopher flew off in a transport of joy to consult with Vespasian, who, from mere tolerance of his beloved master's last "fad," had become the most ardent if unemotional partisan of the same "fad."

It was Vespasian who had provided Christopher with more clothes than he deemed it possible for one mortal boy to wear, who taught him how to put them on, and struggled with him figuratively and literally over the collar question. Vespasian's taste running to a wide margin of immaculate white closely fastened, while Christopher had a predilection for a free and open expanse of neck.

"Look at Mr. Aymer," pointed out the great general's successor sternly. "You never see him with even a turn-down collar, and he lying on his back all the time, when most gentlemen would consider their own comfort."

Christopher, hot, angry and uncomfortable, wondered if Vespasian had insisted on the wearing of those instruments of torture, or if Cæsar really preferred it.

But in spite of small differences of opinion, Vespasian and he were good friends, and he received much instruction from the mouth of that inestimable man. It was he who drilled him in Mr. Aymer's little ways, warned him how he hated to be reminded of his helplessness, and could not endure anyone but Vespasian himself to move him from sofa to chair, and that only in the strictest privacy. How he disliked meeting anyone when wheeled from his own room to the dining-room for dinner, which was the only meal he took in public, and that only in company with his father or very intimate friends. How he avoided asking anyone to hand him things though he did not object to unsolicited help, which Christopher soon learnt to render as unostentatiously as Vespasian himself. Also it was Vespasian who explained to him woodenly, in answer to his direct question, that the scar on Mr. Aymer's forehead was the result of a shooting accident. His revolver had gone off as he was cleaning it, said Vespasian, had nearly killed him, had left him paralysed on one side, so he'd never be better. He added, Mr. Aymer didn't like it talked about. All this and more did the boy learn from this discreet man, but never did Vespasian hint at those dark years when to serve poor Aymer Aston was a work for which no money could pay, when the patient father and much-tried man had secretly wondered whether that fight for mere life that had followed on the ghastly accident had indeed been worth the winning. There was no word of this in Vespasian's revelations. He only impressed on Christopher the necessity of avoiding any expression of pity or commiseration with the paralysed man, and a warning that a somewhat casual manner towards the world, and his entirely undemonstrative way, was no true index of Mr. Aymer's real feelings.

Christopher was himself warm-hearted and given to expressing his joyous feelings with engaging frankness. It could hardly have been otherwise, brought up as he had been by a woman of ardent nature and passionate love for him, but in contradiction to this he had learnt to be very silent over the disagreeables of life and to keep his own small troubles to himself, so that he readily entered into Aymer's attitude towards his own misfortune, and the relationship between the two passed from admiration on Christopher's part to passionate devotion, and from the region of experimental interest on Aymer's part to personal uncalculated affection, and to an easing of a sharp heartache he had tried valiantly to hide from his father. Aymer never questioned him on the past, never even alluded to it. Partly because he hoped the memory of it would dwindle from the boy's mind, and partly for his own sake. But Christopher did not forget. There were few days when he did not contrast the old times with the new, and gaze for a moment across the big gulf that separated Christopher Aston from little Jim Hibbault and the quiet woman absorbed in a struggle for existence in an unfriendly world. He occasionally spoke of his mother to Mr. Aston when they were out together, but he kept his implied promise faithfully with regard to Aymer and made no mention of his former experiences, or of his mother, until one day an event occurred which recalled the black terror under whose shadow they had left London, and necessitated an elucidation of knotty points.

There was in one corner of the garden far away from the house a gap in the high belt of shrubs that jealously guarded the grounds from the curious passerby. In fact the gap had once meant a gateway, but it had been disused so long that it had forgotten it was a gate and merely pretended it was part of the big railings; only it had not got a little wall to stand on. Christopher was fond of viewing life from this sequestered corner. The road that ran by was a main thoroughfare—an ever-varying picture of moving shapes. One morning as he stood there counting the omnibuses—he had nearly made a record count—his attention was attracted by a small boy about his own age or possibly older, who was dawdling along, hands in pockets, with a dejected air. He appeared to be whistling, but if he were, without doubt it was also a dejected air. His was a shabby tidiness that spoke of a Woman and little means. He had sandy hair and light eyes and—but Christopher did not know this—an uncommonly shrewd little face and a good square head, and as he passed by the boundaries of Aston House he glanced at the small fellow-citizen gazing through the railings—rather compassionately, be it said—for he knew for certain the boy inside was longing to get through the gate. That one glance carried him beyond the gate, but he suddenly spun round on his heel, collided with an indignant lady laden with parcels, and stared hard at Christopher. Christopher stared hard at him. Then the boy outside went on his way.

"Jolly like Jim," he ruminated, "but a swell toff, I reckon. Poor little kid."

Christopher, after one shout as the boy went on, tore back through the garden towards the entrance gate, meaning to intercept him there. Such at least was his laudable intention, but half way there his pace slackened; he stood irresolute, kicking a loose stone in the gravel path, and finally strolled off to the stable yard to feed his guinea-pigs.

He was preoccupied and thoughtful for the rest of that day. Mr. Aston was absent, and when evening came and Christopher was still a prey to harassing ideas he decided he must appeal to Cæsar even at the cost of disregarding Mr. Aston's prohibition. He came to this decision as he lay in his usual position on the hearth-rug and was goaded thereto by the approach of bed time.

"Cæsar, could anyone be taken to prison for something he had done ever so long ago—I mean for—for stealing, and things like that?"

"Yes, if he had not been already tried for it. Why do you ask?"

"And if anyone met the person suddenly who had done something would they have to give him up?" persisted Christopher.

Aymer regarded him curiously. He had an unreasonable impulse to check the coming revelation, as he might the unguarded confidence of a weak man, but common-sense prevailed.

"It would depend on circumstances entirely, and the relationship of the two. Are you wanted, Christopher?" he asked in a matter-of-fact tone.

"I was," returned Christopher slowly. "That's why we left London, you know. It was Marley Sartin. He took me out with him. You see," he broke off parenthetically, "I stayed with Martha, that's Mrs. Sartin, all the day while mother took care of a gentleman's house, and sometimes Marley was there, and he taught me things."

"What things?"

Christopher shifted his position a bit, and tossed a piece of wood into the fire.

"Oh, lots of things," he repeated at last, "tricks, and how not to answer, and how to avoid coppers and how to get money. Mother said it was stealing."

The scar on Aymer's forehead was very visible. He took up a paper-knife and ran his fingers along the edge slowly.

"Well?"

The boy looked round, suddenly aware of where he was, of the beauty and comfort around him, of Cæsar's personality, and the incongruity of his admission. However, so it was: facts were facts: it was imperative he should know his own position, even if it was an unpleasing subject. So he went on hastily. "Oh, well, one day he took me out with him for a walk. We went into a big sort of shop with lots of people buying things and he knocked up 'accidental like' (this was evidently a reminiscence of a phrase often used), against a lady and she dropped her parcels and purse and things, and I pretended to pick them up, and if there were only parcels or pennies I really did, but if the money spilt and it was gold I put my foot on it and picked it up for Marley when I could. We made a lot that way. Of course mother didn't know," he added hurriedly, "or Martha. Then one day there was a row and

Marley was caught, and I ran away. You see I was pretty small, and could slip in anywhere. I got back and told Martha, and she cried and told mother, and said as how I should be sure to be took too. So we went away from London that night. I don't know what happened to Martha, but mother said I mustn't go back to London or I'd be taken too."

The grim tragedy of it all, the miserable fate from which the woman had fought so hard to save her child, and the same child's dim appreciation of it struck Aymer with the sharpness of physical pain.

"Marley told me it was only keeping what one found, but mother said it was just stealing, and that Marley was bad. He was good to me anyhow. Martha—Mrs. Sartin—you know—used often to cry about Marley's ways. *She* was always very respectable; her father kept a linen-draper's shop, and she meant to put Sam into a shop. Sam didn't like his father. I saw Sam go by to-day—he's bigger, but it was him and he knew me—and I asked about the being taken up because I thought it wouldn't be safe for me to go about perhaps."

So level and even was his voice that Aymer did not guess the agony of apprehension and fear the boy was holding back behind his almost abnormal self-control, but he did his best to reassure him.

"They would not know you, Christopher, and if they did they would not take you away from me. You were a very little boy then. I could let them know how it happened, and how it could never happen again."

Christopher hid his face in his arms and the room became very silent. The fire crackled cheerfully and strange shadows lived uncertain lives on the ceiling. Aymer put the paper-knife down at last and looked at his charge. He was aware it was a critical moment for them both: also he was quite suddenly aware he was more fond of the child than he had previously imagined. But mostly in his mind was the sickening appreciation of what hours of torture that solitary silent woman must have endured.

"Christopher, old boy, come here," he said quietly.

The boy got up. His face was flushed, hot with his efforts to control himself.

"Do you want the light, Cæsar?"

"No, I want you."

He came unwillingly and sat down on the edge of the sofa, playing with a piece of string.

"You need not be frightened at all," said Aymer. "It is all utterly impossible now, we both of us know that."

"I suppose so."

"You know it. You only did what Marley told you to do. You didn't steal because you wanted money yourself."

But Christopher was doggedly truthful.

"Marley used to give me some for myself, Cæsar, and I liked it and I didn't think it was stealing. It was just keeping what one found."

"But you knew to whom it belonged."

"Not certain sure, Marley said."

"What did your mother say?"

"Just that it was stealing. She said, too, lots of people in the world were thieves who didn't know, and Marley was no worse than many rich men, who just knocked people down to get the best of them. What did she mean, Cæsar?"

"She thought it was as wrong for a rich man to take advantage of a poor man, as for a strong man to attack a weak one, or a cunning man to cheat a simpleton."

Christopher was conscious he had heard something like this before. He nodded his small head sagely. Aymer went on.

"It really means you must never get money at someone else's expense. If you can give them something in return, something equal, it's all right, but it must be equal. That is what your mother believed, and I do too—now."

Christopher regarded Cæsar thoughtfully. He was speculating what he did in return for the golden sovereigns that seemed so plentiful with him.

"We try to give fair exchange," explained Cæsar, answering his thoughts. "The money comes to us out of the big world. And my father gives the world good service in return. You will know how good, some-day."

"Does everybody do things?" sighed his listener, much perplexed.

"Everyone should. You are wondering what I do. My money comes to me before I earn it, from houses—land—I have to see the people who live in my houses have all that is fair and necessary, that the land is in order. Then sometimes we lend other people our money, and they find work for many others, and make more of it. Money is a very difficult thing to explain, Christopher. What I want you to remember now is that you must never take money from other people without giving something in return, because it's stealing."

Christopher, with his usual disconcerting shrewdness, found an unsatisfactory point.

"I don't do anything for the money you give me every week, Cæsar."

Aymer was fairly caught, and wanted desperately to laugh, only the boy's face was so grave and concerned he did not dare. He thought for a moment to find a way out of the difficulty without upsetting the somewhat vague theories he had just crystallised into words.

"But I owe something to the world, and you are a small atom of the world, Christopher, so I choose to pay a mite of my debt that way. Besides, it is a part of your education to learn how to spend money, as much a part as Latin grammar."

Christopher thought it a much pleasanter part and looked relieved.

"I am glad you aren't paying me," he said slowly; "of course it's just my good luck that it happened to be me you pay your debts to. Lots of people aren't lucky like that."

Which was a truth that remained very deeply indented in Christopher's mind. Aymer ordered him to bed, but when he said good-night he kept grip of his hand.

"Why wouldn't you like me to pay you?" he demanded, almost roughly.

The boy got red and embarrassed, but Aymer waited remorselessly.

"I can't do anything," he said, "and if I did I'd hate you to pay me like that. Some day I'll have to pay you, won't I?"

"I should hate that worse than you would," returned Aymer shortly. "There's no question of money between us. I get all I want out of you. Go to bed."

CHAPTER IV

Marden Court lay bathed in the mellow October sunshine. Late Michaelmas daisies, fuchsias, and milky anemones stood smiling bravely in the borders under the red brick walls, trails of crimson creepers flung a glowing glory round grey stone pillar and coping, and in the neighbouring woods the trees seemed to hold their breath under the weight of the rich robes they wore. Marden looked its best in late autumn. The ripeness of the air, the wealth of colour, and the harmonious dignity of the season seemed a fit setting to the old Tudor mansion, with its reposeful beauty just touched with renaissance grace. The glory of the world passes, but it is none the less a glory worth observing.

The Astons regarded Marden as the metropolis of their affections. It was "Home" and any member of the family wanting to go "Home" did so regardless of who might be in immediate possession. Nevil Aston, his wife and two small children and his young sister-in-law lived there permanently, but their position was that of fortunate caretakers, and both the elder Aston and the Wyatts went to and fro at their will.

Nevil Aston was at thirty-two a brilliant essayist and rising historian, and there was a magnificent library at Marden which he professed to find useful in his work. He also was wont to say "Marden was an excellent place in which to work, but a far better place in which to play." He himself did both in turn. A few weeks of furious energy and copious achievement would be followed by weeks of serene idleness from which little Renata, his wife, would arouse him by sheer bullying, as he himself expressed it, driving him by main force of will to the library, setting pen and paper to hand and then placidly consenting to weeks of irregular meals, of absent-minded vagaries, a seeming indifference to her presence, in place of the wholly dependent lovable boyish Nevil of the days of indolence.

It was not till the second autumn after Christopher's introduction to the ménage that the senior Astons decided to desert London for a few months and go "Home." Mr. Aston had been to and fro not infrequently and Nevil Aston had made a few brief visits to town, when Constantia Wyatt had made it her business to see that her gifted brother did not hide his light under a bushel, but little Christopher failed to connect either Nevil or his beautiful sister very closely with his own particular Astons. They were a part of an outside existence with which he was unacquainted, and Marden Court was to him but a name, an unreal place that got photographed occasionally and that Mr. Aston seemed to like. The Astons, probably quite unconsciously, pursued their usual course of leaving Christopher to drift into the stream of their existence without any explanation or attempt to make that existence a clear cut and dried affair to him. He was pleased enough with the idea of the change, once he had ascertained his guinea-pigs might accompany him, and was still more pleased when he was told he would at all events for a time have no lessons to do.

"You'll have plenty to learn though," Aymer had remarked drily when he made the announcement. Christopher refrained from asking for an explanation with difficulty.

Towards the middle of October Nevil Aston, just in the midst of a period of blissful laziness, sauntered down the long walks of the south garden in Renata's wake, occasionally stopping to pick up one or other of the two fat babies who struggled along after their mother, interrupting more or less effectually the business on which she was engaged. A pathetic-eyed yard or so of brown dachshund and a tortoise-shell kitten completed the party. Renata Aston was small and dark, gentle and deliberate of movement, and possessing an elf-like trick of shrinking her entrancing personality into comparative invisibility that bereft one of further vision. She moved from border to border choosing her flowers with care, and looking even smaller than she was in the proximity of her lanky husband, and the plump little babies toddling after.

Presently she came to a stop. All her satellites stopped too. She regarded her trophies critically.

"This is very good for the end of October, you know." She remarked to all the assembled court. "I only want some violets now. Nevil, I wish you'd stop Charlotte picking the heads off the fuchsias: there are no more to come out."

Nevil hoisted his small daughter on his shoulder as the safest way to avoid an altercation and humbly asked if he must pick violets, "they grow so low down."

"You grow so far up," she retorted scornfully. "Max can help me. You can watch with Charlotte. You are very good at watching people work."

"It is not a common virtue," pleaded Nevil, "watchers generally tell the workers how to do it. I never do. Why don't you tell a gardener to pick them, Renata?"

"A gardener! For Aymer?"

"All this trouble for Aymer?"

"It is a pleasure."

"I know just how it will be," he complained mournfully, "the moment Aymer is here you will hound me off to work and I shall see nothing of you at all.

You won't even give me new pens. Charlotte, I should look horrid if I had no hair: be merciful."

Renata smiled and shook her head. "I shall get no more work out of you this side of Christmas, sir. I have no such impossible dreams. Perhaps Aymer won't want either of us now he has got Christopher."

"I wonder now," remarked Nevil, depositing Miss Charlotte on a seat while he took out his cigarette case, "I wonder if you are jealous, Renata."

She flushed indignantly and denied the fact with most unnecessary emphasis, so her husband told her in his gentle teasing way. He turned her face up to his and professed to look stern, which he never could do.

"Confess now," he insisted. "Just a little jealous of Christopher?"

"Well," she admitted, laughing and still pink, "Aymer has never stayed away from us for so long before. I don't know what was the use of his having those rooms done up for himself if he never means to use them."

Renata continued to pick violets, and Max to decapitate those he could find. The dachshund and kitten continued to watch with absorbing interest, and Nevil continued to smoke and to let Charlotte investigate his cigarette case till her mother turned round and saw her.

"You dreadful child!" she cried, "Nevil, just look. Charlotte is sucking the ends of your horrid cigarettes! How can you let her?"

Charlotte was rescued from the cigarettes, or the cigarettes from Charlotte, with considerable difficulty and at the cost of many tears. Indeed her protestations were so loud that nurse appeared and bore her and Max away and silence again reigned in the warm garden between the sunny borders.

The dachshund gave a sigh and flopped down on the path, and the kitten began a toilet for want of better employment. Renata, who had stood aside during the small domestic storm, gazed at her violets gravely as if she were counting them.

Nevil watched her contentedly and did not observe the trouble in her face.

"Nevil," she said at last, "about Charlotte I wonder—do you think—" she stopped and edged a little nearer her husband and slipped her hand in his.

"Well, dear?"

"You don't think, do you, Nevil, that Charlotte is—is getting like Patricia?"

He put his arm round her and drew her down on the seat.

"You dear silly child, no," he said, kissing her.

She seemed only half assured and leant her head against him, sighing.

"It is quite, quite different," he insisted. "Charlotte's temper is just like anyone else's, yours or mine, or anyone's."

"Yours—you haven't got one," she returned with pretended contempt and then lapsed back into her troubled mien, "but I feel so frightened sometimes."

"My dear, be reasonable. Patricia's temper isn't a temper at all. It's—it's a possession—a wretched family inheritance. She can't help it, poor child, any more than she could help a squint or a crooked nose, and she doesn't inherit it from *your* mother but only from your step-father, so why on earth you should imagine it likely to crop up in our family I can't conceive. It's absurd."

He tilted her pretty face up to his again and kissed her. Nevil would like to have killed all his wife's cares with a caress. It is not always a successful method, but it is more efficacious than the world believes.

"Of course I know all that, though Patricia always seems quite like my own sister. I do hope Christopher won't tease her."

"Aymer will see to that."

"Not unless he is reminded. You know he rather loves teasing the poor darling himself."

"Here is the poor darling, herself. Storm over, I suppose, sky serene."

The little girl coming down the path to them was barely twelve, but she looked older. The features were too set, if anything, too regular for her to be called pretty as yet, but an observer must have been very blind to beauty not to see the possibilities shadowed in her face. She had quantities of smooth gold hair, one plait of which, for convenience's sake, was twisted round her little head that was at present too small for its rich burden. Her great dark grey eyes and long lashes had a curiously expectant look as if ever on the watch for some joy or pain to come. In the clearness of her complexion and the good modelling of her little white hands, she did resemble her half-sister, but it was the only likeness between them. She came to them not running, as a child should, but slowly and deliberately.

"Patricia, do come and hear what this dreadful Nevil has let Charlotte do," cried Renata, still under shelter of her husband's long arm. For some reason she seemed anxious to let the child know she was seen and wanted. Nevil smiled and made room on the seat for her to sit by his side.

Patricia stood in front of them, her great pathetic eyes looking from one to the other. She finally addressed herself to Nevil.

"I'm ever so sorry, Nevil," she said with a dejected sigh.

"Of course, of course, it's all right, child," he answered hastily, "come and hear my short-comings. I'm in deep disgrace."

She sat down obediently and the dachshund immediately shifted its quarters and wedged itself in between her feet. She leant forward with her elbows on her knees and gazed absently at the brown head.

"What have you been doing, Nevil, darling?"

"I? Not I, but Charlotte. Don't you know by this time, Patricia, I'm only a scapegoat for the autocrat of the nursery."

"He let Charlotte nibble a cigarette," explained Renata.

"One of my very best."

"It might have been one of his worst, Rennie," suggested Patricia consolingly.

"They are all 'worst' for Charlotte," cried Renata springing up. "I must go and put up my flowers or they'll be here before I'm ready."

She flitted away in the direction of the house. Her husband looked after her with mute sorrow at his own incapacity to melt from vision in that intangible manner—from situations that were too difficult.

He glanced at his little companion, who was making attempts to tie the dachshund's ears round his own neck.

"You won't be able to treat Christopher that way, Patricia," he said contemplatively, "but it will be jolly for you to have a companion of your own age, won't it?"

"Perhaps he won't like me."

"He is quite likely to like you."

"Oh, yes, at first, because I'll make him," she returned with engaging candour, but then her mouth drooped a little, "but when he knows what I'm really like, he won't."

Nevil examined another cigarette carefully to see it had not been nibbled. He was really very fond of his little sister-in-law though occasionally at a loss how to deal with her strange moods.

"Well, we are all very fond of you, anyway, child," he said easily; "as for the temper, you can't really help it, you know, and you'll grow out of it. I'm sure you try to, my dear."

"But I don't try," cried poor Patricia wildly, "I haven't time, I don't know anything about it till it's there and then it's too late. I might just as well have flung that plate at Charlotte as at you to-day. I wonder Renata lets me go in the nursery."

"No, no. You wouldn't be angry with a baby."

She turned to him with a sort of exasperated patience. "That's just it. You don't any of you understand. It does not make any difference, why, who or where. It just comes. I *can't* help it." She kicked her heel on the gravel fiercely.

"Poor little Patricia," said Nevil gently. "I can only say we all love you just the same, and I believe you'll grow out of it." She changed suddenly and flung herself into his arms in a wild transport of tears and childish abandonment. He was in no wise taken aback and soothed her with adroitness born of practice. When she was calm again he sat with his arm round her talking of indifferent things till a clock somewhere near struck three.

"They should be here directly," he said, but made no effort to rise.

"Would Aymer really mind being met?" she questioned.

"He'd rather be left to Vespasian and Tollens."

Tollens was the old butler.

"Won't he ever get used to it?"

"He is afraid of becoming an invalid if he gets hardened to it."

"But he is, isn't he?"

"Not a bit of it. He has perfectly wonderful health. He has massage and all sorts of things to keep him up to the mark. Aymer's as vain as a girl."

"I don't call it vanity. I call it pluck."

Nevil groaned, "Oh, you women, old and young! But you are right—and there are my father and Christopher himself."

Christopher to his great joy had been allowed to drive down with Aymer and Mr. Aston, and had found the journey not one mile too long. Indeed towards the end his early curiosity as to the termination had evaporated and the milestones had come in sight and vanished all too quickly. It had been reassuring to find Vespasian awaiting them at the door with the old butler to whom he was formally introduced as Mr. Aymer's ward. Then having inquired of Tollens of the family's whereabouts, Mr. Aston bore off Christopher for further introductions.

At the entrance to the garden on the long terrace and by the gate leading to the south garden he had paused and looked round with the slow comprehensive glance of one acquainted with every detail. He spoke nothing of his thoughts to Christopher, but the boy was quite acutely aware that Mr. Aston loved this place and was happy to see it again, while he calmly discussed the possibilities of fishing in the lake that lay below like a silver mirror in the clear sunlight.

And in the south garden Nevil and Patricia met them. Patricia, still white and shaken with the past storm, greeted Mr. Aston shyly, but had no qualms about greeting Christopher. He, for his part, was far too shy and too unused to girls' society to notice her mien. He did, however, remember afterwards that she was standing by a great clump of purple starlike flowers and that he thought her the most beautiful thing he had ever seen, excepting, of course, Constantia Wyatt. He made that mental reservation as they walked along together in front of their elders, and then glancing sideways at the wonderful hair again, decided he liked fair hair best. Constantia's was dark. They soon outdistanced the two men who followed at a leisurely pace. Mr. Aston looked after them and said kindly:

"The little girl still gives trouble, I see."

"Occasionally." Nevil made the admission with reluctance. "There was a scene this morning. I don't know what started it. Perhaps I teased her. She flung a plate at me. I don't believe she *can* help it, poor child."

"You mustn't tell her so, Nevil."

"You'd tell her anything you could if you saw her after. She'll grow out of it."

"I hope so."

They fell to talking of the estate, which Nevil was supposed to look after. He did, when he remembered it, but that was not often, and not of late. His father, half exasperated, half laughing, told him he would defer his lecture till later on. Nevil penitently agreed it was only fitting to do so, and slipping his arm through his father's, began to explain to him the rights of a controversy just started in the *Historical Review*. No one was ever angry with Nevil long. His unchangeable sweet temper and gentle judgment of mankind, his entire lack of vanity and the very real ability that was concealed under his elusive personality outweighed the exasperation his irresponsibility and indolence sometimes awoke. He had no enemies among those who knew him, and the bitterest controversy with pen and ink could be brought to a close in an interview. It must, however, be confessed that with pen in hand Nevil was more dangerous than the unwary might imagine. He knew his power with that weapon and when he chose to use it, did so to good purpose with a polished finish to his scathing periods, that made men twenty years his senior hate with fierce passion Aston the writer, as surely as they would end by appreciation of Aston the man after a personal encounter.

Patricia and Christopher having outdistanced their elders proceeded to make friends in their own way. The girl began operations by asking if he would like to see the stables and found it aroused no enthusiasm in him, which was a point to the bad. But he was polite enough to say he would like to go if she wished it, which nearly equalised matters again. She confessed it might be nice to have someone to play with, which Christopher thought very friendly of her, and told her of his guinea-pigs, which would arrive in the evening with Robert and the luggage. That was distinctly a point to the good; they both waxed eloquent over the special qualities of guinea-pigs. Christopher's original two had already increased alarmingly in numbers. He hinted some might even be left at Marden—in a good home. Also he told her he had christened the family by the names of great painters.

"Cæsar taught me the names," he explained, "there is Velasquez—he painted the Don Carlos in Cæsar's room, you know—he's brown all over except for one spot—*my* Velasquez, I mean—and there's Watteau—an awful frisky little beast—and Sir Joshua, who sleeps in my pocket. You'll like Sir Joshua, he's awfully good tempered."

"I know," nodded Patricia wisely, "and he painted Nevil's great grandmother. It's in the drawing-room. Why do you call Aymer 'Cæsar'?"

"Because he always does what he means to do, or gets it done; besides he is—just Cæsar."

"It isn't bad," she said condescendingly, "perhaps I shall call him so myself. I do hope we are going to have tea in his room. It's such a lovely, lovely room."

"So it is in London. The beautifulest room I've seen."

"It's just as nice here," she maintained stoutly, "he planned how it was to be done, and Nevil saw to it. I like this best."

Christopher was too polite or too shy to insist, but he felt doubtful and became impatient to see for himself, so they went indoors to find Patricia's hopes were justified. Tea was served in "Mr. Aymer's" room.

And Christopher was obliged to allow that Patricia had some ground for her statement. It was a smaller room than the one in London, and singularly like it, only the prevailing note was lighter and gayer in tone. Aymer was there, lying on a similar sofa to his usual one, with the familiar cover across his feet.

Renata was making tea, and making Cæsar laugh also. Christopher was uncomfortably conscious it was all new to him and the familiarity only superficial, while it was a well-recognised phase in Cæsar's life. Even Nevil Aston seemed a different person in his easy country dress, and Christopher failed at first to connect the dark little lady at the tea table with him, and only noted she took Aymer his tea, which was his, Christopher's, special privilege, and treated him with a friendly familiarity that nearly bordered on contempt in Christopher's eyes.

Aymer saw the children and called to them. Patricia greeted him with the air of a young princess and drew herself up when he said she had grown, and would soon be a child instead of a baby. Then he faced Christopher round towards Renata, who had suddenly become grave and shy.

"Here is Christopher, so you can approve or condemn Nevil by your own judgment, Renata. Christopher, shake hands with Mrs. Aston."

Christopher did as he was told, but he realised they had been speaking of him and felt on the defensive. However, he sat down as near to Cæsar as he could. They talked of all manner of people and things of which he knew nothing, traditional jokes cropped up, and Aymer's propensity for teasing asserted itself in a prominent manner. Renata never failed to respond and never failed to claim Nevil's protection and to look delightfully shy and dignified and feminine. Presently the children were sent for. To Christopher's indignant amazement they were plumped down on Aymer and allowed to treat him much as if he was a new species of giant plaything. Charlotte, in her efforts to burrow under Aymer's arm, rolled off the edge of the sofa and was deftly caught by Christopher, who deposited her on the floor. She immediately tried to clamber up again, but Aymer could not second her efforts with his left arm.

"Put her up again, Christopher," he said.

But Christopher apparently did not hear, and Mr. Aston, who had been watching, came to the rescue. Christopher slipped away to the window.

"A question of a third baby, I think," said Mr. Aston softly as he rearranged Charlotte, and Aymer, looking sharply at Christopher, laughed.

When Christopher went to bid him good-night, he found Cæsar alone, looking tired and doing nothing, not even reading.

Christopher said good-night gravely.

"It's not very late," remarked Aymer. "Stay with me a bit."

He patted the chair beside him. Christopher with rather a hot face obeyed.

"How do you like Marden?"

"I—I don't know yet. There seems to be a lot of people here."

"It's home, you see. We all come home when we want to see each other and have people round."

"Yes, I suppose everyone wants to see their people sometimes."

"Don't you like seeing people?"

"I haven't any of my own," said Christopher, without looking at him.

"That's unkind. You have us."

Christopher changed the subject.

"Do those—those little children live here?"

"Yes. It's their home. They are rather jolly little kids. What's the matter, Christopher?"

Christopher assured him nothing was the matter.

Aymer continued in his most matter-of-fact voice.

"I'm fond of those babies. To begin with they are Nevil's and they are the only youngsters I am likely to know well. But I'm a greedy person. I had Nevil, Renata, the kiddies—and that delightfully odd Patricia, and it wasn't enough for me. They were all as good as could be to me, but I wanted to be more than an extra in someone's life, so I must needs encumber myself with a troublesome little boy who's even more greedy than myself, apparently."

Christopher sat with his curly head on his hands trying not to give in to the smile that was struggling to express some undefined sense of content which had sprung to life.

"You are a bad, silly boy to be jealous," said Aymer, watching him, half laughing, half affectionately, "you ought to have known for yourself, if they had been enough for me, you wouldn't be here at all."

CHAPTER V

Two events wrote themselves indelibly on Christopher's memory in connection with this first visit to Marden, while the one great matter that began there and influenced his whole after life merged itself into a general hazy sense of happiness and companionship. For it is given to few of us even when we have reached years of discretion to recognise those moments in our lives which are of real, supreme, and eternal importance: moments when the great doors of experience open slowly on silent hinges and we pass in, unconscious even that we have crossed the threshold. But all that happens to our familiar selves, that touches our well-known emotions, and rubs or eases the worn grooves of existence, is heavily underscored in our recollection, and not infrequently we take for mile-stones on the way what were but pebbles on the road.

The two events which Christopher carried in his memory were, however, not unimportant, for both bore on his relationship with the man who was moulding his life. The one episode turned Vespasian's bald statements into real emotional facts, and the other was the first serious collision between the far-off disastrous tutelage of Marley Sartin and the new laws of existence as propounded by Aymer Aston.

Christopher's education made vast strides during that winter. The season proved an unusually mild one. He was out the greater part of each day with Patricia, enduring with remarkable fortitude her alternate contempt and despair over his ignorance of such everyday matters as horses, guns, dogs, desert island games, and such like. When she laughed at him for not being able to ride he shut his teeth hard not to remind her he'd never possessed a shetland pony from birth as she had, also he rose at an unconscionable early hour and rode in the cold winter's dawn round and round the exercising yard with the young grooms, while Patricia was warm and fast asleep in bed. But he had his reward when Mr. Aston, who had heard of his doings from the stud-groom, took him out with him on one of his rounds of inspection to outlying farms.

"The boy's got a good seat, and pluck, Aymer," reported Mr. Aston. "It's more creditable to him because he has had to learn. It's not second nature to him."

It took him less trouble to learn how to handle a gun, and when "off duty" to Patricia, spent a vast amount of time in the electric plant house, learning the A B C of a big dynamo.

Aymer knew all this and made no mention of lessons, for Christopher was backward in more matters than booklearning and the life on a big estate, the infinite variety of interests was all good food for the boy's hungry brain and soul.

He grew apace. Mr. Aston declared he was a changeling and not the thin little urchin he had first encountered by the mile-stone on the Great Road. They never alluded to his life before that, though they all knew of it, and made their own private comparisons and observations.

Christopher became quite attached to the babies so long as they did not intrude on his own particular hours with Cæsar, but he did not get over a certain shy reserve towards Renata.

"She slips into empty places," he said to Cæsar once, and Cæsar laughed at him and told Renata, who coloured and wrinkled her little forehead.

"He is a nice boy," she said, "and I love him for being so good to Patricia. There hasn't been a storm since he came."

One day, when it was too wet for even Christopher to be out, the two children amused themselves by turning out a cupboard in a disused room. It was a perfect stronghold of treasures. Old riding whips, Badminton Magazines (marked Aymer Aston, Christopher noticed), tennis balls, cricket pads, a pair of fencing foils and mask and gloves, a host of sporting trophies from a hare's pad to a wolf's ear labelled "Kronigratz," and last of all a box full of photographs.

Patricia was called away before they could investigate this last treasure trove, and Christopher, not to be alone in the glory of discovery, carried it off to Cæsar's room and lay on the hearth-rug enjoying it till Cæsar, busy working out estate accounts for his father, was at liberty to look too. They were interesting photographs,—to a boy. Mostly of horses ridden, led, alone, jumping, horses galloping, horses trotting, and over and over again a picture of one horse, and rider, who never seemed to wear a hat and had a thick head of hair that looked as if it might be the same colour as Cæsar's. At last he came to a bigger, more distinct photo of the same man and horse. The horse was evidently a polo-pony and was galloping and the man on it in white riding things, with his shirt open at the neck and was swinging a polo stick in his hand. There was no mistaking it this time: it was undoubtedly Cæsar. Christopher gave a little gasp. Cæsar like that, vigorous, active, panting,— Christopher could feel it so—with life and excitement. He scrambled to his knees with the picture in his hand.

"Cæsar, dear Cæsar, look what I've found."

Aymer looked round, saw the scattered photographs, and held out his hand.

"Is it you really? May I have it for myself?"

Cæsar took the card and as he gave it up, Christopher knew he had made a mistake, and got scarlet.

"Where did you find it?" demanded Aymer sharply.

"In the cupboard in the little red room. We were turning it out."

"Yes, it's I. Why shouldn't it be? I wasn't always a cripple, you know."

He tossed the picture back on the rug. The scar stood out white and distinct, and his face was strangely hard and set. A book slipped down on the left side and he tried to catch it with the left hand and failed, and it fell with a bang on the floor.

"May I have it?" asked Christopher meekly from the rug.

"What for? You don't know the horse and you don't know the man. Put it in the fire."

"No, I won't," exclaimed Christopher indignantly. "Cæsar, don't be so horrid, it's—it's—exactly like you."

Cæsar ignored his own command and asked another question instead. "Where did you say you found it?"

"In a cupboard in the little red room. It's such a jolly little room. It isn't used now and there's hardly anything in it, but the cupboards are full of things—lovely things. Patricia and I just explored."

"It used to be my room and the things are all mine. Why haven't they burnt them?" he muttered.

Christopher gathered up the unlucky photographs and put them back in the box. He was dimly conscious he did not want Mr. Aston to come and see them.

"I'm sorry, Cæsar, I didn't know we shouldn't have done it."

"You haven't done any harm, I—I had no business to be cross, old fellow. Come and show me the pictures again, I'll tell you about them."

Christopher sat down on the sofa with the box in his hand. He really did want to know about them if Cæsar wasn't going to be angry. He took out a photo at random.

"That was my first race-horse," said Cæsar. "Her name was Loadstar. She didn't win much, but I thought a lot of her. And that—oh, that's a mastiff I had: he was magnificent, but such a brute I had to kill him. He went for one of the stable boys and I hardly got him off in time. I've got the marks now of his claws: he never bit me. We used to wrestle together."

"Wrestle with a dog?"

"Yes, I used to be fairly strong, you know, Christopher. It was good training throwing him—sometimes it was the other way. But he had to die, poor old Brutus."

"How did you kill him?"

"I shot him," said Cæsar shortly, "don't ask for morbid particulars. Where is another picture?"

"This?"

This was a photo of a horse standing alone in a field and beneath was written, "Jessica waiting to be tamed." Aymer offered no explanation,—if Christopher had looked he would have seen the scar show up again sharply over a frown.

The next was rather a wicked snap-shot of Aymer cover shooting, with what looked suspiciously like a dead fox curled up at his feet.

"It was a wretched little cub I had tamed," he explained, "the little beast used to follow me everywhere. It's really tied up to a tree, but it always lay out as if dead when it heard a gun. I took it out with me to try and get it used to the sound."

There was a picture of Aymer and Nevil riding and coming over a big water jump side by side.

Aymer told him it was at the Central Horse Show and related the triumphs and honours of the day.

But when the polo photograph turned up again Aymer appeared tired of the amusement, and sent Christopher off to meet his father in the brougham at Maidley station, four miles distant. "If someone doesn't go he'll be reading reports and working out figures till he arrives at the door," said Aymer. "It's disgraceful not to know how to take a holiday properly. It's only small boys who ought to work like that," he added severely.

"You haven't given me any work to do, Cæsar," protested Christopher, but Cæsar only laughed.

When the boy had gone, however, Aymer continued to turn over the photographs. It was an extremely unwise proceeding, for each of them called him with irresistible voice back to the past from which he had sworn he would turn his eyes. It was always there with its whispering, mocking echo, but like a good fighter he had learnt to withstand its insidious temptations, and hold fast to the quiet, secure present where all he could know of joy or fulfilment was centred.

But there it was, the great gulf that lay between him and the past, in which were swallowed up the hopes, ambitions, expectations of his vigorous youth, and all the possibilities of a man's life. He had fathomed it to its blackest depth, and seen no hope of escape or rescue. And yet he had escaped, through the devotion and courage of his father. And it was the ever-living recollection of that devotion that helped him to keep his face turned from the other side of the gulf. Only on rare occasions did his strength of purpose fail him, and by some momentary carelessness he found himself caught back into a black hour of bitterness and helpless anger.

There was no one to blame but himself, no power to accuse but his own headlong passion, and the imperious impatience that would take no gift from life but that of his own choosing. There had been a woman and a tangle of events, and his passion-blinded eyes could see no way of disentangling it, and yet how trivial and easy the unravelling appeared now. The quick—not resolve—but impulse that caught him on the crest of his uncontrolled, wild temper, and prompted the shot that missed its intention by a hairs-breadth: the whole so instantaneous, so brief a hurricane of madness, succeeded by the long pulseless stillness of this life of his now.

To do, and not to be able to undo, to hunger and thirst and ache to take back only a short minute of life, to feel sick and blind before the irretrievableness of his own deed, that was still his punishment in these rare hours of darkness.

He had fought for life at first with all that virile strength of his and won this limited existence which, when he first understood its cruelly narrow horizon, he had as ardently longed and sought to lose again, but the life principle that had been so roughly handled was marvellously tenacious, and refused to be ousted from its tenement. Slowly and painfully Aymer had groped his way from desolate despair to something higher than mere placid resignation, to a brave tolerance of himself and an open heart to what life might still offer him.

There was, however, little toleration in his heart at this hour as he lay staring at the photograph, and then suddenly looked round the room he had made so beautiful for himself. It was just as usual, every detail complete, satisfactory, balanced, redeemed too from its own beauty by its strange freedom from detail and its emptiness.

It pleased him well as a rule, but this evening that same emptiness seemed to emphasise his own isolation. He was suddenly conscious of a sense of incompleteness, of some detail left out that should be there—a want he could not measure or define. It was a sort of culminating point in his own grey thoughts. In a gust of his old imperious temper he caught up the photograph and tore it in half, and flung it from him: tried to fling into the fire and failed even in that. The box of photographs fell and scattered on the floor. He turned his head sharply and hid his face in the cushions.

It was very quiet in the room, the fire burnt steadily, and outside the dusk had already fallen. There was a very little knock at the door, but he did not hear it; the door opened with a breath of fresh cold air and a faint scent of violets as Renata entered.

She saw she was unobserved, saw his attitude, and her whole being seemed to melt into an expression of longing compassion. Nevil or his father would have gone away unseen in respect for his known weakness, but Renata for all her shyness had the courage of her instincts.

"May I come and warm myself, Aymer? You always have the best fire in the house."

He did not move for a moment.

Renata knelt by the fire with her back to him and took off her long soft gloves, her bracelets making a little jangling sound. Then she saw the torn picture and picked it up and shook her head disapprovingly. The overturned box lay nearer the sofa. She picked that up too, and began replacing its contents in a matter-of-fact way.

"You can't possibly see things in this light," she remarked. "It is getting quite dark. Do you want a light, Aymer?"

"No," said Aymer abruptly, turning so that he could see her.

She sat down in a big chair the other side of the hearth and began chatting of the very serious At Home she had just attended in Winchester.

The black mood slipped from him, and with it the sense of need and incompleteness. It had melted as snow before a fire the moment he had heard the swish of her dress across the floor, and the breath of violets reached him. He forgot even to be ashamed of his own passing weakness as he watched her. She was all in brown with strange beautiful gold work shining here and there. She had flung back her furs and there was a big bunch of violets in her dress. He watched her little white fingers unfasten them as she talked.

"If they would not think they were amusing themselves, I could endure it," she said, "but they solemnly pretend it's amusement and frivolous at that. One old lady told me gravely, she hardly thought it seemly that the Dean should so lend himself to the pleasures of the world. There, the violets are not spoilt at all. The Dean gave them to me: it's the one thing he can do—grow violets. You shall have them all to yourself." She fetched a silver cup and began arranging them. Aymer ceased to be tired, ceased to be anything but supremely content as his eyes followed her. She went on relating her experience until she had made him laugh, and then she came and sat on a little stool near him.

"May I have the babies down?"

Aymer pretended to grumble.

"You'll go to them if I say no," he complained, "so I have no option."

The bell was rung and the babies ordered to descend.

"Before they come, Cæsar, I'm going to ask you a favour," she said coaxingly, "now you are in a good temper again."

"Was I in a bad one?"

"Dreadful. It mustn't reoccur. It is such a bad example for the children."

"The favour, please; bother the children."

"Cæsar, I'm ashamed of you. Bless them, you meant to say. Well, the favour. Aymer, I am going to start a crêche in Winchester near the big clothing factory. I've talked to the Bishop and he quite approves. I know just the house, but I shall have to buy it, and I haven't enough money for that. I can run it easily if I can only get the premises. What will you subscribe?"

"I haven't any money at all," he replied gravely. "Vespasian takes it all and I don't think he'd approve of crêches, not being a family man."

"Vespasian, indeed." She tilted her chin in the air as Aymer meant her to do, a trifle too much, and the effect was spoilt, but he was well practised in obtaining the exact tilt he admired.

"You can ask him, of course."

"Very likely I will: in the meantime what will you give me?"

"Half a crown. No; five whole shillings, if I have it," he said teasingly.

She considered the matter gravely. "I am not quite sure. I should not like to inconvenience you. Shall we say four and six?"

"No, I will be generous. I'll do this. If you will take the risk of being accused of burglary by Vespasian, I happen to know there is some money in the right hand drawer of the table over there. I don't know how much. Fivepence, perhaps, but you shall have whatever it is."

Renata walked with great dignity across the room and opened the drawer. A little smile hovered about her lips. She picked up a handful of gold and silver and sat down by him to count it.

"It looks an awful lot," he remarked anxiously. "Won't you let me off? Vespasian is always complaining of my extravagance."

"Sh—Sh—" she held up one finger, "ten, eleven, twelve, and two and six, that's thirteen,—no, fourteen and sixpence."

"Leave me the sixpence," he urged plaintively, but she continued counting.

"Seven pounds, four shillings and sixpence. Count it yourself, Aymer."

Aymer counted and gravely pronounced her arithmetic to be correct.

"Thank you, you are a dear." She piled the coins up neatly in little piles on the table by her side. He told her she had better put it in her pocket.

"I haven't one," she sighed.

"You will be sure to forget it, and then Vespasian will get it again."

"Is it likely I would forget seven pounds, four shillings and sixpence?"

But she did. The children arrived and rioted over Aymer. Master Max bumped his head and had to be consoled with his uncle's watch, while Charlotte wandered off on a voyage of exploration alone, and finally sat on the floor by the window with her fat legs straight out in front of her, making a doll of one arm by wrapping it up in her dress, and singing to herself.

"She has quite an idea of time already: listen to her, Aymer."

But Aymer only scoffed at his niece's accomplishments, and then Nevil came in and went down on his knees to kiss his wife, who was much too occupied with her son and heir to move for him. For a moment all three heads were on a level, and it was only when the long Nevil stood up and Renata was reaching up on tip-toe to put some of the violets in his coat that Aymer's sense of completeness vanished. Finally the children were carried off and he was alone again.

"It's a lucky thing for me," he said to himself steadily, "that Nevil married Renata: he might just as easily have married someone I couldn't endure."

When Christopher and Mr. Aston returned they found Aymer whistling and drawing ridiculous caricatures of the family on the back of the *Times*, and he was so outrageously flippant and witty that his father glanced at him suspiciously from time to time.

"Why haven't you let Vespasian light up?" he inquired.

"I'm afraid to call Vespasian. Renata has been raiding and I shall get a lecture. She's left her booty, as I told her she would. Christopher, when you have quite finished pretending it's your duty to draw the curtains, you might run up with this money to her. Put it in that box."

Christopher came forward rather slowly. He swept the money into the box indicated.

"What a lot," he commented.

"Seven pounds, four shillings, and sixpence, and I am now penniless. I shan't even get credit with Heaven. She'll appropriate that."

Christopher ran off with it and meeting Nevil on the stairs gave it into his hand. Renata had gone to dress, and Nevil sauntered in to his wife with her "spoils" at once.

"Seven pounds, four and sixpence," she said gleefully. "For the crêche fund. It was nice of Aymer. I had not meant to worry him to-day, but he wanted distraction."

"I thought Vespasian kept his money. Six pounds four and sixpence, Renata," Nevil remarked, counting the money carelessly. She came over to him, brush in hand.

"You can't even do addition. Nothing but dates! I counted it most carefully, so did Aymer."

"Then he's defrauded you of a pound since."

"Nonsense."

They counted it together, but no amount of reckoning would make seven sovereigns out of six. The silver was correct.

"It must have fallen down," said Renata at last and put it away carefully in her desk.

They were late for dinner, and Mr. Aston pretended to upbraid them and told Renata to take her soup and leave her correspondence alone, for there was a big envelope lying by her plate. It was her father-in-law's contribution to the crêche scheme, Aymer having forestalled her request, and joined forces with his father in a really adequate sum.

Renata got pink with pleasure as she looked at the cheque. She was, however, far too shy to express her real gratitude in words before them all. She smiled at the donor and remarked she would give him a big photograph in a beautiful frame of the first baby admitted to the crêche, to hang in his room as a slight token of her appreciation of his gift.

"It shall take the place of Charlotte," he assured her gravely.

Aymer looked aggrieved.

"May I ask the precise sum, Renata?" he inquired pointedly, "that earns so gracious a reward."

"It's three figures," she answered, regarding the precious slip of paper affectionately before replacing it in its imposing envelope.

"Ninety-two pounds, fifteen and sixpence more," he groaned; "it's a lot for a photograph of a mere baby, but I can't be left out in the cold."

"Perhaps I can let you have one without a frame for less, only father's must be the best."

"Nevil," remarked Aymer severely, "I would call your attention to the fact that your wife is beginning to weigh men's merits by their means."

Nevil only laughed.

"I hear she has raided you of all you possess. Six pounds odd."

"Seven pounds four and sixpence," corrected Aymer. "I should like the correct sum printed in good plain figures on your list, Renata. Being my all, it is a superior present to more pretentious donations."

"Six pounds four and sixpence, however," persisted Nevil.

Aymer looked up quickly.

"Did you count it?"

Nevil nodded.

"It must have dropped," said Aymer slowly. "I'll send it you with the interest, Renata."

But he knew it had not been dropped.

Mr. Aston began telling them of a deputation from the Friends of the Canine Race he had received that day, and no more was said on the other matter.

CHAPTER VI

Although Christopher's habit of acquisitiveness had given Aymer some uneasy moments, yet there had been so far no very serious conflict of the question of meum and tuum. Aymer had sought rather to overwrite the rude scrawl of Marley Sartin than to erase it. The most serious aspect that had shown itself hitherto was Christopher's readiness to accept tips from over-generous callers and even to put himself to ingenious trouble to invite them. Constantia Wyatt was a great offender in this and brought down a severe scolding on her own head from her brother when he at last learnt of Christopher's propensity.

"He does it so neatly and with such a charming, innocent face," pleaded Constantia, half laughing; "it's no harm, Aymer. All boys like tips: I know my boy does."

But she rather libelled Master Basil Wyatt, who, though not averse to a donation, would have scorned to solicit it. Aymer had told Christopher that gentlemen did not do these things and had taken care to keep the boy out of the way of departing visitors. But this had been before his first lecture on the obligations of money, and Christopher had taken that lesson to heart and quite outgrown his childish and perfectly innocent habit of inviting tips.

Aymer was furiously angry with himself for the quick suspicion which connected the boy with the missing sovereign. He tried honestly to put it away from himself as unwarrantable and dangerous. But there it was, a wretched little poisonous thought, tugging at his heart, unreasonably coupled with a recollection of a conversation between Patricia and Christopher that he had overheard one afternoon at tea-time, anent the construction of an amateur brickwork bridge across an inconvenient stream. Patricia had said they could buy bricks at the brick-yard, and Christopher had said he had no money left; it would cost lots and lots and they must wait till pay-day.

He mentioned the loss of the sovereign to Christopher and asked if he had dropped the money on the stairs, and Christopher had composedly answered in the negative, and had volunteered the remark that if it had been dropped in the room it could not have rolled far on the thick carpet. Aymer had been for the moment convinced of the injustice of his own suspicion. He made no attempt to discover any other solution to the problem; rather he evaded what might prove a difficult task, and contented himself with solemnly sending Renata a cheque for the remainder "with interest," and neither Renata nor Nevil spoke of the matter again, at least to him. Nevil may have had his own opinions about it, and if he had they were quite certainly communicated to his wife. The worrying uncertainty, however, proved too much for Aymer, and the following evening when he was alone with his father he told him the story, half hoping to be scolded for harbouring uncharitable suspicions. Now, Mr. Aston had been scrupulous to a fault in avoiding the offer of any suggestions or advice on Christopher's upbringing. He desired above all things to leave Aymer free in his chosen task, but he realised at once this was a point where Aymer was quite as likely to hurt himself as Christopher, and, therefore, that he, Aymer's father, must make an exception to his rule and he did not like it. He began drawing vague lines on his shirtcuff with a pencil, an evil habit of his when uneasy in mind. Aymer watched him with disapproval.

"After all our efforts," he sighed gravely, "you still persist in your old bad ways, sir. How often have I entreated you to remember a poor valet's feelings, and how often has Nevil begged you to recollect the sorrows of the washerwoman?"

Mr. Aston laughed and put away his pencil.

"Nevil once indited an ode to me entitled 'The Lament of the Laundress.' I fear I'm incorrigible."

"What displeases you, sir?" demanded his son after a little pause; "it's no use pretending there's nothing wrong; you only do that when you want to say something you think won't be acceptable."

"Well, then, Aymer, I say this: Christopher is your concern. I don't doubt your power to manage him, but I can speak of yourself, and I tell you it's a very bad thing to live with an unsatisfied suspicion; particularly bad for you. If you don't clear this up you will never feel quite at ease with the boy. It is so already, is it not?"

Aymer admitted reluctantly that it was indeed the case.

"Don't let anything stand between you, Aymer. I am thinking of you, of course," he added hastily.

"Are you sure you are not thinking of yourself?" returned his son, half laughing, half ruefully; and his father flushed a little.

"Perhaps I was," he said humbly. "It would worry me if you were not happy with him."

Aymer laughed outright at that and assured him he knew how to make allowances for his well-known selfishness. But he took his advice and grappled with the difficulty next afternoon. Christopher was mending a rod, seated on the floor as usual.

"We've not found that sovereign," said Cæsar abruptly.

Christopher looked up quickly, and then went on with his work after a brief "Oh!"

"Did you take it, Christopher?"

He asked the question quite slowly and looked at the boy, who got scarlet but went on tying his rod and appeared to be considering the question carefully, weighing it in his mind as it were, and when he answered, it was as deliberately as Aymer had questioned him.

"No, sir."

Aymer felt a sudden sense of relief, for lying had not been one of Christopher's faults. Then almost immediately he found himself wondering first, why the boy was not angry, and secondly, why it had taken so much thought to answer at all. However, he let the matter drop and told himself he was satisfied. Christopher finished mending his rod and then sat still considering deeply. Presently he took out a penny from his pocket and began rolling it on the thick carpet, and, as he had remarked to Cæsar, it did not roll far, try as he would. At last he jumped up with a satisfied mien and went out. Cæsar heard him whistling as he went down the passage and felt easier in his mind. Renata and the babies paid their usual visit after tea, and Miss Charlotte, after a brief conversation with her uncle, slid off the sofa and trotted away to the end window, where she appeared to be diligently playing hide-and-seek with herself. Suddenly her elders were startled with a prolonged cry of anguish and Renata flew to the rescue.

"I tan't find it; naughty mousie taken my booful golden penny," sobbed Charlotte in her mother's arms. Renata could make nothing of her grief and persisted in thinking that she was hurt, and cuddling her. Aymer, listening attentively, said suddenly to Renata in his imperious way:

"Give Charlotte to me, Renata, and take baby away."

Renata obeyed meekly. People had a weak way of obeying Aymer on occasions, even against their will.

"Now, Miss Charlotte," said Aymer, when the young lady was safely deposited by him, "tell me about it. What golden penny was it?"

But Charlotte got suddenly red and stopped crying.

"Were you playing with it yesterday in the window?" asked her uncle.

Charlotte nodded.

"Was it your penny or mine?"

"Wasn't nobody's, only mummy's. You *said they* were for her. Charlotte wasn't naughty."

"Did you find it on the floor?"

"No."

"Where then?"

"Dey was all in nice itty rows on the table. I only taken one pitty goldy penny. Mummy gives me goldy pennies always."

"Sovereigns for playthings, Renata. That's very immoral."

"No, only new halfpennies. Charlotte didn't know any better, Aymer."

"And you played with it in the window there and left it there."

"Is I naughty?"

"Not very naughty—if you tell me. Did you leave it there?"

Charlotte's lip trembled. "I putted it to bed in the curtain by a mousehole, and it's all gone, naughty mousie."

"Go and see, Renata, if there's a hole there."

"Please," said Charlotte gravely.

"Please what?"

"Please go and see."

Aymer laughed. "I beg your pardon, Renata. Please will you mind looking for the mousehole?"

"I tan't see the mousehole," put in Charlotte, "I only 'tend it."

But Renata looked all the same. There was no mousehole and no golden penny.

"It is all right," explained Aymer in answer to his sister-in-law's troubled look. "I know all about it. Don't worry your little head. We will give Charlotte another golden penny, or a silver one. Only," he added, regarding his small niece severely, "Charlotte must not touch anyone's pennies again, not mummy's or Uncle Aymer's, or anyone's. It is not dreadfully naughty this time, but it would be next time—*dreadfully* naughty."

Charlotte opened her eyes very wide.

"Would you be dreffly angry?"

"Yes, and very unhappy. I shouldn't let you come to see me any more."

At that Miss Charlotte flung her arms round his neck, protesting she wasn't naughty and Uncle Aymer must love her. Peace was at last restored and

Aymer drew pictures of innumerable mice carrying off golden pennies and only sent the children away when Christopher came in.

He gave no hint to Christopher that he had solved the problem of the lost money and discovered the boy's own compromise between truth and dishonesty. He was anxious to see whether Christopher's moral standard was really satisfied with the same compromise or not. So he treated him as far as he could in his natural manner during the next few days, but found it a little difficult. Fond of Christopher as he was, this was just one of those points where the enormous difference between the child of one's own self,—of self plus the unknown—and the adopted child of others, became visible. The fault was so inexplicable to Aymer, so utterly foreign to his whole understanding, that he had nothing but contempt for it, whereas, had Christopher been his own son, love would have overridden contempt with fear.

Christopher, with his uncanny, quick intuition of Aymer's innermost mind, was not deceived by his ordinary casual manner, and became, to Aymer's secret satisfaction, a little suppressed and thoughtful.

It was at this point the boy had his first introduction to poor little Patricia's temper.

The two children had been riding and returned home by way of the brook over which their ambitious dreams had already built a bridge. Patricia, who was in rather a petulant mood, reproached Christopher rather sharply for having got rid of his last month's pocket money so prematurely. "Just like a boy," she said, wrinkling her nose contemptuously. She had five whole shillings left of her money and when Christopher could double that they were to go to the brick-yard and bargain.

"Haven't you any at all?" she questioned impatiently.

Christopher, who was examining the proposed site, did not answer at once, and she repeated her question.

"I have some," he confessed unwillingly.

"Well, can't we start with that. You said you hadn't any on Monday. How much is it?"

But Christopher declined to answer.

Patricia persisted in her point. If Christopher had *any money* they could begin the bridge next day. Christopher said he'd see about it.

Patricia, much exasperated, said she should go home, and her companion proposed to make the ponies jump the brook. She was too angry to answer him, but she set her pony at it, and the pony, instead of rising to the jump on command, very cautiously stepped into the stream and splashed across. It is to be feared Christopher laughed. Patricia cantered on, having seen, with much satisfaction, the other pony behave in precisely the same way. But the end was not the same. Christopher wheeled the pony round and tried again, tried eight times and failed and succeeded at the ninth. It was characteristic of him that he did not lose his temper, but had kept on with a sort of dull, monotonous persistence that must have been very boring to the equine mind.

Then he galloped after Patricia, and catching her up at the lodge gates retailed his triumph gleefully. Perhaps he was a shade too triumphant, for he was still in disgrace, and she had not spoken. At all events by the time they had dismounted and were returning to the house through the garden, she was in a fever of irritation, and Christopher, blissfully ignorant of the fact, was just a tiny bit inclined for private reasons of his own, to emphasise his own good spirits. He never noticed the clenching and unclenching of her small hands or saw the whiteness of her tense averted face, and he began teasing her about her pony and her weight. "Nevil must buy you a brand new one, up to your weight," he suggested, "you've broken Folly's spirit evidently."

He was standing on the steps, just one step below her, and he looked back laughing. On a sudden, with no word or sound of warning, she turned and cut at him with her riding whip, her little form quivering with the grip of the possessing demon. The lash caught him across the face and he fell back against the wall gasping, with his hand up. Luckily it was but a light whip and a girl's hand, but the sting of it blanched him for an instant. The flaming colour died from Patricia's face as suddenly as it had come, and with it the momentary fury. She stood gazing at her companion a moment, and when he looked up half terrified, half angry, she turned quickly and ran down a grass path, dropping her whip as she went.

Christopher stood still, rubbing his smarting cheek gingerly, wondering vaguely what he would say if it showed. He had heard from others as well as from Patricia herself, of the child's fearful paroxysms of rage and had rather scoffed at it—to her. But at this moment he was far nearer crying, very near it, indeed, to be strictly truthful. He was really concerned for Patricia, and also he was a little—unnecessarily—ashamed of his own collapse under the sudden attack. Probably she thought it worse than it was. He walked slowly down the grass path between the yew hedges and picked up the whip as he went. Patricia was not on the tennis court nor in the summer-house, nor in the rose-garden, so he turned his steps to the wilderness, as the rough wooded slopes on the northern side of the garden were called. He knew her favourite spots here and presently came on her huddled up on an old moss-grown stone seat, her head in her arms. She was quite still, she was not even crying, and Christopher felt a little frightened. What if she were still angry like that? However, the chances were against it, so he went up and sat down by her.

"Patricia, don't be silly," he commanded. "What did you run off like that for? You didn't hurt—not much," he added truthfully—he had taken to being very exact about the truth of late.

"Go away," said Patricia. "I don't want you. I don't want anyone. You don't understand."

"Well, someone's got to understand," persisted the boy in a high-handed way. "You aren't going to be let get in tempers with me and then sulk about it afterwards. Don't be silly. Sit up." Patricia's golden hair lay about her like a veil. He pushed it aside and tried to pull her hands away from her face, for he was getting really a little frightened at her manner. Some instinct taught him that her misery was as exaggerated and bad for her as her temper, and he was dimly afraid of leaving her alone, as was the custom of her little world after one of her outbreaks.

Patricia suddenly sat up. There were black rims round her great sad eyes already and her face was red and white in patches from the pressure of her hands.

"You said I hadn't hurt you," she gasped, gazing at the dull red mark of which Christopher was already almost unaware.

"Does it show? What a beastly nuisance. I said it didn't hurt much, Patricia. Not at all now. I'm sorry I was such a baby." He put his arm round her and she leant her head against him too exhausted to care whether he thought her a baby or not.

"It must be jolly exciting having a temper like that," he said, thoughtfully. "It wouldn't be half so bad if you meant it."

She sat bolt upright and stared at him.

"Why?" she demanded breathlessly.

"Because if you meant it you could take care *not* to mean it, silly. You'd look out. But you don't mean it. You didn't mean to hurt me then till you did it. It's much worse for you."

She drew a long breath.

"Oh, Christopher dear, how clever you are. No-one ever understood that before. They all say, 'well, anyhow, you don't mean it,' as if that made it better."

"Stupid, of course it's harder to help what you don't mean than what you do."

"But I can't help it."

Christopher gave her a little shake. "Don't be silly. You will have to help it, only it's harder. You can't go on like that when you are big—ladies don't—none I've seen. It's only—" he stopped.

"Only what?"

"Women in the street. At least—some, I've seen them. They fight and scream and get black eyes and get drunk."

"Christopher, you are hateful!" She flared up with hot cheeks and put her hand over his mouth. "I'm not like that, you horrid boy. Say I'm not."

"I didn't say you were," said Christopher with faint exasperation. "I said it reminded me—your temper. Come along in."

She followed very unwillingly, more conscious than he was of his disfigured face.

And Renata met them in the hall and saw it and got pink, but said nothing till Patricia had gone upstairs. Christopher was slipping away too—he never found much to say to Mrs. Aston—and of late less than ever. However, she stopped him.

"Have you been quarrelling, Christopher?" she asked deprecatingly with a little tremor in her voice.

Christopher assured her not.

"You have hurt your face."

"The branch of a tree," he began shamefacedly, and stopped lamely.

"I'm so sorry."

No more was said. Renata was conscious of her own failure to get on with Christopher, but she put it down entirely to her own shyness, which interfered now in preventing her overriding his very transparent fib in Patricia's defence. She went away rather troubled and unhappy. But Christopher, a great deal more troubled and unhappy, looked out of the hall window with a gloomy frown. His own words to Patricia that she had so sharply resented, about the women he had seen fighting in the street, had called up other pictures of the older life, pictures in which Marley Sartin figured only too distinctly. He felt uncomfortably near these shifting scenes. Like Patricia, he wanted to deny the connection between himself and the small boy following in the wake of the big man through crowded streets and long vistas of shops. He did not wish to recognise the bond between little Jim Hibbault and Christopher Aston. But the pictures were very insistent and the likeness uncomfortably clear. At last, with no more show of emotion or will than if he were going on an ordinary errand, he walked slowly down the corridor to Cæsar's room. He had entirely forgotten about Patricia now and was taken aback by Cæsar's abrupt inquiry about the mark or his face.

"It was an accident," he said hurriedly, and then plunged straight into his own affairs.

"Cæsar, I have something to give you."

He held out his hand with a sovereign in it.

Cæsar took it and, after glancing at it casually, put it on the table, looking hard at Christopher, who got red and then white.

"It couldn't have been the sovereign you lost," he said earnestly. "I didn't take any of that money, really, Cæsar. I found this on the floor by the window. It couldn't have rolled all that long way from here. It must be another."

He was pleading with himself as much as with Cæsar, desiring greatly to keep faith with his own integrity, though something in Cæsar's face was driving him from his last stronghold.

"You didn't ask me if I'd found a sovereign," he pleaded desperately, "you asked me if I had taken one of Mrs. Aston's sovereigns, and I hadn't, because how could it have got to the window from here?"

Cæsar's face flushed a dusky red. He spoke in a hard, constrained voice.

"Charlotte took one of the sovereigns as a plaything when we were not looking and hid it under the curtain in the window. To her it was only a toy, but to you—"

He made a last effort to keep control of his temper and failed. The storm broke.

"But to you—" he repeated with a curiously stinging quality in his voice as if the words were whipped to white heat by inward wrath—"to you a sovereign is no toy, but a useful commodity, and your code of honour—do you call it that?—is doubtless a very convenient one. It is far too subtle a code for my poor intellect, but since you appear able to justify it to yourself it is no concern of mine."

Christopher stood still and white under this ruthless attack: all his energies concentrated in keeping that stillness, but at the back of his mind was born a dull pain and sharp wonder, a consciousness of the Law of Consequence by which he must abide, and henceforth accept as a principle of life. There was too great confusion in his mind for him to weigh his instinctive action and subsequent behaviour against what, to Aymer, was the one and only possible code of honour. For the present it was enough that in Aymer's eyes that action was mean, despicable and contemptible. The Law of Consequence he dimly realised worked from the centre of Aymer's being and not from the ill-trained centre of his, Christopher's, individuality.

"In future," went on Aymer, still too furiously angry to weigh his words or remember they were addressed to a child, "if I have occasion to make any inquiries of you we will have a distinct understanding as to whether we are speaking with the same code or not. You can go."

Christopher turned blindly away, and was stopped at the door. "As for the sovereign, which must be very precious to you, considering the price you were ready to pay for it, I will have it pierced and put on a chain, so you can wear it round your neck. It would be a pity to lose anything so valuable."

Christopher turned with indignant protest in every line. However Aymer might talk of their separate codes of honour, he was, nevertheless, dealing out a punishment adequate to the infringement of his own code, and to Christopher it appeared unjust and cruel. For the moment it was in him to remonstrate fiercely, but the words died away, for such a protest must of necessity be based on an acceptance of this divided code, and to that he would not stoop. It was some poor consolation to pay the penalty of a higher law than he was supposed to understand. He turned again to the door and got away before a storm of tears swamped his brave control.

When Charles Aston returned that night he found Aymer in a very irritable mood. Nevil, in his gentle, patient way, had been doing his best to soothe him, but in vain. When Aymer was not irritated, he was bitter and sarcastic, even his greeting to his father was short and cold. It was clear some event in the day had upset his mental equilibrium, and Christopher's absence (he did not even appear to say "good-night") gave Mr. Aston a clue to the situation.

Nevil was wading through a book on farm management, which bored him considerably. His part was to read long extracts which Aymer was comparing with some letters in the "Field." They continued their employment and Mr. Aston sat down to write a letter. From time to time he paused and heard Aymer's sharp, unreasonable remarks to his brother. A memory of the old bad days came so forcibly to Mr. Aston that he laid aside his pen at last and sat listening with an aching heart. He knew those quick flashes of temper were a sign of irritation brought to a white heat. Presently, after one remark more unjustifiable than ever, Nevil looked across at his father with a little rueful grimace, and seeing how grave was Mr. Aston's expression he made another valiant effort to keep peace and ignore the abuse, and went on reading. The subject under discussion was the draining of a piece of waste land, and when the long article came to an end, Nevil in his dreamy way summed up the matter by saying it was a very picturesque corner of the estate and a pity to spoil it.

Aymer flung the papers down violently.

"That's all you care for, or are likely to care for," he said brutally. "I know I might as well let the estate go to the dogs as try and improve it. Once my father and I are dead, you'll turn it into a damned garden for your own use."

For one second Nevil's face was a study in suppression. He got up and walked across the room, his hands shaking.

Mr. Aston spoke sharply and suddenly.

"Aymer, pull yourself together. You are taking advantage of your position. What circumstances do you imagine give you the right to trample on other people's feelings like this, whenever something or other has put you out? It's outrageous! Keep your temper better in hand, man."

It was so obviously deserved, so terribly direct, and at the same time so calculated to hurt, that Nevil turned on his father with reproachful eyes, and then perceiving his face, said no more.

Aymer became suddenly rigid, and lay still with waves of colour rising to and dying from his face, and his hands clenched.

Mr. Aston waited a moment and then said apologetically and hurriedly, "I'm awfully sorry, Aymer."

"Oh, it had to be done," responded Aymer, turning his face to him with a rueful smile. "I'm a brute. Nevil, old fellow, you ought to give him a V. C. or something; he is positively heroic."

"Don't be an idiot," retorted his father, blushing for all his fifty-eight years, because of a grain of truth in his son's words. For indeed it sometimes requires more courage to be brutal to those we love than to be kind to those we hate.

"Go away, Nevil," continued Mr. Aston good humouredly, "I'll look after Aymer."

Nevil departed, with secret relief, the atmosphere was a little too electrical for his liking.

When he had gone, Mr. Aston went over to his elder son and sat on the edge of the sofa.

"What's really the matter, old chap?" he asked gently.

Aymer related the whole history of the sovereign, Christopher's confession and the subsequent events.

"I dare say he was quite honest about his point of view," he concluded petulantly, "but because I could not see it I lost my temper with him."

His father sat thoughtfully considering the carpet.

"It will be a little hard on Christopher," he said at length, very slowly and without looking up, "if every time he has the misfortune to remind you of his father you lose your temper with him."

Aymer turned sharply.

"What do you mean, sir?"

"I think," went on the elder man steadily, "I think, Aymer, it was not only Christopher's hazy ideas of honour and honesty that angered you, but he forced on your notice the fact that he was his father's son, that he had in him the germs of that quality which has made his father what he is—a successful man. Isn't it so?"

Aymer did not answer. It was true, he knew, however great his wish to disown it. Something of the self-dissatisfaction that had numbed poor little Christopher fell to his share. He felt his father was a little hard on him—he could not really understand his relationship to the boy.

"It is not quite fair on Christopher, is it?" said Mr. Aston very gently, "at least that is how it strikes me. I do not want to interfere between you, but I do want you to do yourself full justice in dealing with him."

Aymer looked suddenly up at his father and laughed. "It is evidently not only Christopher who is in disgrace to-day," he said ruefully. "I wish I could in turn upbraid you with unfairness, but Christopher has the pull over me there."

He held out his hand. It was a great concession in Aymer to show even this much demonstration of feeling unasked, and it was appreciated.

"You might say good-night to Christopher when you go upstairs," Aymer said casually a little later, and his father nodded assent, by no means deceived by the indifferent tone. Both Aymer and Christopher slept the better for his ministrations that night.

CHAPTER VII

At the end of February the elder Astons returned to town and Marden Court was no longer mere vague locality to Christopher, but the "home" of those he loved, the centre piece of their lives, and he had a share in it himself.

Still he was very happy to find himself back at Aston House. Its many deserted rooms, the long, silent corridors and its strange spacious emptiness lent themselves to his robust imagination more easily than the living friendly warmth of the old house, brimful of actualities. He re-explored every corner of house and garden in the first days of return, interviewed the staff collectively and individually, from Warren the butler, to the new scullery boy. He rearranged his books and hunted up half-forgotten treasures, slid down the shiny banisters fifty times a day and dispelled the silent lurking shadows with a merry whistle and a laugh that woke an echo in quiet rooms. But he regretted Patricia. It would have been very pleasant to take his turn at showing her round—Patricia had only been in London once,—and there would have been plenty to show her. Lessons, however, recommenced almost at once and Christopher was left with little time for regrets. Life fell back into its old grooves with the solitary difference that those grooves seemed deeper worn and more familiar than he had imagined. The months no longer only presented possible problems; he could consult his memory as to what had previously been at such a time or in like conditions.

He was also given much greater liberty now and encouraged to go out by himself, and to do errands for Mr. Aston or Aymer. It was a proud day for him when Aymer first sent him to The House with a letter for Mr. Aston, who was acting secretary on a Committee at the time. Christopher had had to wait and had sat outside a Committee room door and watched men go to and fro, men whose faces were dimly familiar to a student of illustrated papers, and men who were strange, but all men doing something in return for the good things the world had given them. Such at least was Christopher's innocent belief. Aymer did not disillusion him.

He used to recount his small adventures to Cæsar in the evenings and was encouraged to form his own conclusions from what he had noticed and to confirm existing ideas from actual life. Such conclusions and ideas were naturally often childish and illogical, but Cæsar never appeared to find them laughable and would give careful and illuminating consideration to the most chaotic theories.

The everlasting problem of riches and poverty, happiness and misery often came uppermost, and on this point Christopher was assuredly, but quite unconsciously, as illuminating to Aymer as Aymer was to him. There were certain points of view, certain lines of thought with regard to the attitude of these "under-world" people, which Christopher knew without knowing how, and which, flashing out unexpectedly, would dissolve philanthropic theories wholesale. Aymer would retell them to his father afterwards, who in turn would bring them out in his quiet, unexpected way in one of those wonderfully eloquent speeches of his that made the whole list of "Societies" court him as a dinner guest and speaker, and political coteries sigh with pained surprise at his refusal to stand for Parliament.

Christopher, indeed, possessed to a full degree the power of absorbing the mental atmosphere in which he lived and of becoming a sort of visible incarnation of it. Places and people who had thus once found expression in him could always bring to the surface again that particular phase of existence they had originally stamped on his mind. The Christopher who wandered amongst the wharfs and warehouses in that vague region across the river, remembered and was concerned over quite different matters to the happy boy who rode every morning in the Row with Mr. Aston.

There were many people to and fro to Aston House: Men who were a power in the world; men who would be so, and men who had been, as well as many of no note at all. They came to consult Charles Aston on every conceivable thing under the sun, from questions of high politics to the management of a refractory son. They did not always take his advice, nor did he always offer it, but they invariably came away with a more definite sense of their own meaning and aims, and somehow such aims were generally a little more just, a shade more honest, or a little higher than they had imagined when they started out. Charles Aston was still alluded to by men of high repute as "the man who might have been," yet many there were who, had they considered it carefully, might have said to themselves that "might have been" was less well than "has been." Very occasionally he entertained and Constantia came to play hostess for him. On these occasions Aymer rarely appeared at dinner, but a few privileged guests visited him afterwards and kept alive the tradition that Charles Aston's son, that poor fellow Aymer, was an even more brilliant conversationalist and keener wit than his father. But as a rule very few from the outside penetrated as far as the Garden Wing of Aston House, and Aymer and Christopher continued to lead a peaceful and uninterrupted existence there.

Christopher continued to occupy his leisure with a prodigious number of pets and the construction of mechanical contrivances for their convenience, in which he showed no little ingenuity. There were occasionally tragedies in connection with the pets which were turned to good account by the master of their fate even at the expense of his own feelings—and fingers—as on the occasion when he cremated a puppy-dog who had come to an untimely end. Cæsar objected to this experiment, and when the next catastrophe occurred, which was to a guinea-pig, a more commonplace funeral had to be organised.

But this tragedy became curiously enough linked with a new memory in Christopher's mind, of more lasting importance than the demise of "Sir Joshua Reynolds" of the brown spots.

It happened this-wise. Sir Joshua having stolen a joyous but unsafe hour of liberty fell a victim to the cunning of the feline race. Christopher rescued the corpse and heaped tearful threats of vengeance on the murderess, and then tore into Cæsar's room to find sympathy and comfort. He tumbled in at the window with Sir Joshua in his arms, and flung himself on Cæsar before he had observed the presence of a visitor—a stranger, too. He was a big, florid man, with a good-natured face and great square chin, and he was standing with his back to the fire, looking very much at home. He gave a slight start as Christopher tumbled in, and a queer little cynical smile dawned on his face as he watched the two.

"Hallo, Aymer, I didn't know you had—"

"Go and get ready for tea, Christopher," interrupted Aymer peremptorily, "and take out that animal. Don't you see I have a visitor?"

Christopher, who had just perceived the stranger, hardly disguised his lack of appreciation of so inopportune a caller, and went out to see what consolation could be got out of Vespasian. When he returned, tidy and clean, even to Vespasian's satisfaction, he found the two men talking hard and slipped quietly into his seat behind the little tea-table hoping to be unobserved; but Cæsar called him out of it.

"Peter," he said, "let me present my adopted son to you. Christopher, shake hands with Mr. Masters."

The big man and the small boy looked at each other gravely, and then Christopher extended his hand. Aymer looked out of the window and apparently took no notice of them.

"How do you do, sir?"

"What's your name besides Christopher?" demanded the visitor. He had queer, light blue, piercing eyes that were curiously unexpressive and looked through one to the back of one's head, but, unlike Mr. Aston's kind, steady gaze, that invited one to open one's soul to it, the immediate impulse here was to pull down the blinds of one's individuality in hasty self-defence, and realise, even in doing it, that it was too late.

"Aston," said Christopher, rather hastily, escaping to the tea-table.

Peter Masters looked from him to Aymer with the same queer smile.

"Good-looking boy, Aymer," he said carelessly. "You call him Aston?"

"We've given him our own name," said Aymer steadily, "because it saves complications and explanations."

"A very wise precaution. What are you going to do with him eventually?"

"I hardly know yet. What were you saying about the strike?"

They fell to discussing a recent labour trouble in the Midlands, and Christopher gathered a hazy notion that their visitor employed vast numbers of men who were not particularly fond of him, and for whom he had not only no affection, but no sort of feeling whatever, except as instruments of his will.

Christopher was very glad he was not one of them; he felt rather hostile to the big, careless, opulent man who spoke to Aymer with a familiarity that Christopher resented and had already apparently forgotten his own small existence.

The forget was but apparent, however, for presently he turned sharply to the boy and asked him if he had ever been down a coal mine. Christopher, putting control on his own hot curiosity to explore the subject, answered that he had not, and gave Mr. Masters his second cup of tea without any sugar to emphasise his own indifference to the questioner, who unfortunately never noticed the omission, but drank his tea with equal satisfaction.

"Ever been over an iron foundry?" persisted Mr. Masters, with the same scrutinising gaze.

Cæsar was playing with his favourite long tortoise-shell paper-knife; he seemed unusually indifferent to Christopher's manners, nor did he intervene to save him from the string of sharp questions that ensued.

Christopher made effort to answer the questioner with ordinary politeness, but he was not communicative, and Mr. Masters presently leant back in his chair and laughed.

"Young man, you'll get on in the world," he said approvingly, "for you've learnt the great secret of keeping your own counsel. I prophesy you'll be a successful man some day."

Christopher was not at all elated at the prospect. He was wondering why Aymer drank no tea, also wondering how long the visitor meant to stay. There seemed no sign of departing in him, so Christopher asked if he might go and bury the guinea-pig with Vespasian's help. Aymer nodded permission without speaking.

"A cute lad," remarked Mr. Masters; "what are you going to do with him?"

"I do not know yet."

"Put him in the iron trade. 'Prentice him to me. There's something in him. Did you say you didn't know who his father was?" He shot one of his quick glances at Aymer.

The tortoise-shell paper-knife snapped in two. Aymer fitted the ends together neatly.

"No, I didn't," he answered very deliberately. "I told you he was my adopted son. I adopted him in order to have something to do."

"Oh, yes. Of course, of course." A slow smile spread over his big face. "Think of Aymer Aston of all men in the world playing at being a family man!"

He leant back in his chair and laughed out his great hearty laugh whose boyish ring, coupled with the laugher's easy careless manners, had snared so many fish into the financial net.

"They'd like to make a family man of me again—do their dear little best—but I'm not such a fool as they think me. Men with brains and ambitions don't want a wife. You miss less than you think, old chap," he went on with the colossal tactlessness habitual to him when his own interests were not at stake; "a wife plays the devil with one's business. I *know*." He nodded gloomily, the smile lost under a heavy frown.

Aymer put down very carefully the broken toy he had been playing with. Peter's elephantine tread was so great that it had almost overstepped its victim. At all events Aymer gave no outward sign that he felt it except in his deepened colour and a faint straightening of the lips.

"What on earth do you do with yourself?" went on Peter thoughtfully; "the care of a kid like that doesn't absorb all your brains, I know."

"What would you recommend me to do?" asked Aymer quietly.

"With your head for figures and your leisure you should take to the Market. Have a machine and tapes fitted up in reach, and, by Jove! in a quiet spot like this, out of the way of other men's panics and nonsense, you could rule the world."

"The Market, I think you said."

"Same thing. Think of it, Aymer," he went on eagerly and genuinely interested in his proposition, whether spontaneous or not. He began walking up and down the room, working out his idea with that grasp of detail that had made him the millionaire he was.

"You could have the instruments and a private wire fixed up along the wall there, and your sofa by them. A clerk over there: it would be a sort of companion. You've plenty of capital to start with, and wouldn't have to lose your head at the first wrong deal. Of course you'd want someone the other end, a figurehead and mouthpiece, and someone to show you the lines, start you off; I'd be pleased to do it. We could make a partnership concern of it, if you liked."

There was a quick sidelong glint in his eyes towards Aymer as he came to a stand near the sofa.

"What particular results would you expect?" inquired Aymer, knowing the only plan to keep the enthusiast at bay was to humour him.

"Why, man, you might be the greatest power in the world—you—the unseen, unknown, mysterious Brain—you would have time—you would escape the crazy influences that ruin half the men 'on 'Change'—and you've got the head for it. Calculation, nerve, everything. It would be just the thing for you. You'd forget all about not being able to walk in a week. I wonder why none of us have thought of it before."

"I'm getting used to it after twelve years," said Aymer, with shut teeth; "the objection to your scheme is that I do not happen to want money."

"Power, power, man," cried the other impatiently. "Money is just metal, its value lies in the grip it gives you over other men, and if you don't even care for that, there's the joy of chancing it. And you were a born gambler, Aymer, you can't deny that," he laughed heartily, but also again came the quick sidelong glint of his eyes. "Think of it, old fellow," he said carelessly, dropping his enthusiastic tone, "it would be a good deal better for you than doing nothing. It's such wicked waste."

For the first time Aymer winced.

"I'll think of it, and let you know if it's likely to be entertained. I have the boy, you know; that gives me something to do."

"Poof! Let him bring himself up if you want to make a successful man of him. The more he educates himself, the better he'll get on. If you do it, you'll make him soft. *I* know! Public School: University: Examinations, and £200 a year if he's lucky. That's your education! All very well if you are born with a golden spoon in your mouth and can afford to be a fool. If you can't, better learn to rough-and-tumble it in the world. Education doesn't make successful men."

"You were not exactly uneducated, Peter," said Aymer drily.

Peter grinned.

"Ah, but I was a genius. I couldn't help it. It would have been the same had I been born in the gutter. No, I believe in the rough-and-tumble school to make hard-headed men."

"Well, for all you know, Christopher may be a genius, or be born with a golden spoon in his mouth."

The other looked up sharply.

"Nevil has a boy of his own, hasn't he?"

"Don't be a fool if you can help it, Peter. Other people have golden spoons besides the gilded Aston family."

Peter shrugged his shoulders. "It's no business of mine, of course, but the boy looks sharp. Pity to spoil him. Ha, Ha. I don't spoil mine."

He got up yawning and sauntered over to the fireplace and so did not see Aymer's rigid face go white and then red.

"I've got a boy—I think it's a boy—somewhere. Daresay you've forgotten. You weren't very sociable, poor old chap, when it happened. About a year after your accident. He's about somewhere or other. Oh, I back my own theories! I don't suppose he's a genius, so the rough-and-tumble school for *him*."

"You know the school?"

"I can put my hand on him when I want to—that's not yet. The world can educate him till I'm ready to step in."

"If he'll have you."

Peter chuckled. "He won't be a fool—even if he's not a genius. Well, you think of my proposition, I'll go halves."

"How you have disappointed me, Peter. I thought you called from a disinterested desire to see me after all these years."

"Twelve years, isn't it? Well, you look better than you did then. I didn't think you would come through—didn't think you meant to. I'm sorry to miss Cousin Charles. He doesn't approve of me, but he's too polite to say so, even in a letter. How does he wear?"

"Well, on the whole. He works too hard."

The other spread out his hands.

"Works. And to what end? I'm glad to have seen you again. It's like old times, if you weren't on that beastly sofa, poor old chap."

"Perhaps you will call again when father is in," said Aymer steadily, with a mute wonder if a square inch of him was left unbruised.

"To tell the truth, I'm rarely in London. I work from Birmingham and New York, and calling is an expensive amusement to a busy man."

"Produces nothing?"

"Yes, a good deal of pleasure. It's worth it occasionally."

He stood over his cousin, looking down at him with quite genuine concern and liking in his eyes. His size, his aggressiveness, his blundering disregard of decency towards trouble, everything about him was on such a gigantic scale that one could not weigh him by any accepted standard. Aymer knew it, and notwithstanding Peter's unique powers of hurting him to the soul, he made no attempt to scale him, but met him on his own ground and ignored the torture.

"What has it cost you exactly, this visit?"

Peter considered quite gravely.

"Let me see. I was to have seen Tomlands. He's ceding his rights in the Lodal Valley Affair and his figure goes up each day." He considered again. "Three thousand," he answered with a wide grin.

"I am abashed at my value," said Aymer gravely. "I daren't ask you to come again now."

"Oh, I'll have an extravagant fit again, some day. Where's the boy?" His hand was in his pocket and Aymer heard the chink of coin.

"At work, or should be. Don't tip him, please, Peter. He has as much as he needs."

"How do you know? A boy needs as much as he can get. Well, don't forget my advice. Don't educate him."

He was gone at last. Presumably to gather in the Lodal Rights before their value further increased.

Charles Aston did not betray any particular sorrow at missing the visitor.

"It's rather odd his turning up again now after forgetting our existence so long," he remarked, frowning. "Of course we've had correspondence—not very agreeable either."

"I can hardly wonder at his not coming to see me, at all events. It's nearly twelve years since we met, and I wasn't very polite to him that time," said Aymer wearily.

"There was a reasonable excuse for you."

"I'm afraid I did not consider reason much in those days, sir. If he'd been a saint in disguise I should have behaved like a brute just the same."

Charles Aston came and stood looking down with a kind, quiet, satisfied smile. The attitude was the same as Peter Masters' and Aymer, remembering it, smiled too.

"What did he really want, Aymer? He never came for nothing."

"To induce me to go on the Stock-Exchange in partnership with him, I think. Thought it would be less boring than lying here all day with nothing to do."

Charles Aston opened his mouth to protest and shut it resolutely, turned and walked down the room ruffling his hair, so that when he went back to Aymer, his iron-grey thatch was more picturesque than neat.

Aymer laughed.

"Who's lost his temper now?" he demanded.

His father looked in a glass and, perceiving the devastation, attempted to remedy it.

"I'm awfully sorry," he said with much contrition, "but I can't keep my temper over Peter. Has he improved?"

"Not a bit. He doesn't hurt, father, he's too big," he paused a moment, "he saw Christopher."

Mr. Aston gave Aymer a scrutinising glance.

"It was unavoidable, I suppose."

"I did not try to stop it."

"And the result?"

"There was no result except he appeared impressed with his mental capacity."

Mr. Aston ruffled his hair again in a perturbed manner.

"Didn't he see his likeness to his mother, Aymer?"

"Apparently not. It's not so strong as it was. He offered me advice on his upbringing."

"Did he?" with an indignant shake of the head.

"All in good faith," said Aymer steadily, "he said he didn't approve of education; as a proof of his sincerity, he cited the line he was taking with his own boy."

There was a silence.

"He said he could put his hand on him when he liked." Aymer's voice was quite level and inexpressive, but his father leant forward and put his hand on his, saying hastily.

"He always says that. He believes it just a matter of money. It was his one answer to all my remonstrances. When he wanted him he could find him—not before. Aymer, I wish I'd been at home. Why did you see him?"

"I could hardly refuse; it would have been churlish—unpolitic. I did not know why he came. He was evidently struck with Christopher."

He laughed a little unsteadily, but his father smothered a sigh and watched him with curious solicitude. The unwritten law that Christopher had learnt so well had been very heavily infringed, and Charles Aston had no liking for the man who had infringed it, though he was his first cousin.

He was weighing in his mind what his son must have suffered in that interview, and trying to see if it could have been foreseen and prevented.

Peter and Aymer, who was only five years his junior, had been great friends in the far-off days before the tragedy, but the former was too nearly, though half unconsciously, connected with that to be a possible intimate for Aymer now. The possibility of his turning up in this casual manner, ignoring with ruthless amiability all that had passed, had really never occurred to either father or son, and they were both unprepared for a narrowly escaped crisis. But Aymer was evidently not going to own frankly how great had been the strain and how badly he had suffered under it. He set his pride to heal his bruised feelings, however, applauding himself secretly for not betraying to his cousin the torture to which he had unintentionally put him. But he could not, having done this, altogether put it from him, and the subject of Peter Masters cropped up next morning when Christopher was sitting on the edge of Cæsar's bed.

Aymer asked him abruptly what he thought of the visitor of the previous day.

"I don't like him at all. I think he's beastly," was Master Christopher's emphatic verdict.

"He is my second cousin, his mother was an Aston, and he is one of the richest men in England, if not quite the richest. He is thought rich even in America."

"And horrid, too, just the same: only perhaps I oughtn't to say so as he is your cousin," added the boy with sudden confusion.

Aymer regarded him with an introspective air.

"He is a strange man, though many people don't like him. We were great friends once."

Christopher opened his eyes very wide.

"*You*—and Mr. Masters?"

"Yes—when I was a young man like others. We quarrelled—or rather I quarrelled—he came to see me when I was first—ill," he jerked the word out awkwardly, but never took his eyes from Christopher's face. "I was perfectly brutal to him. That's twelve years ago. Most men would never have spoken to me again, but he doesn't bear malice."

"He wouldn't mind what anyone said to him," persisted Christopher; "fancy your being friends!"

"You like me best then?"

Master Christopher caught up a pillow and hurled it at him, and then made a violent effort to smother him under it.

"I think you're almost as nasty—when you say things like that, Cæsar."

"Then retreat from my company and tell Vespasian his baby is waiting to be dressed."

Vespasian found his master in one of his rare inconsequent moods, talking nonsense with provoking persistence and exercising his wits in teasing everyone who came in his way.

Vespasian smiled indulgently and spent his leisure that day in assisting Christopher to construct a man-of-war out of empty biscuit boxes and cotton reels, for he was dimly possessed of the idea that the boy was in some way connected with his master's unusually good spirits.

CHAPTER VIII

It was not until Christopher had passed his fourteenth birthday that he came face to face once more with the distant past. He had crossed Westminster Bridge to watch the trams on the other side, and from there, being in an adventurous mood, he had wandered out into vague regions lying beyond, regions of vast warehouses, of narrow, dirty streets and squalid houses, of sudden palaces of commerce towering over the low tide of mean roofs. Suddenly turning a corner, he had come on a block of "model dwellings," and an inrush of memories brought him to a standstill before the giant ugly pile.

There, on the topmost floor of the east corner of Block D, had lived Martha Sartin, and Marley Sartin, packer at one of the big warehouses near, also Jessie Sartin and numerous other Sartins, including Sam, who was about Christopher's age; there in the dull asphalt court Sam and Christopher had played, and up that steep stairway had climbed in obedience to husky shouts from over the iron railings of the top landing.

It was all so vivid, so unaltered, so sharply set in Christopher's mind that he had to look down at his own immaculate blue suit and unpatched boots to reassure himself he was not waiting for Martha's shrill order to "come up out of the dirt." But assured once more of his own present personality he could not resist exploring further, and went right up to the foot of the iron staircase and looked up. It was all just as sordid and dirty and unlovely as ever, though he had not known before the measure of its undesirableness. Leaning over the railing of the top landing was an untidy-looking woman in a brown skirt and half-fastened blouse. She looked over into the yard and shouted in a voice that made Christopher jump.

"Jim, come up out of the dirt, you little varmint!"

And Christopher, erstwhile Jim, leant against the wall and felt his head was whirling round. Then he inspected himself again, but at that moment a shock-headed dirty mite of four years brushed past him and began to clamber up the stairs, pushing his way through the horde of small babies on each landing and squealing shrilly, "I'm coming, Mammie."

Christopher went too. He could not possibly have resisted the impulse, for assuredly it was Martha's voice that called—called him back willy nilly to the past that after all was not so far past except in a boy's measure of time.

A dark-eyed, decent-looking woman passed him on the stair and looked at him curiously; further on a man, smoking a pipe, took the trouble to follow him to the next floor in a loafing fashion. The small Jim, out of breath and panting with the exertion of the climb, was being roughly dusted by an undoubted Martha when Christopher reached the topmost landing. She was stouter than of yore, and her hair was no longer done up in iron curlers as of old, also a baby, younger than Jim, was crawling out of the room on the right. But it was Martha Sartin, and Christopher advanced a friendly hand.

Mrs. Sartin gazed at the apparition with blank amazement. She could connect the tall, pleasant-faced boy in his spotless suit and straw hat with nothing in her memory. He did not look as if he could belong to the theatre at which she was a dresser, but it seemed the only solution.

"Are you come from Miss Vassour?" she asked doubtfully.

"Don't you know me, Mrs. Sartin?"

"Know ye? No. How should I?"

"I'm Jim Hibbault."

"Garn!"

"Yes, I am really." Poor Christopher began to feel embarrassed and a little disappointed.

He *was* Jim Hibbault at that moment and he felt queerly lonely and stranded.

Martha pulled down her sleeves and went to the inner door.

"Jessie, come out 'ere," she screamed.

Christopher felt his heart go thump. He had almost forgotten Jessie, yet Jessie had been more to him than Martha in other days. It was Jessie who had taken him for walks, carried him up the steep stairs on her back, shared sweets with him, cuffed her brother Sam when they fought, and had finally taken little Jim Hibbault back to his mother when the great clock in the distance struck six,—Jessie, who at eleven had been a complete little mother and was at sixteen a tall, lanky, untidy girl who had inherited the curling pins of her mother and whose good-natured, not ill-looking face was not improved thereby.

She came to the doorway and stood looking over her mother's arm at Christopher.

"Ever seed 'im afore?" demanded Mrs. Sartin.

"Well I never, if it ain't Jimmy!" cried Jessie, beaming, and Christopher could have embraced her if it were in accordance with the custom of his years, and he felt less inclined to bolt down the stairs out of reach of his adventure.

Neither of the two women expressed any pleasure at his appearance. Mrs. Sartin accepted her daughter's recognition of their visitor as sufficient evidence it was not a hoax, and asked Christopher in.

The room, though the window was open, smelt just as stuffy as of old, and a familiar litter of toys and odds and ends strewed the floor. Christopher missed the big tea-tray and Britannia metal teapot, but the sofa with broken springs was still there, covered as it had ever been with the greater part of the family wardrobe.

Christopher sat in the armchair, and Mrs. Sartin, having plumped the baby into its chair, sat down by the door. The small Jimmy pulled at her apron. Jessie leant against the wall and giggled. No one said anything. Christopher began to wish he had not come.

"I never could remember the name of this place," he began at last, desperately. "I just came on it by accident to-day, and remembered everything all at once."

"Shilla Buildings, that's what it's called," said Mrs. Sartin nodding her head. "Block 7, C. Door."

Silence again. A strict sense of etiquette prevented either of the feminine side of the company from uttering the question burning on their tongues.

"I did see Sam once, a long time ago," Christopher struggled on, "but I could not catch him." He got red and embarrassed again.

"'Ows your Ma?" asked Mrs. Sartin at last.

"She's dead," explained Christopher very gravely, "five years ago now—more."

"Lor'. To think of it. I never thought she was one to live long. And she went back to her friends after all, I suppose."

It was not a question: it was only a statement to be confirmed or contradicted or ignored as the hearer liked.

"She died in the Union at Whitmansworth," said Christopher bluntly. "I lived there afterwards and then someone adopted me. Mr. Aymer Aston, son of Mr. Aston. Perhaps you know the name."

Mrs. Sartin appeared to consult an imaginary visiting list.

"No, I can't say as I do. Do you, Jessie?"

Jessie shook her head. She had ceased to look at their visitor; instead, she looked at his boots, and her cheeks grew red.

"I thought I would like to see if you were still here."

"Very good of you, I'm sure." It was not meant ironically, it was solely addressed to the blue suit and brown boots, but it nearly reduced the wearer of these awe-inspiring clothes to tears.

For the moment, in the clutch of the past, with associations laying gripping hands on him and with his curious faculty of responding to the outward call, Aston House and the Astons became suddenly a faint blurred impression to Christopher, less real and tangible than these worn, sordid surroundings. Had anyone just then demanded his name he would undoubtedly have responded "Hibbault." He felt confused and wretched, alive to the fact that little Jim Hibbault had neither people nor home nor relations in the world, if these once kindly women had no welcome for him.

"I heard you call Jim," he hazarded at last, in an extremity of disconcerted shyness.

Mrs. Sartin eyed the four-year-old nestling in her apron and pulled him from cover.

"Yes, that be Jim. We called 'im Jim arter you. He was born arter you an' your ma went away."

He longed to ask after Marley of unhappy memory, but the possibilities were too apparent for him to venture, so silence again fell over them.

At this precise juncture of affairs a shrill whistle was heard ascending the stairway, growing momentarily louder and louder till it became earsplitting in intensity as it arrived on landing No. 6. The author of it pulled open the door and the whistle tailed off into a faint "phew" at sight of the embarrassed group. The new-comer was a thin-faced lad with light sandy hair cropped close to his square head. He had light, undetermined eyes that were keen and lively. Christopher had beaten him in the matter of size, but there were latent possibilities in his ill-developed form.

Christopher sprang up and rushed forward, then suddenly stopped.

"Ullo, mother, didn't know as 'ow you 'ad swell company this arternoon. I'd 'ave put on my best suit and topper," he grinned affably as he deposited on the floor a big basket he carried.

"Oh, I say, Sam—don't you know me either?" began poor Christopher.

He wheeled round, stared hard, and a broad smile of recognition spread over his face.

"Why, if it ain't Jim," he cried and seized his hand with a fervour that set Christopher aglowing and strangely enough set him free from the clinging shadow of his lost identity. *This* was tangible flesh and blood and of the real authentic present.

"Well, I'm blowed," ejaculated Sam, stepping back to look at his erstwhile companion, "to think of you turning up again such a toff. No need to ask what sort of luck came *your* way. My. Ain't 'e a swell, just."

But unlike the women, he was unabashed by externals. He demanded "tea" of his mother that very moment, "cos 'e 'adn't no time for dinner and 'is bloke 'ad sent 'im round to get a bit o' somethink now," at a slack hour.

"Greengrocer business, Clare Street," he explained. "Seven shillings a week. Not a bad old cove. What d'yer say about yourself?"

He had the whole history out of Christopher in five minutes.

The women listened and flung in "Well, I never's," and "Who'd 'ave thought it's" from time to time and thawed into ordinary human beings under Sam's convivial example. In the end Sam offered sincere if oddly-expressed congratulations, and disappeared into the back kitchen to wash his hands. Jessie, too, vanished mysteriously, eventually returning minus the curling pins and plus a row of impossible curls and a bright blue blouse bedecked with cheap lace. Mrs. Sartin meanwhile tidied up by kicking the scattered toys under the sofa.

"Them sisters what looks arter the poor is always givin' broken rubbish to the children," she exclaimed. "Not but what they mean it kindly, but it makes a heap of muck to clear up."

Christopher nodded his head comprehendingly, by no means so hurt at her ingratitude as a real Christopher Aston might have been.

The good woman bustled about, and eventually the family drew up round the tea table. The cloth might have been cleaner, the cups and saucers have borne a longer acquaintance with water, and there was a spoon short, though no one was so ill-mannered as to allude to it. Jessie unobtrusively shared hers with her mother under cover of the big tea-pot. There was bread and a yellow compound politely alluded to as butter, and a big pot of jam. The younger Sartins gorged silently on this, all unreproved by a preoccupied mother. Mrs. Sartin, indeed, became quite voluble and told Christopher how she was now first dresser at the Kings Theatre and how Jessie was just taken on in the wardrobe room.

"Which is uncertain *hours*," Mrs. Sartin explained, "but it's nice to be together in the same 'ouse, and one couldn't want a kinder gentleman than Mr. X. to do with. I've been there ten years and never 'ad a cross word with 'im. And 'e was that good when Marley was took, and never turned me off as some of 'em do." She stopped suddenly under the stress of Sam's lowering countenance. Jessie hastily passed her bread, "which I thanks you for, but will say what I was a-goin' to, for all Sam's kicks under the table," continued the hostess, defiantly regarding her confused offspring.

The confusion spread to Christopher, who looked at his plate and got red. Sam pushed back his chair; there was a very ugly scowl on his face. His undaunted mother addressed herself to their guest.

"No woman ever 'ad a better 'usband than Marley, though I ses it, but Sam here 's that 'ard 'e won't let me speak of my own man if 'e can 'elp 'it. 'Is own father, too. Ah, if 'e 'ad 'ad a bad father, Sam would 'ave know what to be thankful for."

"I'm thankful 'e's gone," burst out Sam, with sudden anger. "I asks you, 'ow's a cove to get on when he's 'itched up to a father wot's done time? Why, old Greenum gave me a shillin' a week less than 'e ought, cos why, 'e knew I couldn't 'old out with a father like that," and he eyed his mother wrathfully.

"A better 'usband no woman 'ad," sobbed Mrs. Sartin. "When 'e came out 'e didn't seem to get no chance and so...."

"Is he in London?" asked Christopher, nervously gulping down some tea.

"No—sloped," said Sam, shortly, "cribbed some other chap's papers I guess—went abroad—we don't know—don't want to, either."

The fierce hostility and resentment in the boy's voice made it clear to Christopher this was evidently a subject better dropped. He seized the chance of directing Jessie's attention to Master Jim Sartin, who was brandishing the bread-knife, and plunged hastily into a description of the doings of Charlotte and Max. Mrs. Sartin accepted the diversion, but kept an anxious eye on Sam, who ate hard and seemed to recover some of his ordinary composure with each mouthful, much to Christopher's amazement. By the time tea was finished he was himself again. There was no lingering then. He went back to work. Christopher said he must go too, and bade the family good-bye. The farewell was as cordial as the welcome had been cold and he clattered downstairs after Sam with many promises to come again.

The two boys talked freely of the passing world as they went through the streets, in the purely impersonal way of their age, and it was with great diffidence and much hesitation Christopher managed to hint he'd like to buy something for the kiddies.

Sam grinned.

"Sweets," he suggested. "They eat 'em up and leave no mess about."

Christopher turned out his pockets. There was an unbroken ten shillings, three shillings and some coppers.

They walked on a while gravely and came to a stand before a confectioner's window.

"Cake," suggested Sam, with one eye on his companion and one on the show of food within.

"A sugar one?"

"They cost a lot," said Sam shaking his head, but he followed Christopher inside. Christopher boldly demanded the price of a small wedding cake elaborately iced. It was five shillings.

He put down the money with a lofty air and desired them to send it without loss of time to Mrs. Sartin's address.

The woman stared a little at the oddly assorted couple, but the money rang true and the order was booked.

As they hurried towards Clare Street, Christopher diffidently asked if there was anything Mrs. Sartin would like, and Sam's sharp wits seized the occasion to please his mother and Christopher and serve himself at the same time.

"Come on to my place and send her some lettuce," he suggested. "Mother's main fond of lettuce. We've got some good 'uns in this morning."

It was strictly true; it was also true that Master Sam had outstayed his meal-time and a new customer might help to avert the probable storm awaiting him, as indeed it did.

Mr. Gruner, greengrocer, was standing at the door of his shop looking both ways down the street at once, owing to a remarkable squint, and his reception of Sam was unfriendly, but quickly checked at the sight of his companion, whose extraordinary terms of intimacy with his errand boy rendered the good man nearly speechless. The young gent, however, ordered lettuces and green peas with a free hand and earned Sam's pardon, as anticipated by that far-sighted youth.

The two boys said good-bye and Sam made no hint as to the possibilities of a future meeting, neither did Christopher, embarrassed by the presence of the greengrocer. He also would be late and hurried off, hoping he might still be in time to give Aymer tea and relate his adventures. He had no misgivings at all as to Cæsar's approval of his doings.

As he came out into a main thoroughfare again he passed a big cheap drapery establishment and something in the gaudy, crude colouring there displayed brought him to a standstill. Jessie was still unprovided with a present. The two had exchanged very few words, but she by no means loomed in the background of the picture. He stood staring at the window and fingering the remaining coins in his pocket. One section of the shop front was hung with gaily-coloured feather boas. He was dimly conscious he had seen Mrs. Wyatt wear something of the sort in soft grey. There was a blue one that was the colour of Jessie's blouse, or so Christopher thought, hanging high up. He did not admire it at all, but it suggested Jessie to him and after a moment's consideration he boldly pushed through the swinging doors and marched up the shop.

"I want one of those feather things in the window," he announced to the shop-walker's assiduous attentions.

He was delivered over to the care of an amused young woman, who proceeded to show him feather boas of all descriptions and qualities. Christopher was adamant.

"I want a blue thing that's hanging up in the window, last but one on the top row," he insisted, disdaining to look at the fluffy abominations spread around him. He was sure they were not like the thing Constantia wore now, but it was too late to retreat.

The young woman showed him one she declared was identical.

"I want the one in the window," he persisted doggedly.

In the end he got it, paid for it, saw it packed up and addressed, and quenching sundry misgivings in his heart, marched out of the shop and treated himself to a bus homeward.

It is perhaps not out of place to mention here that Jessie had no misgivings as to the real beauty of the present. She had sighed long for such a possession, and having never seen Mrs. Wyatt's delicate costly wrap, was perfectly content with her own and applauded Christopher's taste loudly.

CHAPTER IX

Christopher continued to visit the Sartins and to find considerable pleasure in Sam's companionship, who on his few holidays was only too glad to explore the grey river and its innumerable wharfs with Christopher. Sam was already a fair waterman; he at least spent all his scant leisure and scantier pennies in learning that arduous profession.

Once Mr. Aston visited Block D. with Christopher, and lingered behind gossiping to Mrs. Sartin while the boy went to meet Sam, expected home to tea. Sam got nothing out of his mother anent that conversation except the information that Mr. Aston was "a real Christian gentleman, who knew what trouble was, and don't you make any mistake, but as 'ow Mr. Christopher was a lucky young gentleman."

Mr. Aston also found time to visit Sam's master, though on this occasion he was not accompanied by Christopher, who, indeed, chanced to be on the river with Sam Sartin that afternoon.

It must not be imagined that Christopher had no other friends than the humble Sartins. Besides the Wyatt household, half a dozen families with boys of his age welcomed him gladly enough, but though he was on good terms with these and though not one of the boys could afford to despise him as an antagonist in any sport, yet none of them contrived to have more than a very superficial idea of Christopher Aston. They took to him at once, but he remained just the good-natured, jolly acquaintance of the first day, never more, if never less. Christopher, indeed, though he confessed it to no one, not even to Aymer, felt a little cut off from this pleasant clan, who held the same traditions, the same experiences, and who went through the same training at their various schools, who led indeed a life that differed essentially from Christopher.

He was never conscious of any lack of company. The Astons, old and young, were companions who answered to every need of his energetic mind. He made giant strides in his studies in these days and passed beyond the average into the class of those of real ability. All his well-earned holidays were spent at Marden, where there was always Patricia as a most admirable playfellow.

It was when Christopher was a little over fifteen and Patricia about the same age that the first definite result of their companionship came about.

On the other side of the lake at Marden Court the high road, sunk between a low wall on one side and the upsloping land on the other, ran directly eastward and westward, joining eventually a second Great Road of historic importance to Christopher Aston. The rough ground beyond the road was covered with low scrub, and dwarf twisted hawthorns, with a plentiful show of molehills. Here and there were groups of Scotch firs, and the crest of the hill was wooded with oaks and beeches and a fringe of larches, with here and there a silvery black poplar.

Christopher and Patricia were fond of this rough land that lay beyond the actual park. In early days it had made a glorious stage for "desert islanders," with the isle-studded lake to bound it, whose further shore for the nonce melted into vague mistiness. Later on, when desert islands were out of fashion, it was still good ground to explore, and through the woods away over the hill one came to a delectable wide-spread country, where uncultivated down mingled with cornfields and stretches of clover, a country bounded by long, spacious curving lines of hill and dale, tree-capped ridges and bare contours, with here and there the gash of a chalk pit gleaming white.

Just at a point where a stretch of down-land ran into a little copse, was a small barrow. A round green mound, memento of a forgotten history that was real and visible enough in its own day, as real as the two children of "the Now," with whom the spot was a favourite camping ground.

Patricia, who knew all about barrows from Nevil, used to invent wonderful stories of this one, to which Christopher lent a critical attention, adding here and there a practical touch.

It was he who first suggested exploring the mound, and one day they dragged heavy spades thither and worked hard for an hour or two without great result, when suddenly Patricia began shovelling back her pile of brown earth with feverish haste.

"I don't like it. It is horrid," she panted in return to Christopher's protests. The idea of desecration was so strong on her that when her companion still indignantly protested, the black passion leapt up to life and she flung round at him.

It was then that Christopher made his discovery. He saw the mad flare in her face and flung his strong arms round her from behind, and held her against him with her hands in his gripped fast to her breast.

"Steady on, Patricia," he said sharply, "don't get frightened. You aren't going to get wild this time."

There was no alarm or anger in his voice and a queer, new note of firmness and force. She struggled ineffectually a moment and then came the dangerous quietness that waited a chance.

He could feel her muscles strained and rigid still.

"Patricia," he said quite loudly, "drop it. I won't have it, do you hear? You *can* stop if you like now, and you've got to."

- 83 -

She bent back her head and looked at him, her child face old and worn and disfigured with her still burning fury. She looked right in his eyes: his met hers steady and hard as flints, and through the blind passion of her look he saw her soul leap up, appealing, piteous, and by heaven-taught instinct, he answered that.

"It's all right, Patricia, you are safe enough. I'm not going to let you make a fool of yourself, my dear; don't be afraid. Stop thinking. Look at the dark shadows over there—on the cornfield. They'll cut that next week."

Little by little he loosed his grasp on her as he felt the tension slacken, and presently she stood free, still dazed and bewildered. Christopher picked up a spade and whistled.

"All the same, you are right, Patricia," he said thoughtfully, "it does seem a shame to disturb the old Johnny, and creepy too. I'll fill up."

He continued to work hard, watching her out of the corner of his eye, but talking cheerfully. Presently she took up her spade and made a poor pretence of helping him, but she said nothing till they had done and he suggested a return.

"Do you mind resting a bit, first?"

Her subdued voice called for a scrutinising glance. Then he dropped his spade and flung himself on the grass by her side. A little wind swept up the downland to them, making the brown benets nod in a friendly fashion. The purple scabious, too, nodded cheerfully. Patricia picked one and began stroking it with her fingers. Christopher lay on his back and whistled again softly, watching a lark, as he had watched one five years ago, when a small boy, by the side of the Great Road.

"Christopher, how did you do it?" demanded Patricia abruptly.

"Do what?"

"Stop me."

"I didn't. You stopped yourself."

"I never have before."

"Then you ought to have. You see you can, if you only will think."

"I *can't* think."

"But you did," he insisted, with some reason.

"Because you made me. I'd have been much angrier with anyone else—it was like—like—holding on to a rock, when the water was sucking one away."

"Bosh," said Christopher, sitting upright suddenly.

"Look here, Patricia, it was only that I made you take time to think: no one, even you (he put in rudely enough), could be silly enough to make such a little idiot of yourself if you *thought* a moment. Everyone seems to take it for granted you'll go on being—stupid—or else they are afraid to stop you, and I—well I won't have it, Patricia, that's all. You must jolly well learn to stop."

His boyish words were rougher than his voice, just as his real feeling in the matter was deeper than his expression of it, and secretly he was a little proud of his achievement and felt a subtle proprietorship over his companion that was not displeasing.

Patricia slipped her arm in his and leant her golden head against him.

"Christopher, I want to tell you all I can remember about it. I don't know what anyone else has told you."

"All right, fire away," returned Christopher resignedly.

"The only thing I can remember at all about my father is seeing him get into rages like that with my mother. I can remember him quite well, at all sorts of times; he was very big and fair, and splendid, but always everything I remember ends in that. And I can remember getting in a rage when I was quite little and seeing my mother turn white, and she jumped up and ran out of the room crying out to Renata. My father was killed hunting when I was six years old and mother died when I was nine years old. Renata was married then, you know, so I came to live with her and Nevil. But always I remembered when I was naughty like that, my mother used to look frightened and go away and our old nurse used to come and scold me and watch me till I could have killed her. Renata, darling Renata, used to talk to me after and make me promise to try and be good, but she, too, was really afraid when I was bad. I suppose they had both had so bad a time with father." She stopped, gazing out at a misty half-understood tragedy, whose very dimness woke a faint echo of terror in her heart, for she was as surely the daughter of the woman who had suffered as of the man who had caused the suffering.

"That's all," said Patricia, with a sudden movement, "everyone always takes it as part of me. Nevil says I'll outgrow it. I don't—and Renata cries."

"And I scold you. Anyhow, it isn't part of you in my eyes, but just a beastly sort of thing which you let get hold of you, and then it isn't you at all. It's all rot inheriting things, though of course, if you *think* so—" this young philosopher on the much-debated subject shrugged his shoulders.

"But I don't think so, I don't want to think so," cried poor Patricia; "it's just because you don't think it that you made me feel I can stop it. Oh, Christopher, go on believing I can help it, please."

"But I do. Of course I do. It's a beastly shame anyone ever suggested anything else to you. Come along home, Patricia, it will be tea-time."

This was the establishing of a covenant between the two. Whether it was from the suggestion or the dominant will of the boy himself, or both causes combined, Patricia began to gather strength against her terrible inheritance and, at all events in Christopher's presence, actually did gain some show of control over her fits of passion.

The first of these times, about six months after the covenant on the barrow, Nevil was present. Renata and one of the children had been there also, but Renata had seen the queer pallor creep up in her sister's face before even Christopher had guessed and had straightway hurried off with Master Max, a proceeding which usually precipitated events.

Then Christopher flung down his work and caught her clenched hand in his.

"Stop it, Patricia," he said imperiously.

Nevil held his breath. It was a tradition in the Connell family that interference invariably led to a catastrophe. In his indolent way he had taken this belief on trust, the "laissez faire" policy being well in accordance with his easy nature.

However, tradition was clearly wrong, for after one ineffectual struggle, Patricia stood still and presently said something to Christopher that Nevil did not catch, but he saw the boy free her and Patricia remained silently looking out of the window. Christopher turned to pick up his book, and for the first time remembered Nevil was present and grew rather red. Nevil had watched them both with a speculative eye, for the moment an historian of the future rather than of the past. He said nothing, however, but having discoursed a while on the possibility of skating next day, sauntered away.

He came to anchor eventually in Aymer's room, and sat smoking by the fire, his long legs crossed and the contemplative mood in the ascendency. His brother knew from experience that Nevil had something to say, and would say it in his own inimitable way if left alone.

"Christopher's a remarkable youth," he said presently.

"Have you just discovered it?" said Aymer drily.

"He is no respecter of persons," pursued Nevil quietly; "by the way, has it ever struck you, Aymer, that he'll marry some day?"

"There's time before us, yet. I hope. He isn't quite sixteen, Nevil."

"Yes, but there it is," he waved his hand vaguely. "I think of it for myself when I look at Max sometimes."

Aymer wanted to laugh out loud, which would have reduced his brother's communicative mood to mere frivolity, and he wished to get at what lay behind, so he remained grave.

"There's Patricia, too," went on Nevil in the same vague way. "She, too, will do it some day. It's lamentable, but unavoidable. And talking of Patricia brings me back to Christopher's remarkableness."

He related the little scene he had just witnessed in his slow, clear way, made no comment thereon, but poked the fire meditatively, when he had finished.

Aymer, too, was silent.

"You are her sole guardian, are you not?" he asked presently.

"With Renata. I wonder, Aymer, if anyone could have controlled that unhappy Connell?"

Aymer ignored the irrelevant remark.

"Renata does not count. Nevil, would you have any objections—as her guardian?"

Nevil strolled across to his brother and sat on the edge of his couch. He took up a sandy kitten, descendant of one of Christopher's early pets, and began playing with it, attempting to wrap it up in his handkerchief.

"If you would mind, we will guard against the remote contingency at which you hint, by keeping Christopher away when he is a bit older," said Aymer steadily.

"My dear Cæsar, it's not I who might object—it's you. You know what Patricia is, poor child. I thought it might not fit in with your plans. She hasn't a penny of her own, though, of course, Renata and I will see to that." He knotted the handkerchief at the four corners and swung it to and fro to the astonishment of the imprisoned kitten.

"Christopher has nothing either," said Aymer almost sharply, "and I shall see to that, with your permission, Nevil. That unfortunate kitten!"

Nevil released it. It scampered over the floor, hid under a chair and then rushed back at him and scrambled up his leg.

"Indeed, if things turn out as I hope, I shall have to provide for him," went on Aymer steadily, "indeed I wish to do so anyway. It will mean less for Max, but—"

"What a beastly ugly kitten," remarked Nevil suddenly with great emphasis, placing the animal very gently on the floor again.

"Don't swear, Nevil," retorted Aymer with a little ghost of a smile.

"Very well," answered his brother meekly, "but it is. Aymer, don't be an ass, old fellow—Max won't want anything."

He lounged out presently before Aymer could make up his mind to vex him further with the question of Max's inheritance.

The property set aside for the use of the son and heir of the Astons provided a very handsome income, the original capital of which could not be touched. In early days Aymer had found the income barely sufficient for his wants. He spent it freely now—the Astons were no misers, but his father and he managed to nearly double the original capital and this was Aymer's to do with as he would. Apparently he meant it for Christopher. It was one of Nevil's little weaknesses that he could not endure any reminder of the fact that to him and his small son would the line descend, and that his brother's was but a life interest, and his position as his father's heir a merely formal matter of no actual value. Poor Nevil, who was the least self-seeking of men, could not endure any reminder of his elder brother's real condition of life.

CHAPTER X

There was a certain princely building in Birmingham where all the business connected with the name of Peter Masters was transacted. On each floor were long rooms full of clerks bending over rows of desks, carrying on with automatic regularity the affairs of each separate concern. Thus on the ground floor the Lack Vale Coal Company worked out its grimy history, on the second floor the Brunt Rubber Company had command, on the fifth the great Steel Axle Company, the richest and most important of all, lodged royally. But on the very topmost floor of all were the offices devoted to the personal affairs of Peter Masters, and through them, shut in by a watchful guard of head clerks, was the innermost sanctum, the nest of the great spider whose intricate web stretched over so great a circumference, the central point from which radiated the vast circle of concerns, and to which they ultimately returned materialised into precious metal—the private office, in short, of Peter Masters.

The heads of each separate floor were picked men—great men away from the golden glamour of the master mind—each involved in the success or failure of his own concern, all partners in their respective firms, but partners who accepted the share allotted to them without question, who served faithfully or disappeared from the ken of their fellow-workers, who were nominally accountable to their respective "company," but actually dependent on the word and will of the great man up above them. None but these men and his own special clerks ever approached him. Some junior clerk or obscure worker might pass him occasionally in a passage, or await the service of the lift at his pleasure; they might receive a sharp glance, a demand for name and department, but they knew no more of this controller of their humble destinies.

It was a marvellous organisation, a perfected system, a machine whose parts were composed of living men.

The owner of the machine cared much for the whole and nothing for the parts. When some screw or nut failed to answer its purpose, it was cast aside and another substituted. There was no question, no appeal. Nuts and screws are cheap. The various parts were well cared for, well oiled, just so long as they fulfilled their purpose; if they failed in that—well, the running of the machine was not endangered for sentiment.

Apart from this business, however, Peter Masters was a man of sentiment, though the workers in Masters's Building would have scorned the idea. He had expended this sentiment on two people, one, his wife, who had died in Whitmansworth Union, the other Aymer Aston, his cousin, who on the moment of his declared union with Elizabeth Hibbault, had fallen victim to so grim a tragedy. His "sentiment" had never spread beyond these two people, certainly never to the person of his unseen child, whom, however, he was prepared to "discover" in his own good time.

His wife had left him within a year of his marriage, and whatever investigations he may have privately made, they were sub rosa, and he had persistently refused to make public ones. She would come back, he believed, with an almost childish simplicity in the lure of his great fortune,—if she needed money,—or him. That she should suffer real poverty or hardship, lack the bare necessities of life, never for a moment occurred to him. Why should she, when his whole fortune was at her disposal—for her personal needs?

People who knew him a little said he had resented the slight to his money more than the scandal to himself when Mrs. Masters disappeared. They were in the wrong. Peter's pride had been very cruelly hurt: she had not only scorned his gold, but spurned his affection, which was quite genuine and deep so far as it went, but since he had never taken the world into his confidence in the matter of his having any affection to bestow, he as carefully kept his own counsel as to the amount it had been hurt, and continued his life as if the coming and going of Mrs. Masters was a matter of as little concern as the coming or going of any other of the immortal souls and human bodies who got caught in the toils of the great Machine.

As for the expected child, let her educate it after her own foolish, pretty fancy. When it was of an age to understand matters, the man of Power would slip in and claim his own, and he never doubted but that the dazzle of his gold would outshine the vapid illusions of the mother, and procure for him the homage of his offspring. Such was the mingled simplicity and cuteness of the man that he never for one moment allowed to himself there was any other possible reverse to this picture, this, the only thought of revenge he harboured, its very sting to be drawn by his own good-natured laugh at her "fancies." So he worked on in keen enjoyment, and the dazzle of the gold grew brighter as the years passed away unnoticed.

Peter Masters sat in the innermost sanctuary of the Temple of Mammon. It was a big corner room with six windows facing south and east, with low projecting balustrades outside which hid the street far down below. The room had not a severely business-like aspect, it rather suggested to the observer the word business was translatable into other meanings than work. Thus the necessary carpet was more than a carpet in that it was a work of Eastern art. The curtains were more than mere hangings to exclude light or draught, but fabrics to delight the eye. The plainness of the walls was but a luxury to set off the admirable collection of original sketches and clever caricatures that adorned them. One end of the room was curtained off to serve as a dining-room on necessity. No sybarite could have complained of the comfort of the chairs or the arrangement of the light. The great table at which Peter Masters sat, was not only of the most solid mahogany, but it was put together by an artist in joinery—a skilful, silent servant to its owner, offering him with a small degree of friction every possible convenience a busy man could need. The only other furniture in the room was a gigantic safe, or rather a series of little safes cased in mahogany which filled one wall like a row of school lockers, each labelled clearly with a letter.

Peter Masters leant back in his chair and gazed straight before him for one moment—just that much space of time he allowed before the next problem of the day came before him—then he rang one of the row of electric bells suspended overhead.

Its short, imperious summons resounded directly in the room occupied by the head clerk of the Lack Vale Coal Company, and that worthy, without waiting to finish the word he begun writing, slipped from his stool and hurried to the office door of his chief, where he knocked softly and entered in obedience to a curt order. The room was a simplified edition of the room on the top floor; everything was there, but in a less luxurious degree, and the result was insignificant. The manager of the Lack Vale Coal Company, who sat at the table, was a hard-featured, thin-lipped man of forty-five, with thin hair already turning grey, and pince-nez dangling from his button hole.

"Mr. Masters's bell, sir," said the clerk apologetically.

Mr. Foilet nodded and his thin lips tightened. He gathered up a sheaf of carefully arranged papers and went out by a private door to the central lift.

Peter greeted him affably and waved his hand to the opposite chair.

"You have Bennin's report at last?"

"Yes. He apologised for the delay, but thought it useless to send it until he had investigated the gallery itself."

"That's the business of his engineers. If he is not satisfied with them he should get others."

Mr. Foilet bowed, selected a paper from the sheaf he carried and handed it over. Peter Masters perused it with precisely the same kindly smiling countenance he wore when studying a paper or deciphering a friendly epistle. It was not a friendly letter at all, it was a curt, bald statement that a certain rich gallery in a certain mine was unsafe for working, though the opinion of two specialists differed on the point. The two reports were enclosed, and when all three reports were read Peter asked for the wage sheet of the mine. There was no cause of complaint there.

"The articles of the last settlement between the firm and the men have been rigorously adhered to?" questioned Masters, flinging down the paper.

"Rigorously. I will say they have taken no advantage of their success."

Peter smiled. "It is for us to do that. Mr. Weirs pronounces the gallery fit for working. The seam is one of the richest we have. What improvements can be done to the ventilation and propping before Monday are to be done, but the gallery is to be worked then, until the new shaft is completed. Then we will reconsider it."

Again Mr. Foilet bowed, but his hand fingered his glasses nervously.

"And if the men refuse?" he questioned in a low voice, with averted eyes.

Peter Masters waved his hand.

"There are others. Men who receive wages like that must expect to have a certain amount of danger to face. Danger is the spice of life." He leant back in his chair, humming a little tune and watched Mr. Foilet with smiling eyes. Mr. Foilet was wondering whether his chief was personally fond of spice, but he knew better than to say more. He left the room with a vague uneasy feeling at his heart. "A nice concern it will be if anything happens before the New Shaft's ready," he muttered; "if it wasn't for his wonderful luck, I'd have refused."

So he thought: but in reality he would have done no such thing.

The manager of the Stormby Foundry, which was a private property of Mr. Masters's, and no company, was the next visitor. He was a tall lank Scotchman with a hardy countenance and a soft heart when not fretted by the roll of the Machine. The question he brought was concerning the selling of some land in the neighbourhood of the works, for the erection of cottages.

"Surely you need no instructions on that point, Mr. Murray," said Peter a little more curtly than he had spoken to Mr. Foilet.

"There are two offers," said the Scotchman quietly. "Tennant will give £150 and Fortman £200."

"Then there is no question."

"Tennant will build decent cottages of good material and with proper foundations, and Fortman—well, you know what Fortman's hovels are like."

"No, I don't," said Peter drily. "He has never been my landlord."

Mr. Murray appeared to swallow something, probably a wish, with difficulty.

"They are mere hovels pretending to be villas."

"No one's obliged to live in them."

"There are no others," persisted Mr. Murray desperately, imperilling his own safety for the cause.

Masters frowned ominously.

"Mr. Murray," he said, "as I have before remarked, you are too far-sighted. Your work is to sell the ground for the benefit of the company, which, I may remind you, is for your benefit also. You have not to build the cottages or live in them. If the people don't like them they needn't take them. I do not profess to house the people. I pay them accordingly. They can afford to live in decent houses if they like."

"If they can get them," remarked the heroic Mr. Murray.

Peter smiled, his anger apparently having melted away.

"Let them arrange it with Fortman, and keep your obstinacy for more profitable business, Murray, and you'll be as rich as I am some day."

There was nothing apparently offensive in the words, yet the speaker seemed a singularly unlovable person as he spoke them, and Murray did not smile at the compliment, but went out with a grave air.

Neither he nor his business lingered on Peter's mind once the door had closed behind him. Peter got up and lounged to the window. He stood a while looking down into the street below with its crowd of strangely foreshortened figures. On the opposite side of the wide street was a shop where mechanical toys were sold, a paradise for boys. As Peter watched, a chubby-faced, stout little man with a tall, lanky boy at his side came to a stand before the windows. Peter knew the man to be one of the hardest-headed, shrewdest men in the iron trade, and he guessed the boy was his son. Both figures disappeared within the shop, the elder with evident reluctance, the younger with assured expectation. Peter waited a long time—a longer period than he would have supposed he had to spare, had he thought of it. They emerged at last in company with a big parcel, hailed a hansom and drove away. Peter looked at the clock and chuckled. "To think Coblan is that sort of fool. Well, that youngster will add little to the fortunes of Coblan and Company. Toys!" He turned away from the window, and, seated again at his desk, began to scribble down some dates on a scrap of paper. Then he leant back in his chair thoughtfully.

"Hibbault says that boy has just got a rise in that berth of his in Liverpool. I'll let him have a year or so more to prove his grit. I suppose Hibbault's to be trusted, but I might write to the firm and ask how he gets on! However, Aymer's boy shall have the vacancy!"

Therefore he took up his pen again and wrote the following brief letter:

Princes Building, Birmingham, April 10.

Dear Aymer:—

Are you going to 'prentice that boy of yours to me or not? I've an opening now in the Steel Axle Company, if you like to take it.

Yours,
Peter Masters.

PART II

CHAPTER XI

Despite his honest intention never to stand between Christopher and any fate that might serve to draw him into connection with his father, Aymer had a hard fight to master his keen desire to put Peter's letter in the fire and say nothing about it. Surely, after all, he had the best right to say what his adopted charge's future should be. It was he who had rescued him from obscurity, who had lavished on him the love and care his selfish, erratic father, for his own ambitious ends, denied him. Aymer believed, moreover, that a career under Peter's influence would mean either the blunting if not the utter destruction of every generous and admirable quality in the boy, or a rapid unbalanced development of those socialistic tendencies, the seeds of which were sown by his mother and nurtured in the hard experience of his early days. Besides this, Peter's interest in the boy was probably a mere freak, or at the best, sprang from a desire to serve his cousin, unless by any remote chance he had stumbled on a clue to Christopher's identity.

This last suspicion wove itself like a black thread into the grey woof of Aymer's existence. His whole being by now had become concentrated in the boy's life. It was a renewal of youth, hopes, ambitions, again possible in the person of this child, and for the second time a fierce, restless jealousy of his cousin began to stir in the inner depths of Aymer's being, as fire which may yet break into life beneath the grey, piled-up ashes which conceal it.

He sought help and advice from none and fought hard alone for his own salvation through the long watches of a black night—fought against the jealousy that prompted him to hedge Christopher about with precautions and restrictions which, however desirable they might seem to his finite wisdom, yet were, he knew, only the outcome of his smouldering jealousy, and might well grow to formidable barriers for Christopher to climb in later years. Aymer fought, too, for that sense of larger faith that in the midst of careful action yet leaves room for the hand of God and does not confound the little ideas of the builder with the vast plan of the Great Architect.

So the letter—the little fact which stood for such great possibilities—was shown to Christopher, to whom it was a mere nothing, to be tossed aside with scorn.

"I don't want to be under him," he commented indignantly, "I don't care about his old axles," and then because Cæsar was silent and he felt himself in the wrong, he apologised.

"All the same, I don't want to go to him unless you particularly wish it, Cæsar," he insisted.

But Cæsar did not answer directly.

"You are certain you want to be an engineer?" he asked at length.

"Certain,—only—" Christopher stopped, went over to the window and looked out.

They were in London and it was an evening in early spring. There was a faint primrose glow in the sky and a blackbird was whistling at the end of the garden. The hum of the great town was as part of the silence of the room.

Now at last must come the moment when Christopher must speak plainly of his darling purpose that had been striving for expression these many months, that purpose which had grown out of a childish fancy in the long ago days when his mother and he toiled along the muddy wearisome roads, or wended painfully through choking white dust under a blazing sun—

"Mother, how does roads get made here in the country, are they made like in London?"

"Yes, Jim, they were made somewhere by men, not over well, I think, for walkers such as we are."

"I'll make roads when I'm big," announced Jim, "real good ones that you can walk on easily."

So Christopher broke his purpose to Cæsar abruptly.

"I want to be a Road Engineer."

"A what?"

"A Roadmaker. To make high roads,—not in towns, but across countries. Roads that will be easy to travel on and will last." Again he stopped, embarrassed, for the vision before him which he only half saw, made him hot and confused. Yet it was a good vision, perhaps that was why—a picture of countless toiling human beings travelling on his roads all down the coming ages, knowing them for good roads, and praising the maker. But he was a boy and was abashed at the vision and hoped Cæsar did not guess at it. Cæsar, however, saw it all more clearly than Christopher himself and was not abashed but well content.

The boy went back to Cæsar's side. The thing was done, spoken of, made alive, and now he could plead for it, work to gain his end,—also there was a glow in his face and a new eagerness in his manner.

"Oh, Cæsar, do say it's possible. I always wanted to do it, even when I was a little chap, and watched men breaking stones on the road."

"It's quite possible, only it will want working out. You must go abroad—France—Germany—I must see where to place you."

"Yes, I must learn how they are made everywhere, and then—then there must be roads to be made somewhere—in new countries if not here."

They talked it out earnestly; Cæsar himself caught the boy's enthusiasm, and the moment Mr. Aston came in he too was drawn into the discussion and offered good advice.

Thus Christopher's future was decided upon as something to be worked out quite independent of Peter Masters and his millions. Perhaps because he had seen the vision which covered Christopher with shy confusion, Aymer became very prosaic and practical over the details, and Mr. Aston was the only one of the trio who gave any more thought to the boy's dream on its sentimental side. He used to sit in the evenings watching the two poring over maps, letters and guidebooks, thinking far thoughts for them both, occasionally uttering them.

"I wonder," he remarked one night, "if you know what a lucky young man you are, Master Christopher, not only in having a real wish concerning your own future—which is none too common a lot—but in being free to follow it."

Christopher looked up from the map he was studying.

"Yes, I know I'm lucky, St. Michael. It must be perfectly horrible to have to be something one does not want to be. I suppose that's why lots of people never get on in the world. It seems beastly unfair."

"Yet I've known men to succeed at work for which they had no original aptitude," returned Mr. Aston quietly.

"Mightn't they have succeeded better at what they did like?"

"That is beside the mark, so that they did not fail altogether. I knew a soldier once," he went on dreamily, "just a private. A good chap. He was a soldier because he was born and bred in the midst of a regiment, but his one passion was music. He taught himself a little instead of learning his drill. In the end he deserted and joined a German band. That argues nothing for his musical taste, you say. He just thought it a stepping-stone, but it was a tombstone. He was quite a smart soldier, too."

"Well, I think it was jolly hard lines on him to have to be a soldier at all, if he didn't like it. He wanted a Cæsar to help him out. I think all fellows ought to have a chance, there should be someone or something to say, 'what do you want to be?'"

"You'd be surprised how few could answer. Prove your point yourself anyway, my dear boy. Succeed."

"I mean to," said Christopher with shut teeth and an intonation that reminded both men of Peter Masters himself.

"We are all of us Roadmakers of one kind or another," went on Mr. Aston meditatively, "making the way rougher or smoother for those who come after us. Happy if we only succeed in rolling in a few of the stones that hurt our own feet."

"You *are* rather like a steam roller," remarked Aymer quietly, "it hadn't struck me before."

Mr. Aston rumpled his hair distractedly and Christopher giggled.

"I wasn't talking of myself at all," said Mr. Aston hastily. "I was merely thinking of you making things smooth for Christopher. You are much more like a steam roller than I am. You are bigger."

Christopher began to laugh helplessly, and Aymer protested rather indignantly.

"I deny the likeness. But if rolling has to be done, it is better to do it heavily, I suppose. Whose roads shall we roll, Christopher?"

Christopher looked up, suddenly grave.

"What do you mean, Cæsar?"

"You say everyone should have a chance and my father insists we are bound by some unknown Board of Guardians to level our neighbours' roads, so where will you start?"

"On Sam Sartin!"

He sat upright, his face glowing, looking straight at Cæsar. Cæsar's tone might be flippant, but if he meant what Christopher supposed him to mean, he must not let the golden opportunity slip.

"I thought Sam was in a greengrocer's shop," said Cæsar in a drawling, indifferent manner.

"So he is. But would anyone be in a greengrocer's shop if they could be in anything else? When we were kids, he and I, we used to plan we'd be Lord Mayors—A greengrocer!"

"An honest and respectable calling, if a little dirty," murmured Mr. Aston. "The greengrocers, I mean not the Lord Mayors."

"Sam's got a head on his shoulders. He's really awfully sharp. He could be anything he liked," urged Christopher. "Could you help him, Cæsar?"

"You might if you liked."

"Make what I like of him?"

"No. Most emphatically, no. Make what he likes of himself. A crossing sweeper, if he fancies that. Buy him a crossing and a broom, you know."

"But really, what he likes; not joking?"

"Sober earnest. I'll see to-morrow, and tell you. Now, will you kindly find that place you were looking for when we were so inopportunely interrupted with irrelevant moralisings."

"I won't do it again," said his father deprecatingly. "I apologise."

Aymer gravely bowed his head and the subject was dropped. But when they were alone that evening, Mr. Aston reverted to it.

"What are you going to do with Sam Sartin?" he asked, "and why are you doing it?"

"Sam must settle the first question himself," said Aymer, idly drawing appalling pictures of steamrollers on the fly-leaf of a book, "as to the second—" he paused in his drawing, put the book down and turned to his father.

"Christopher's got the makings of a rabid socialist in him. If he's not given good data to go on he will be a full disciple when he's twenty-one, all theories and dreams, caught in a mesh of words. I don't want that. It's natural too, for, after all, Christopher is not of the People, any more than—than his mother was." He examined his pencil critically. "She always credited them with the fine aspirations and pure passions of her own soul, instead of allowing them the very reasonable and just aspirations and ambitions that they have and should be able to reach. Sam may be an exception, but I don't think he is. I'm quite ready to give Christopher a free hand to help him, provided he knows what he wants himself."

"To provide an object lesson for Christopher?"

"Yes, precisely."

"Is it quite fair on Sam?"

Aymer looked up quickly.

"He benefits anyway."

"Possibly; but you do not care about that."

"Christopher does."

"Ah, yes. Christopher does. That is worth considering. Otherwise—"

"Otherwise?"

"How far are we justified in experimenting with our fellow-creatures, I wonder?"

CHAPTER XII

It was a day of expectancy—and promise—of blackthorn breaking into snowy showers, and of meadows richly green, blue sky and white cloud—and a sense of racing, headlong life joyously tremulous over the earth.

The boys had met at Paddington Station, Sam Sartin by no means abashed at his own appearance in an old suit of Christopher's, and wearing, in deference to his friend's outspoken wishes, a decorous dark-blue tie and unobtrusive shirt. He looked what he was—a good, solid, respectable working lad out for a holiday. Excitement, if he felt it, was well suppressed, surprise at the new world of luxury—they travelled down first—was equally carefully concealed. The code of manners in which he was reared was stringent in this particular.

Christopher, on the contrary, was in high spirits. Sam had watched him come down the platform, out of the corner of his eye, with a queer sense of proud possession. He would have liked to proclaim to the world that the young master there, who walked like a prince, was his own particular pal. Yet he pretended not to see him till Christopher clapped him on the shoulder with a warm greeting.

"I've got the tickets. Come on," said the giver of the treat. "I say, what a day, Sammie—if it's good in London what will it be in the country?"

"Cold, I shouldn't wonder. What's the matter with London?" said the cockney sarcastically.

"Old Bricks and Mortar," retorted Christopher gaily. "You'll know what's the matter with it when you come back. It's too jolly small."

"Big enough for me. But the country's well enough to play in. I say, Mr. Christopher, I've been thinking, we may not find any boats. It's early."

"Oh, I've seen to that," said Christopher with the faintest suspicion of lordliness in his voice. "I wrote to the man I know at Maidenhead to have a boat ready—a good one."

Sam grinned. "My, what a head-piece we've got, to be sure."

The other flushed a little. "It was really Cæsar who suggested it," he owned.

Sam had never been down that line before, so Christopher pointed out the matters of interest. They found their boat ready at Maidenhead, bestowed their coats in the bow and settled themselves. Christopher insisted on Sam's rowing stroke. Sam thought politeness obliged him to refuse, but he ultimately gave in. He retrieved the little error in manners by handling his oar in a masterly way. "Stroke shaping well," Christopher heard the boatman say as they went off.

The wind on the river was cold enough and, in spite of the bright sun, cut through them. But half an hour's steady pulling brought them into a glow and mood to enjoy themselves. Christopher called for a rest. Sam looked over his shoulder.

"Tired?"

"No," responded the other, laughing, "but we didn't come down just to row 'eyes in boat'; I want to look at the world."

"Nothing but green fields and trees and cows."

"I like cows."

"I don't."

Nevertheless he desisted from work, and they drifted on. Christopher was bubbling over with a great secret that was to be the crowning episode of the day. It would be fatal to divulge it too early, so he plunged into friendly discussions and they rowed on happy in the physical exertion, the clean, fresh air and the smiling earth.

It was not till after lunch that Christopher decided the great matter must be broached, to allow time to discuss it in full detail. They had changed places and he was stroke now. He pulled with a slower swing but greater power than Sam and for some time bent to his work in silence, thinking over what he was going to say. He took a rapid mental survey of Sam's present life and future, of what it held and more especially of what it did not hold; the limitations, the lack of opportunity, the struggle for existence that left no room for ambitions or hopes. And he, with Cæsar's help, was going to change all that, and open the gates of the world wide for him. If the thought were exhilarating, it had also a serious side. He was not afraid, he was too young for that, but he had sense enough to know it was a big thing to uproot a life and plant it in a new spot more congenial to growth.

Mr. Aston's words to him that morning came back with puzzling insistence. "Remember," he had said in his kindly way, "no two people see life through the same glasses. Don't be surprised if Sam's make you squint." What did he mean? It was just because he, Christopher, was not sure of Sam's real ambition that he was to be given the choice. He amused himself while cogitating over it, tasting like an epicure the flavour of the good wine to be drunk presently. Sam complained he was a bad stroke, and they changed again. This better suited his plans. He could see the town boy's thin sloping shoulders bend evenly before him. Sam was no athlete in build, but his passion for rowing had stood him in good stead and developed muscle and endurance.

"He'll choose something in boats," thought Christopher, mentally picturing Sam as captain of a great liner and then as an alternative, as an admiral of the Fleet, and so came the crucial point.

"Sam, if you had your choice, what would you be?"

"Dunno."

"But think. I want to know. A greengrocer like Mr. Gruner? Ho, ho!" he shouted out wholesome laughter.

Sam grinned. He was less ready to laugh. Life had taken toll of that birthright already.

"I hate vegetables. Beastly, dirty things," he said prosaically. "No, I wouldn't be a *green*-grocer."

"Well what? An engineer? A doctor, lawyer, parson?"

"Why not a king now?" scoffed Sam.

"Not enough situations vacant. I mean it, really. What would you be if you were as free to choose as I am?"

"If I were you, you mean."

"No, not that. If you could choose for yourself as I have."

Sam rowed on stolidly. "Dunno that it's much use bothering," he said indifferently. "I'm doing all right, though it's not what I'd choose."

It had seemed an easy, insignificant task to break the news five minutes ago, but either Christopher had taken the wrong approach or it was a stiffer job than he had fancied. He became uneasily conscious his own part in it could not be overlooked, that he was doing something that evilly-disposed persons might even call magnanimous or philanthropic. His face grew red at the thought.

"Sam," he said as naturally as he could, "it happens you can choose, you see. Choose anything you like. Cæsar's given me a free hand. We are both to start life just as we like. What shall it be? I've told you my choice."

The narrow form in front never slackened its stroke, but pulled on mechanically, and at last spoke a little gruffly.

"Say. You're kidding me, you know."

"I'm not. Dead earnest."

Again the boat shot on, but Christopher stopped rowing. Sam looked back over his shoulder.

"You're lazy. Why don't you pull?"

Christopher obeyed mechanically. He knew he could afford to be patient now.

"Easy," said the stroke at last.

There was a smooth reach of water before them. Low meadows with reddish muddy banks lay on either side, no house or any living soul was in sight. Sam rubbed his hands on his trousers, looked back at his friend and away again.

"You mean you'll start me in any trade I like? 'Prentice me?"

"Any trade or profession."

"What do you do it for, anyhow?"

"Cæsar suggested it. He said I might if I liked."

"Well, why do you do it?"

"Does it matter?"

"I want to know certain."

Christopher looked embarrassed. "Weren't we kids together? Besides, it seems to me every chap ought to have a chance of working on the job he likes best. It's only fair. It's jolly rough on a fellow to have to do just what comes along whether he's fit for it or not."

"Seems to me," said Sam meditatively, "a good many jobs would want doing if everyone did what they liked."

"Oh, science would step in and equalise that," returned Christopher, hastily quoting from some handbook and went on to further expound his creed.

Sam concluded he had been listening to spouters in the Park, but he was sharp enough to recognise beneath the crude boyish creed the kindly generous nature that prompted it.

"So Cæsar says you've just to choose. We'll see you through."

"He must be jolly rich."

"Well, that's why he's rich, isn't it, to be able to do things."

"I don't see what he gets out of it anyhow."

"He doesn't want anything, you silly."

"I want to think this out," said Sam, "there is something I've always wanted since I was a kiddy, but I want to think. Row on."

This was intelligible and encouraging. Christopher's sense of flatness gave way a little. He pulled steadily, trying to make out what had so dashed him in Sam's reception of the great news. He had not yet learnt how exceptional is the mind that can accept a favour graciously.

After nearly ten minutes' silence Sam spoke again. "Well, then, I'd like to be a grocer," and straightway pulled furiously.

"What?" gasped Christopher, feeling the bottom story of his card house tottering to a fall.

"It's like this. I don't mind telling you—much—though I've never told nobody before. When I was a bit of a chap, mother, she used to take me out shopping in the evenings. We went to pokey little shops, but we used to pass a fine, big shop—four glass windows—it has six now—and great lights and mahogany counters and little rails, and balls for change, tiled floor, no sawdust. Every time I saw it I says to myself, 'When I'm a man I'll have a place like that.' I tried to get a job there, but I couldn't—they made too many family inquiries, you see," he added bitterly; "well, if I could get 'prenticed to a place like that ... might be head man some day...." He began whistling with forced indifference, queerly conscious that the whole of his life seemed packed in that little boat—waiting. The boat had drifted into a side eddy. Christopher sat with his head on his hands, wondering with his surface consciousness if the planks at his feet were three or four inches wide, but at last he brushed aside the last card of his demolished palace and recalled his promise to Cæsar to leave Sam as free and unbiased in choice as he had been himself.

"That would be quite easy to manage," he said with assumed heartiness, "it's—only too easy. Only you must be a partner or something. Oh, oh. A white apron. I'll buy my tea and bacon of you when I've a house of my own!"

"All right," grinned Sam. "I'll have great rows of red and gold canisters and—and brass fittings everywhere—not your plated stuff for me—solid brass and marble-topped counters. But it won't come off," he added dejectedly, "things like that never do."

"But it will," persisted Christopher impatiently, "just as my going to Dusseldorf is coming off."

"You don't get 'prenticed for nothing," was the faithless rejoinder.

Christopher joggled the boat and shouted: "You sinner, if you won't take my word for it I'll smash you."

"All right—keep cool, I'm only having you on, Chris. Oughtn't we to turn now?"

They expended their excitement and emotion in rowing furiously, and landed again at Maidenhead in time for tea. Then Christopher broke the further news to Sam that he was to return with him to Aston House and see Cæsar. He overcame with difficulty Sam's reiterated objections, and they walked from Paddington, Christopher keeping a strict guard over Sam lest he should escape.

But Sam's objections were more "code" than genuine. He was really anxious to hear the wonderful news confirmed by more responsible lips than Christopher's—not that he disbelieved his intentions, but he still doubted his powers. He grew very silent, however, as they turned in at the beautiful iron gates of Aston House. He had never managed to really connect his old friend with this wonderful dignified residence that he knew vaguely by sight. He had had dim visions of Christopher slipping in by a side entrance avoiding the eyes of plush-breeched lords-in-waiting. But here was that young gentleman marching calmly in at the big front doors nodding cheerfully to the sober-clad man waiting in the hall who called Christopher "Sir."

Sam successfully concealed under an expression of solid matter-of-factness the interest and curiosity that consumed him. He looked straight before him and yet saw all round. He accepted the whole calmly, but he wanted to sit down and stare.

Christopher explained that they were to have dinner together in his own sitting-room as soon as they had seen Aymer.

They went through the swing doors down the long corridor leading to Aymer's room, and Christopher stopped for a moment near a window.

"I never come down here in this sort of light," he said with a little catch in his voice, "without thinking of the first evening I came. How big it all seemed and how quiet."

"It is quiet," said Sam in a subdued whisper.

In another moment they were in Aymer's room.

"Hullo, Cæsar. Here we are, turned up like bad pennies."

Christopher pulled Sam across the room to the sofa. Sam would have been not a little surprised had he known that it cost Aymer Aston a great deal more effort to see a new face than it cost him to look at this Cæsar of whom he had heard so much.

The "code" slipped from his mental horizon and left him red and embarrassed, watching Christopher furtively to see what he would do.

"Here's Sam, Cæsar. I've told you all about him and he may just have heard your name mentioned—possibly—" laughed Christopher seating himself on the sofa and indicating a chair to his friend.

Aymer held out his hand.

"Yes, I've heard of you, Sam. Sit down, won't you?"

Sam sat down, his hands on his knees, and tried to find a safe spot on which to focus his eyes.

"Now, isn't it a jolly room," began Christopher triumphantly, "didn't I tell you?"

"It's big," said Sam cautiously.

"Christopher, behave yourself. Don't mind his bad manners, Sam. It's sheer nervousness on his part, he can't help it."

A newspaper was flung dexterously across his face.

"Which gives point to my remark," continued Aymer, calmly folding it. "Well, have you enjoyed your day? Madness, I call it, the river in March!"

Christopher plunged into an account of their jaunt to which his companion listened in complete bewilderment, hardly recognising the simple pleasures of their holiday in their dress of finished detail and humour.

"Is that a true account?" asked Aymer, catching the tail of a broad grin.

"I didn't see the water-rat dressing himself, or the girl with the red shoes," said Sam slowly. "My, what a chap you are, Christopher, to spin a yarn. Wish I could reel it off to mother and the kids like that."

He found himself in a few minutes discoursing with Aymer on the variety and history of his family. It was not for some minutes or so that the great subject was approached.

"I suppose," said Aymer at last, "I need not ask if you and Christopher have been discussing his little plan for your future. What do you think of it, Sam?"

Christopher got up and walked to the window. Minute by minute a sense of overwhelming disappointment and shame obliterated the once plausible idea. It was not only an opportunity missed, it was wasted, thrown away. What glory or distinctions, what ambitions could be fulfilled in the narrow confines of a grocer's shop—a nightmare vision of an interminable vista of red canisters, mahogany counters, biscuit boxes and marble slabs, swam before his eyes. It was no use denying it. It was a cruel disappointment ... and what would Cæsar think?

Meanwhile Sam, in answer to Aymer's questions, had stumbled out the statement he thought it a rattling fine thing for him and was very much obliged.

"And you know your own mind on the point?" demanded Aymer, watching him closely.

Sam coughed nervously. "Yes, I always knew what I wanted to be. I told him," with a backward jerk of his head towards Christopher.

This was better than Aymer had expected. A boy with an ambition and a mind of his own was worth assisting.

"Well, what is it. Will you tell me too?"

Sam looked at him out of the corner of his shrewd eyes. "It's you as is really doing it, sir?"

"What is it?"

"It's like this," began Sam, hesitating; "it costs money,—my top ambition; but it's a paying thing and if anyone would be kind enough to start me on it I'd work off the money in time. I know I could."

"I'm afraid Christopher hasn't quite explained," said Aymer quietly; "it's not a question of investing money on your industry. I don't expect him to pay back the cost of starting him in life. You are to start on precisely the same ground."

Sam got red. "He—he belongs to you—it's different," he began.

"What is your ambition?"

"Grocery business. I've told him. Ever since I was a bit of a chap that high I've wanted it. I never could get a job in a shop, but if I was regularly apprenticed now—if that wasn't too much?"

Aymer's glance meandered thoughtfully to the distant Christopher, still staring out of the window; a shadow of a smile rose to his lips.

"Yes, that would not be difficult to manage, Sam. How old are you?"

"Over sixteen, sir. There's money in grocery, sir. I could pay it back. I'm sure I could."

Aymer lay still, thinking. "What sort of schooling have you had? Not much? Passed the fifth standard young?"

"But it takes a long time for a 'prentice to work up," said Sam, watching him eagerly.

"I'm thinking of another way," said Aymer slowly. "Christopher."

He rejoined them, standing by the grate and kicking the logs into place. He did not look at Aymer.

"Sam has been telling me of his wishes," said Aymer. "I think them quite excellent, but I've not quite decided on the best way to carry them out. Go away and get your dinner and come back to me afterwards."

The boys departed, and once in Christopher's den, the host turned to his guest questioningly.

"Well, what do you think of Cæsar?"

"He's a stunner, a jolly sight more sensible than you, Chris. But I say," he added in a grumpy, husky voice, "is he always like that?"

"Like what?"

"On a sofa. Lying down."

"Yes," said Christopher shortly. He had become almost as sensitive on that point as Aymer himself.

"He must get a bit tired of it. Didn't he ever walk?"

"Yes, of course. It was a shooting accident. Shut up, Sam, we all hate talking of it."

The dinner that was served immediately somehow impressed Sam more than any other event of the day. He had occasionally had a meal in a restaurant with Christopher, and once had been in a dining-room at an hotel, but it all seemed different to this intimate, comfortable dinner. The white napery, the shining silver and delicate glass and china, the serving of the simple meal was a revelation of his friend's life, for Christopher took it all as a matter of course and was unabashed by the presence of the second footman who waited on them.

There was soup, and cutlets in little paper dresses, tomatoes and potatoes that bore no resemblance to the grimy vegetables Sam dispensed daily. Then came strange bird-shaped things, about the size of sparrows which Christopher called chicken and which had no bones in them, cherry tart, with innumerable trifles with it, afterwards something that looked like a solid browny-yellow cake, which gave way to nothing when cut, and tasted of cheese. Finally there was fruit, that was a crowning point, for Sam knew what pears cost that time of year, and said so.

Christopher laughed. "These come from Marden," he explained. "Marden's noted for pears; they have storages of different temperatures and keep them back or ripen them as wanted. The fire's jolly after all, isn't it?"

He stretched out his long legs to the fender, a very contented young Sybarite for the moment.

"I say, Chris," said Sam abruptly, "I must tell you though you'll think it pretty low of me. But after you came and told us you were living here with Mr. Aston I used to ask people about him. One day I came round here and ... somehow I never took it in. I knew in a way you lived here, but I didn't know it was like this...." He stumbled over his words in an embarrassed fashion.

"Like what?" demanded Christopher shortly.

"Well, I thought you was here like a sort of servant—not with them exactly—I see now, I never took it in before—you with your own rooms and walking in at the front door and ordering dinner and them blokes in the hall saying 'sir' to you—oh, lor'."

"I told you they had adopted me," said the other, frowning and rather red.

"I ought to have taken it in, but I didn't," continued Sam humbly, "and then you ask me here—and are going to give me a chance—Oh, lor',—what's it all for, I want to know? What does it mean?"

Christopher got up and walked away. Had Sam but known it, his chance in life was in dire peril at that moment. Seldom had Christopher felt so angry and never had he felt so out of touch with his companion. Why on earth couldn't Sam take his luck without wanting reasons. It was so preposterous, in Christopher's eyes, to want any. In the old days Sam had been ready to share his scant pennies and toys with his small friend. The offer of a ride in a van from the warehouse where Sartin senior worked would have included both of them or neither. What was the difference? What was the use of having plenty if not to share it with a friend?

To his credit he did not allow Sam to guess his irritation, but suggested a return to Cæsar's room.

"Didn't it take you an awful long time to get used to all this?" inquired Sam, as he followed him.

"I forget. No, I don't though. I hated it rather at first, the clothes and collars and having to change and be tidy, and all that, but I soon got used to it. Here we are."

Mr. Aston was there too now. Sam was duly introduced and behaved with great discretion. He was far less abashed by Mr. Aston than by Aymer, whose physical condition produced a shyness not inherent in the youth.

Mr. Aston talked to him in a friendly gossiping way, then looked across at Aymer with a faint nod.

Aymer unfolded his scheme of carrying out Sam's ambitions to a fruitful end. He was to go for a year to a commercial school, and after that to be put into a good firm as pupil or 'prentice with a chance of becoming a junior partner with a small capital if he did well.

"If you don't do well, of course it's off," concluded Aymer, rather wearily, "the future is in your hands, not ours: we only supply an opportunity."

Sam said stolidly he quite understood that: that he was much obliged, and he'd do his best.

"It will be a race between you," remarked Mr. Aston, looking from one boy to the other, "as to whether you become a full-fledged grocer first or Christopher a full-fledged engineer."

But late that night when Mr. Aston was bidding Aymer good-night, he remarked as he stood looking down at him:

"You have done a good piece of road-making to-day, old man."

"No, I haven't," retorted Aymer, rather crossly. "I've only supplied material for someone else to use if they like."

"Just to please Christopher?"

But Aymer did not answer that. Mr. Aston really needed no answer, for he knew that long ago Sam's mother had made smooth a very rough piece of road for another woman's feet, and that woman was Christopher's mother.

CHAPTER XIII

A thin, sickly-looking woman in a dingy black dress sat by the roadside with a basket of bootlaces and buttons at her feet. She rested her elbows on her knees and gazed with unseeing eyes at the meadowland below.

The burst shoe, the ragged gown, and unkempt head proclaimed her a Follower of the Road, and the sordid wretchedness that reached its lowest depth in lack of desire for better things, was a sight to force Philanthropist or Socialist to sink differences in one energetic struggle to eradicate the type. If she thought at all it was in the dumb, incoherent manner of her class: at the actual moment a vision of a hat with red flowers she had seen in a shop window flickered across her mind, chased away by a hazy wonder as to how much supper threepence halfpenny would provide. That thought, too, fell away before a sudden, shrewd calculation as to the possible harvest to be gleaned from the two people just coming over the brow of the hill.

These two, a boy and a young man, were walking with the swinging step and assurance of those who have never bent before grim need.

"Young toffs," she decided, and wondered if it were worth while getting up or not.

The young man was listening eagerly to the equally eager chatter of his companion, and they walked quickly as those who were in haste to reach a goal until they were level with the tramp woman, who watched them with speculative eyes. The boy, who was about twelve years old, was as good a specimen of a well-trained, well-nurtured boy as one might find in the country, the product of generations of careful selection and high ideals, active, brimming over with vitality and joyousness, with clear-cut features perhaps a trifle too pronounced for his age. But the elder of the two, who was twenty-one and might by appearance have been some few years older, was a far stronger type. There was a certain steady strength in the set of his square head, in the straight look of his dark eyes. It was a face that might in time be over-stern if the kindly humorous lines of the mouth should fade. The tramp woman saw nothing of this. She only observed their absorption in each other and abandoned hope of adding to her meagre fortune.

Max Aston's quick blue eyes saw her and were averted instantly, for she was not a pleasing object. But at sight of her the shadow of some dominant thought drove every expression from his companion's face but pity: and the pity of the strong for the weak lies near to reverence.

He crossed the road abruptly, his hand in his pocket. Max dawdled after him. The woman looked up with awakened interest.

"It's a long road, kind sir, and poor weather," she began in a professional drawl, and then stopped. The young face looking down on her had something in its expression to which she was not accustomed. It was as if he checked her begging for very shame. She noticed dully, he held his cap in his hand.

He said nothing at all, but dropped a coin in her hand and went on, followed by Max, who was a little puzzled.

The woman looked after them and forgot she had not thanked him. She wished the moment would repeat itself and the young gentleman stand before her again. She had not taken it all in—taken *what* in, she hardly knew.

She looked at the coin and it gleamed yellow in her hand. It was half a sovereign. Oh, what luck, what luck! It was a mistake of course—he had thought it was a sixpence no doubt, but he had gone, and she had it.

A vista of unlikely comforts opened before her, even the hat with red flowers was possible. It was careless of him though.

She got up suddenly and looked down the hill. The two were still in sight—the boy had stopped to tie his boot-lace.

She looked at the half-sovereign again, and then set off at a shuffling slipshod trot after them. They had resumed their walk before she reached them, but the boy looking back, saw her, and told the other, who wheeled round sharply, frowning a little.

"'Ere, please sir, I wants to see yer," she gasped, out of breath, choking a little with unwonted exertion. Christopher went back to her and waited gravely. She opened her hand and the half-sovereign glinted again in the light.

"Expect yer made a mistake, didn't yer, sir?" she asked in a hoarse whisper, and saw a wave of hot colour under his brown skin.

"No," he said awkwardly, "I hadn't anything else. It was good of you to trouble to come though. Go and get some new boots and a good supper. It's bad going on the roads in autumn. I *know*, I've done it."

She gasped at him bewildered, her hand still open.

"Yer a gentleman, yer are,"—her tone hesitated as it were between the statement of a plain fact and doubt of his last words.

"Winchester is three miles on. You can get decent lodgings out by the Station Road to the left as you go under the arch. Good-bye." He raised his hat again and turned away. The woman looked after him, gave a prolonged sniff and limped back up the hill.

Max looked at Christopher out of the corner of his eye, a little doubtfully. He had not come near, fastidiousness outweighing curiosity.

"What did she want—and why did you take your hat off?"

Christopher grew hot again.

"Oh, she's a woman, and my mother and I tramped, you know."

Max did not know, and intimated that Christopher was talking rot.

Christopher decapitated a thistle and explained briefly, "Cæsar adopted me straight out of a workhouse. My mother and I were tramping from London to Southampton, and she got ill at Whitmansworth, the other side of Winchester, and died there. The Union kept me till Mr. Aston took me away. I thought everyone knew."

Embarrassment and curiosity struggled for the mastery in the young aristocrat by his side.

"And you really did tramp?" he ventured at length.

"Yes, for a time, but we were not like that. My mother was—was a lady, educated, and all that, I think, only quite poor. She understood poor people and tramps. We used to walk with them, talk to them. They were kind."

"And if Cæsar hadn't adopted you?"

"I should be a workhouse porter by now, perhaps," laughed Christopher lightly and then was silent. A picture of the possible or rather of the inevitable swam before his eyes; a picture of a hungry, needy soul compassed by wants, by fierce desires, with the dominant will to fulfil them and no means, and the world against him. He did not reason it out to a logical conclusion, but he saw it clearly.

Max concluded the subject was not to be discussed and went on with an explanation of why Christopher had not been met in state after four years' absence.

"The motor was to come for you, but it's gone wrong, and Aymer said you'd rather walk than drive, and we were not quite certain of the train. Do you really hate driving, Christopher?"

"Yes, I always think the horses will run away. Aymer knows that. Is it really four years since I was here, Max?"

"Yes, at Christmas. You never came down when you were in town two years ago. It was a beastly shame of you."

"I'd only two months and Cæsar wanted me. That was before I went to Switzerland, wasn't it? They know something about road-making there, Max, but I've learnt more in France."

"And all about motors, too?" questioned Max eagerly. "Can you really drive one?"

Christopher laughed. "I've won a race or two, and I've got a certificate. Perhaps it won't pass in England."

"Will you teach me to drive? I just long to: but St. Michael says no—though he doesn't mind Geoffry Leverson teaching me to shoot. He's home now, you know, and comes over most days, and when Patricia won't play golf, he takes me shooting."

"Patricia's taken to golf then?"

"Yes. Geoffry says she's splendid, but I expect that's just to make her play up."

They had turned off the highroad now and were in the fields following a path on the side of the sloping meadows. The mist that hung over the river did not reach up to them and Christopher could see the thick foliage of the woods opposite, splashed with gold and russet, heavy with moisture. The warm damp smell of autumn was in the air. He took a long breath and squared his shoulders.

"It's good to be back. To think of its being four whole years."

"And two since you've seen any of us. Are you going away again, Christopher?"

"In the spring. There's St. Michael."

He was waiting by a stile leading into a wood that gave quicker access to Marden Court, and he came forward to meet them with undisguised pleasure.

Charles Aston had rendered but small homage to time. He was as erect and thin as ever, hair perhaps a little white, but the kind eyes had lost nothing of their penetrating quality.

Christopher's welcome could not have been warmer had it been his own father. Max went ahead to find Charlotte and left the two to come on together.

"How is Cæsar?" demanded Christopher, the moment they were alone.

"Can't you wait for his own report?"

"I want yours." There was an urgent insistence in his voice, and Mr. Aston looked at him sharply.

"Well, he is decidedly better since he came down here, and I want him to stay, Christopher, to give up London in the end perhaps altogether."

"He has not been well then?"

"I have not thought so: but what made you suspicious, my dear boy?"

"His letters have been over-witty and deliberately satirical. Just the sort of things he says when something is wrong."

Mr. Aston nodded.

"Yes, I felt that. There seemed nothing physically wrong, but I felt he must have more people round him."

"And you?"

"Oh, I stay here too, and go up and down when needs must."

"And the Colonial Commission? How will it get on without you?"

"Oh, they easily found a better man. As I explained to Cæsar, I was only asked as a compliment," he answered simply.

Christopher kept to himself his dissent from this, and was silent a moment, thinking how this man's life was spent to one end; and desirable as he felt that end to be, he was of age now to feel a tinge of regret for all that had been and still was sacrificed to it. An infinitesimal sacrifice of personal feeling and convenience was demanded of him now, if he were to second St. Michael's attempt to keep Aymer from Aston House and teach him to permanently regard Marden Court as home, for dearly as Christopher loved Marden it was only there he was awake to the apparently indisputable truth that he was not one of that dear family who had done their best to make him forget once and for all that obnoxious fact. His sense of proprietorship in Aymer and of Aymer's in him was undeniably stronger in town than in the country, and this not entirely because Nevil was to all intents master of Marden, but rather that there Aymer himself was less isolated, merged more into the general family life, and became again part of the usages and traditions of his own race.

Mr. Aston, without actually speaking the words, had conveyed to Christopher his own dread lest some day Aymer might be left alone, stranded mentally and physically in the great silent London house that was their home by force of dear companionship. Christopher saw it in a flash, saw it so clearly that he involuntarily glanced at his companion to assure himself of the remoteness of that dread chance. Hard on this thought pressed the knowledge that neither of these two men who had done so much for him made the least claim on his life or asked ought of him but success in his chosen line—and that knowledge was both sweet and bitter to him.

"Cæsar will be far better satisfied when you are actually started at work," Mr. Aston went on. "He lives in your future, Christopher, he is more impatient for this training period to be over than you yourself."

"Because I am training and have no time to think. The first real step is coming. I have a good chance, only I must tell him first."

He quickened his steps insensibly, for the thought of Cæsar waiting was like a spur even to physical effort, and even so his mind outraced his feet, till it came full tilt against a girl coming directly from its goal and momentarily obliterating it by her very presence.

"Oh, Christopher, Christopher," Patricia cried, holding out both hands. "How long you have been! I began to think you never would come again!"

Christopher, taking her hands, felt it was a long two years since they parted and that time had made fair road here meanwhile. His thoughts outpaced his feet no longer, but kept decent step with the light footfall beside him.

Mr. Aston, following, noted it all, and first smiled and then sighed a little. The smile was for them and the little sigh for Aymer waiting within.

He found, however, little reason to repeat his sigh during the next few weeks, for Christopher was in constant attendance on Aymer, and gave but the residue of his time to the rest of the little world. His suspicions as to Aymer's well-being vanished away, for the latter betrayed by no outward sign the sleepless nights and long days spent in wrestling with intangible dread of impending evil and the return of almost forgotten black hours. Indeed, Christopher's steady dependable strength and vigorous energy seemed to renew belief and confidence in the man with whom life had broken faith. He was jealously greedy of Christopher's company, though he sought to hide this under a mask of indifference, and he made a deliberate attempt to keep him near him by the exercise of every personal and social gift he possessed. It was not enough for him to hold his adopted son's affection by the bond of the past, it was not enough to be loved by force of custom, his present individuality struggled for recognition and won it. Deliberately, skilfully and successfully he bound Christopher to him by force of personality, by reason of being what he was as apart from all he had done.

None of the household grudged him his triumph or resented their own dismissal from attendance in the West Room. The women-kind once more superfluous to Cæsar's well-being, resumed their wonted routine with generous content.

Patricia's routine appeared to consist very largely of golf in which she and Geoffry Leverson could undoubtedly give Christopher long odds. Christopher, however, was undaunted, and the few hours he did not spend in Aymer's company, he spent toiling round the links points behind Patricia, play she never so badly. Geoffry complained bitterly to Patricia in private that she was spoiling her game, but she, indifferent to her handicap, continued to play with Christopher and to ignore promised matches with Geoffry whenever her old playmate chose to set foot on the green.

At length Geoffry could stand it no longer and protested loudly when Christopher challenged her, that it was the third time she had put off a return match. Christopher withdrew his challenge at once and declared he would infinitely rather watch a match. Patricia demurred and pouted, whereupon he sternly insisted that promises must be kept.

She played Geoffry and beat him by one point, secured by a rather vicious putt, then lightly requesting him to take her clubs back to the Club House with his, she summoned Christopher to take her home. Geoffry had not protested again. He took early opportunity to challenge Christopher instead and reaped a small revenge of easy victories, half embittered, half enhanced by Patricia's plainly expressed annoyance with the vanquished one. He knew she would have condoled with him had he lost.

So the weeks slipped by unnoticed and autumn merged into winter. Christmas came and went—with festivities in which both Patricia and Christopher took active part.

Christopher read and studied, but did nothing definite, and the New Year slipped along with rapid, silent foot. It was Cæsar who at length broke up the pleasant drifting interlude and he did it as deliberately as he did everything else, urged by his haunting desire to see Christopher finally committed to the future he had chosen.

"Why don't you go and see those road experiments they are trying in Kent?" Aymer asked one day.

"Frost-proof roads? They are no good. It was tried in Germany. What I would like is to run down to Cornwall and see how the Atlantic Road stands the winter, only it's such a beastly way down by train."

"It would certainly interfere with golf?" returned Cæsar drily.

"I'm beginning to play. Leverson says if I work really hard I may do something in a few years. Patricia says I shan't even if I live to be as old as Methuselah; so I must stick to it to prove her wrong."

"That's highly desirable, of course. All the same she might leave you a little leisure to play round with your hobby. You mustn't work too hard or Sam will beat you yet."

"How is Sam?"

"He came to see me before I left town. He is doing well. They will take him in as junior partner in a year or two. I always said he'd do better than you." He sighed profoundly.

"What a pity you didn't adopt him instead of me," retorted Christopher teasingly. "Is it too late to exchange? Buy him a senior partnership and leave me a free lance."

And because Aymer did not reply at once to his familiar nonsense, he turned quickly and surprised a strange look in the blue eyes, a fleeting, shadowy love, passionate, fierce, jealous. It lost itself almost as he caught it and Aymer drawled out in his indifferent tone:

"It really might be worth considering. For then I could go back to London and he could come home every night. Besides, Sam really appreciates me."

But it was Christopher who had no answer ready this time.

The look he had surprised gripped his heart. It revealed something hitherto unguessed by him. He came and sat on the edge of the sofa, and though he spoke lightly as was his manner, his voice and eyes belied his words.

"On the contrary, Sam does not appreciate you at all. He regards you as an erratic philanthropist with a crank for assisting deserving boys."

"A just estimate."

"Not at all. It is wrong in every particular."

"Prove it."

"You are not erratic; you are methodical to a fault. You are not a crank; therefore not a philanthropist. And you show a lamentable disregard to the moral qualities of those to whom you extend a helping hand."

"Jealousy."

"Jealousy of whom, please?"

"Of Sam."

Christopher considered thoughtfully.

"I believe you are right," he returned at last in a tone of naïve surprise. "How stupid of me not to have guessed before. I had always tried to think you helped him to gratify me. It was a great strain on my credulity. Now I understand."

"It had nothing to do with you at all," retorted Cæsar irritably, shifting his position a little, whereby a cushion fell to the ground. With a gust of petulance he pitched another after it, and then in rather a shamed way, told Christopher to ring for Vespasian to put the confounded things right.

But Christopher did no such thing. He put his strong arm round Cæsar, raised him, and rearranged the refractory cushions, talking the while to divert attention from this unheard-of proceeding.

"I shall go to London to-morrow and study Sam in order to oust him from your fickle affections," he announced. "Seriously, Cæsar. I ought to be running round seeing things a bit."

And Cæsar, having brought him to the conclusion he wished, signified his entire approval.

The following morning when Christopher came in to bid Cæsar good-bye, he found Mr. Aston also there, standing by the fire with a humorous smile on his face in evident appreciation of some joke.

"Christopher," said Aymer severely, "I have something important to say to you."

Christopher drew himself up to attention as he had learnt to do when under rebuke as a boy.

"If you are going to make a habit of running up and down to town and the ends of the earth on ridiculous business and worrying everyone's life out with time-tables (it was notorious Christopher never consulted anyone about his comings and goings), you must understand you cannot use Renata's carriage and pair for your station work. Max's pony is not up to your weight, neither is the station fly. I find on inquiry my father occasionally requires his motor for his own use; anyhow, it is not supposed to get muddy. So you had better buy one for yourself."

He held out a blank signed cheque.

Christopher looked from one to the other. It was the dream of his life to possess a motor, but this free gift of one was overwhelming.

"Of course," went on Cæsar hastily, "I shan't give you a birthday present too. It's to get out of that, you understand. You are twenty-one, aren't you? And it's only half mine, the other half is from St. Michael. I don't know where your manners are, Christopher; I thought I had brought you up to be polite. Go and thank the gentleman nicely."

Christopher turned to Mr. Aston, but he was beyond words. He could only look his overwhelming gratitude.

"It's not I," said that gentleman, hastily. "I only told Cæsar I'd like to go shares—the lamps or bells or something. Get a good horn with a good rich tone."

Christopher took the cheque with shaking fingers.

"I can't thank you, Cæsar, it's too big. Why didn't you let me earn it?"

"I wanted to prove to you the justice of Sam's opinion of me. Hurry up; you'll miss your train if there is one at this hour at all."

"You've not filled up the cheque."

"Not I. From what I know of your business methods you'll get what you want at half the price I should. I'm not going to let St. Michael fling away good money."

In his excitement Christopher forgot to wait for Patricia, who had promised to walk to the station with him. (Cæsar's complaint anent the horse vehicles was even more unfounded than his grievance over the time-table.) But seeing him start, she ran after him and made some candid and sisterly remarks on his behaviour and was only mollified by a full explanation of his unwonted state of elation. The rest of the walk was spent in discussing the merits of various species of motors.

CHAPTER XIV

Christopher spent the whole of the day inspecting possible motors, perfectly aware all the time of the one he meant to purchase, but in no wise prepared to forego the pleasures of inspection. Sam was not free that evening, so he dined with Constantia Wyatt, whose elusive personality continued to remove her in his eyes far from relationship with ordinary women. She was going to a "first night" at His Majesty's Theatre as a preliminary to her evening's amusement, and her husband, honestly engrossed in work, seized on Christopher at once as an adequate substitute for his own personal escort. He would meet her with the carriage after and go with her to the Duchess of Z—, but it would be a great help to him to have a few early evening hours for his book; so he explained with elaborate care.

"Basil is so deliciously mediæval and quaint," Constantia confided to her young cavalier as the carriage drove off; "he quite seriously believes women cannot go to a theatre or anywhere without an escort, even in our enlightened age. I assure you it is quite remarkable the number of parties we attend together; people are beginning to talk about it. If it's impossible for him to come himself he always seems to have hosts of cousins or relations ready to take his place. Oh, charming people; but quite a family corps, a sort of 'Guard of Honour,' as if I were Royalty—and really, at my time of life."

She turned her radiantly beautiful face to Christopher. She was indeed one of those beloved of time and it seemed to Christopher as he saw her in the crude flashing glare from the streets without, that the past ten years which had made of him a man had left her a girl still, but since he was as yet no adept at pretty speeches he kept the thought to himself and said shyly:

"It is not a question of age at all."

"You, too, think me incompetent to look after myself?"

"It is not a matter of competence either, is it? I mean, one can easily understand that Mr. Wyatt is proud of being your...." He stopped lamely.

"Finish your sentence, you tantalising boy."

"Your caretaker, then," he concluded defiantly.

"Delicious," she clapped her hands softly. "I thought you were going to say 'proprietor.'"

"It is you who are the proprietor of the caretaker, isn't it?"

"The new cadet is worthy his commission," she pronounced with mock gravity.

"It is a great honour, especially since I am not one of the family."

He never forgot this in her presence. It was as if an overscrupulous remembrance of hard days forced him to disclaim kinship with anything so finely feminine as Constantia Wyatt; as if he found no right of way from his own world of concrete fact into that delicate gracious world of illusions in which he placed her. Such barriers did not exist for her, however, and thence it came that it was to Constantia that Christopher spoke most easily of his relationship to the Aston family.

She put aside his disclaimer now, almost indignantly.

"You belong to Aymer. How can you say you do not belong to us, when you have been so good for him?"

His main claim on them all lay in that, that he was and had been good *for* the idolised Aymer Aston. He recognised it as she spoke and was content, for the proud generosity of his nature was built on a humility that had no underprops of petty pride.

"That was quite unpremeditated on my part," he protested whimsically; "you are all far too good to me. I can never explain it to myself, but I accept it, and realise I am a real millionaire."

Constantia Wyatt started slightly. Christopher noticed the diamonds on her hair sparkle as she leant forward.

"How did you discover that?" she asked in a low voice.

"My fortune? I was only ten when I came to Cæsar, but I must have been a very dense child indeed if I had not known even then that the luck of the gods was mine—if I had not been sensible of the kindness—"

His voice was low also and he fell into his old bad habit of leaving his sentence unfinished—hardly knowing he had expressed so much.

Constantia gave a sigh of relief, and Christopher again was only aware of the twinkling diamonds, of melting lines of soft velvet and fur, a presence friendly but unanalysable. They passed at that moment a mansion of a prince of the world of money, and she indicated it with a wave of her fan.

"Supposing, Christopher, you could realise some of your imaginary fortune for *his*?"

"Heaven forbid. Think how it was made."

"The world forgets that."

"You do not forget," he answered quickly; "besides it's much nicer to be adopted than to fight other people for fortune."

"I thought all boys liked fighting."

"Not if there's anything better to be done. A Punch and Judy show or a funeral will stop the most violent set-to. I've seen it times, when I was a boy in the street. Sam and I raised a cry one day of 'soldiers' to stop a chum being knocked down. Then we ran."

"Oh. Christopher, Christopher, can't you forget it?"

He shook his head.

"I don't want to. It wouldn't be fair to Cæsar. Also I couldn't."

"Some day you will marry, and perhaps she will rather you should forget."

"No, she won't, she is far too fond of Cæsar."

He stopped abruptly. For one brief moment the great voice of the streets and the yellow glare died away; he was blinded by a bewildering white light that broke down barriers undreamed of within his soul. Then the actual comparative darkness of the carriage obscured it and he found himself again conscious of the scent of roses, the sheen of satin and soft velvet, and his heart was beating madly. He had stumbled over the unsuspected threshold, surprised the hidden temple of his own heart, and this, inopportunely, prematurely, and, to his everlasting confusion, in the presence of another.

He clanged to the gates of his inner consciousness in breathless haste and set curb on his momentary shame and amazement. The break was so short his companion had barely time to identify the image disclosed when his voice went on with quiet deliberation.

"Or will be when she appears. A case of 'if she be not fair to "he," what care I how fair she be.'"

Constantia with rare generosity offered no hindrance to the closing of the door and discreetly pretended she had not been aware it had opened. Yet she smiled to herself and decided it was quite a desirable image and very advantageous to Aymer. Also, she reflected with pleasure, she had predicted the result from Patricia's and Christopher's intimacy, to her father years ago.

The piece at the theatre was a modern comedy which did not greatly interest him, indeed, he was more concerned in keeping his attention from that newly-discovered temple within than in unravelling the mysteries of the rather thread-bare plot of the play. Being, however, quite unaccustomed to dealing with this dual condition of mind it is to be feared he was a little "distrait" and mechanical of speech. Constantia allowed him the first act to play out his mood and then with charming imperiousness claimed his full attention, gained it, and with it, his gratitude for timely distraction.

Half way through the play he remembered this was the theatre at which Mrs. Sartin and Jessie were employed. He mentioned the fact to Mrs. Wyatt, who remarked gravely their names were not on the programme. Christopher equally gravely explained quite briefly. If he found nothing surprising in his own interest in these friends of the past, he never made the error of imagining they would be of interest to newer friends. There was a certain independence in his attitude towards all affairs that touched him nearly, which even at this early age made him a free citizen of the world in which he chanced to move. This attitude of mind was more in evidence to-night than he had imagined. Personally, he quite appreciated the fact he was sitting in a box with one of the loveliest women in London, and that she was everything that was charming and nice to him, but it never occurred to him that half the men in the theatre would have given a big share of their worth to be in his place; he was almost childishly unconscious of the envious glances he earned. Constantia was not: neither was she blind to his attitude of personal content and impersonal oblivion. It amused her vastly, and she compiled an exceedingly entertaining letter to Aymer on the strength of it.

"He handed me over to Basil in the vestibule afterwards," she concluded, "with the most engaging air of having been allowed a special treat and fully appreciating it, and departed straightway to conduct Mrs. Sartin, dresser at the theatre, to her house in the wilds of Lambeth. He owned it in the most ingenuous way, seeing nothing whatever of pathos in it. Does he lack sense of humour?"

Aymer, ignoring the rest of the letter, refuted this query with pages of vigorous sarcasm, to the complete delight and triumph of his sister.

Christopher, having ascertained from a suspicious doorkeeper that Mrs. Sartin would not be free for twenty minutes, cooled his heels in a dark, draughty passage with what patience he could.

He seized on Mrs. Sartin as she came unsuspectingly down a winding stair, and bore her off breathless, remonstrating, but fluttering with pride, in a hansom.

"I'm only up for a few days," he explained. "Sam dines with me to-morrow and I want you to come out somewhere in the afternoon. Crystal Palace, or wherever Jessie likes."

Mrs. Sartin's face and Mrs. Sartin's person had expanded in the last few years and her powers of expressing emotion seemed to have expanded with her person. Disappointment was writ large on her ample countenance.

"Well, now, if that isn't a shame and a contrariwise of purpose. I've taken a job, Mr. Christopher, for that blessed afternoon. I've promised to dress Miss Asty, who is making a debût at a matiny at the Court. Eliza Lowden, she was goin' to dress her, but she can't set a wig as I can."

"What a nuisance. But, anyhow, Jessie isn't engaged, is she?"

For an instant he had a glimpse of Mrs. Sartin's full face, dubious, questioning, even hostile, but to him it was merely the result of flickering light and conveyed nothing.

"I don't rightly know," she said slowly, "maybe she doesn't care much for gadding about."

"Rubbish," he retorted contemptuously, "if you can't come, Jessie must anyway."

Mrs. Sartin held firmly to the carriage door and the oscillation of the cab caused her to nod violently, but it was not in assent to Christopher's proposition. She appeared to be turning something over in her slow mind.

"I don't know but what I could arrange with Eliza," she remarked.

"Of course you can, like a good woman; and you and Jessie come up to Aston House at one o'clock and say where you'd like to go, and we'll go."

Martha demurred. "Mr. Aston won't like it."

"Won't like what?"

"Our comin' to 'is 'ouse, like as if we 'ad any claim on you."

"Do I or you know Mr. Aston best?" he demanded imperiously. "Claim indeed. Martha, you dear old stupid, where would I be now, if you hadn't taken my mother in?"

"That were just a chance, Mr. Christopher, because I 'appened to be comin' 'ome late and your pore ma was took bad on the bridge as I crossed, and bein' a woman what 'ad a family, I saw what was the matter."

"What was it more than a chance that Cæsar in looking for a boy to adopt stumbled on the son of someone he used to know?"

Again the oscillation made Mrs. Sartin nod vigorously. She bestowed on her companion another of those shrewd, dubious glances, began a sentence and stopped.

"Yes. What were you saying?" asked Christopher absently.

"You've come quite far enough, Mr. Christopher," she announced, with the air of a woman come to a decision, "you just tell that man on the top to stop and let me out. Thanking you all the same, but I don't care to be seen driving 'ome this time of night and settin' folks a-talking. You set me down, there's a dear Mr. Christopher."

She got her way in the matter of dismissing the cab, but not in dismissing Christopher, her primary desire, lest an indiscreet tongue should prompt her to say more than was "rightful," as she explained to Jessie.

"For if the dear innocent don't see 'ow the land lays, it isn't for me to show 'im, and Mr. Aymer so good to Sam."

"Maybe you are all wrong," said Jessie shortly.

Mrs. Sartin sniffed contemptuously.

The Sartins no longer inhabited Primrose Buildings, but were proud inhabitants of a decent little house in a phenomenally dull street, sufficiently near the big "Store" to suit Sam's convenience. Sam himself came to the door and, late as it was, insisted on walking back with Christopher into the region of cabs, and, becoming engrossed in conversation, naturally walked far beyond it.

"This partnership business," began Sam at once, "I do wish, Chris, you'd get Mr. Aymer to make it a loan business. I'd be a sight better pleased."

"I can't for the life of me see why," Christopher objected with a frown. "It's only a matter of a few hundred pounds, and if Cæsar chooses to spend it on you instead of buying a picture or enamel, or that sort of toy, why should you object. It's not charity."

"Then what is it?" demanded Sam, "because I'm not a toy. Don't fly out at me, Chris, be reasonable. I'm as grateful to him as I can be, and I mean to use the chance he's given me all I can. But this partnership business beats me. It's all very well for him to do things for you. Of course he couldn't do less; but how do I come in?"

A drunken man reeled out of a house and lurched against Christopher, who put out his hand to steady him without a word of comment, and when the drinker had found his balance, he turned again to Sam with sharp indignation.

"He could do a jolly sight less for me and still be more generous than most people's fathers. There's no 'of course' about it."

Sam stared stolidly in front of him.

"That's just it. It's one thing to do it for someone belonging to one, and another thing to do it for a stranger," he persisted.

"Well, that's just how I feel, only I don't make a fuss. It's Cæsar's way, and a precious good way for us."

They parted at last with no better understanding on the vexed subject, and Christopher, once back at Aston House, sat frowning over the fire instead of going to bed. Why all of a sudden had this question of his amazing indebtedness to Aymer been so persistently thrust on him. Hitherto he had accepted it with generous gratitude, without question, had recognised no room for speculation, allowed no play to whispers of curiosity. It was Cæsar's will. Now he was suddenly aware, however he might close his mind, others speculated; however guard his soul from inquisitiveness, others questioned, and it angered him for Cæsar's sake. His mother had never spoken to him of the past, never opened her lips as to the strange sacrifice she had made for her unborn child, except once when they were hurriedly leaving London by stealth, after the episode with Martha Sartin's rascally husband. Mrs. Hibbault had remarked wearily: "I wonder, Jim, shall I spend my life taking you out of the way of bad men?"

When he asked her if she had done it before she answered: "I took you from your father." It was the only time he remembered her mentioning that unknown father; he recollected still how her face had changed and she had hurried her steps, as if haunted by a new suspicion.

It gave him quite unreasonable annoyance that these thoughts intruded themselves to-night, when he wanted to give his full attention to the wonder and glory of the discovery he had made in Constantia Wyatt's company. That was, indeed, a matter of real moment. How had he contrived to be blind to it so long? He had not reached the age of twenty-one without entertaining vague theories concerning love, and having definitely decided that it had nothing to do with the travesty of its name which had confronted him on his wanderings. Neither taste nor training, nor the absorbing passion for his work had left him time or wish to explore this field which roused only an impatient contempt when thrust on his notice. Of Love itself, as before stated, he held vague theories: regarding it rather as a far-off event which would meet him in future years and land him eventually at Hymen's feet. And here he found all such theories suddenly reversed. The first moment the idea of marriage was presented to his notice the vision of the only possible bride for him stood out with quite definite distinctness. Instead of Love being a prelude to the thought of Marriage, that thought had been the crashing chords that had opened his mind to Love. But the Love had been already there, unrecognised. He found he could no way now imagine himself as apart from Patricia. To eliminate her presence from his heart was to lose part of his individuality; to separate his practical life from her was as if he wantonly destroyed a limb. Away from her actual presence and before this dual conception of themselves he was of assured courage, thankfulness and strange joy, but the moment his thoughts flew to her in concrete form, to Patricia Connell at Marden Court, he experienced a reversion: his confidence was gone, the assured vision became a very far-away possibility, a glory which he might hardly hope to attain.

Very slowly this latter aspect blotted out the first triumphant joy of his discovery. Mundane things, such as Renata Aston's wishes, Cæsar's consent, and even the person of Geoffry Leverson interposed between Patricia and him. This mood had its sway and in turn succumbed to an awakening of his dormant will and every fighting instinct. Patricia must be his, was his potentially, but he recognised she was not his for the asking. He would have to acquire the right to say to Cæsar, "I want to marry Mrs. Aston's sister." Aymer might easily make the way smooth for him, if he would. He had no reason then for believing he would oppose the idea. Yet Christopher knew that in the gamut of possible needs and desires the one thing he could not freely accept from Cæsar's hands was his wife. His life was before him, before Patricia too. When he reached this point in his deliberation he made a sudden movement. The fire had gone out and it was very cold. Christopher decided it was time to go to bed.

CHAPTER XV

Jessie proved by no means averse to "gadding about," as her mother expressed it. She and Mrs. Sartin turned up punctually at Aston House, though laden with an air of desperate resolve. On their way they had both cheerfully concealed some tremulous qualms and neither had ventured to express a dormant wish that Mr. Christopher had chosen some other spot for lunch than the lordly, sombre, half-opened house. It was not until they stood beneath the great portico that their vague discomfort got the upper hand, and Mrs. Sartin agreed without demur to Jessie's suggestion that they should seek a smaller entrance. As they were turning away the great door swung open and Christopher came out.

"How jolly of you to be so punctual," he cried, greeting them warmly. "Where were you off to? Did you think I wasn't at home because the blinds were down? They don't open all the house for me," he added, leading the way through the great hall. "I live on the garden side."

Mrs. Sartin had no mind to hurry: she wanted to take in the solid beauties as she passed. Jessie plucked her nervously by the sleeve seeing Christopher was outpacing them, and terrified of being left in that labyrinth of corridor without a guide. However, once within the sunny little room with its homely comforts and Christopher's kindly self for host, they regained their wonted composure.

The smallness of the staff left in charge at Aston House gave Christopher an excuse for dispensing with the services of Burton, the footman, and the meal was a great success. It never occurred to the host to think these good kind friends of his in any way out of place here. His sense of humour was quite unruffled, nay, he was even genuinely pleased to see the good, ample Martha, the strings of her black bonnet untied, her face wreathed in smiles, vigorously clearing out a tart dish, and Jessie's homely features lit up with passive enjoyment, her brown eyes shining beneath the ridiculous curls.

They had chosen the Hippodrome for their afternoon's amusement, and there was plenty of time after lunch to show them some of the glories of Aston House. Christopher led them through the shrouded rooms, but the treasures he displayed to view were not so much those of artistic merit as those which had pleased his own boyish fancy years before. Passing down a corridor he stopped by a remote closed door. Jessie was examining some Wedgewood plaques a little way off. Christopher looked at Mrs. Sartin with a queer little smile.

"When I was a kid," he said rather shamefacedly, "I used to play that my mother was going about the place with me. You see there were no womenfolk, and the pretence seemed to help things. I used to make it seem more real by always starting here, and pretending that was her room. It was the only door that was always locked."

"Lor', what a queer idea!" ejaculated Mrs. Sartin, gazing suspiciously at the closed door.

Christopher laughed. "Oh, I've been in since; there's nothing there but newspapers, quite a dull little room. But it was an odd fancy. My feeling was so strong I used to take her round and show her things I've shown you to-day. I always wanted to show them to someone instead of the real treasures, which are rather dull, you know."

Mrs. Sartin said again it was very queer. She followed Jessie and Christopher reluctantly with backward glances towards the door, full of puzzled suspicion. When they were again in the hall it was time to start for the Hippodrome, and there was a great deal of patting of hats and tying of strings before a Venetian mirror.

But Aymer Aston's room, with its world-famed pictures, was unvisited.

When the Hippodrome performance was over and he had seen his guests safely homeward, Christopher called on Constantia Wyatt and found her in. She seemed in no wise surprised to see him, but asked him promptly when he was going down to Marden.

"I don't know," he said slowly, his eyes on the fire, "I don't think I shall go back yet."

Constantia rang the bell and told the footman she was not at home, and then drew her chair up to the fire and made Christopher some fresh tea.

"Is London proving so very attractive?" she inquired.

"I shan't stay in town. I think I shall go abroad again. I want to think."

"Dear, dear. Is Marden such a bad atmosphere for the intelligence?"

He coloured up boy-like and then laughed.

"There are too many clever people to help one think there. Also there is a man in Belgium trying some private road experiments. I want to help him."

"What will Aymer say to it?"

"He thinks I've been idle long enough."

"And the man in Belgium will help you to think?"

"I'm afraid that's my own job."

Constantia rose and wandered round the room, vaguely touching a flower here and there and presently came to stand behind her visitor's chair. She was thinking how young he was, and how strong, and that Patricia was a fortunate girl. Her eyes were very soft and kind as she bent over his chair and touched his shoulder with her fingers.

"Christopher, you are in love!"

Very young indeed, was her inward comment on his startled wondering face turned to her.

"How do you know?" he asked, making no denial of the fact. Denial would have savoured of disloyalty to his new kingdom.

She laughed gently. "Don't you even know that? What a lot I could teach you if Aymer would hand you over. Listen, Master Christopher, love is the only thing men want to think about alone, just as it's the only thing a woman never wants to keep to herself. You could think to much better advantage at Marden but it's no use telling you so. You won't believe it."

"I do believe it, only it's not a question of *my* advantage, you see."

"There spoke Aymer's pupil. Remember roads take a good deal of making and short cuts were made for—lovers."

She returned to the fire and stood there looking at him with an interest that surprised herself: a tall, gracious presence whose knowledge of his secret hurt not one bit, so clearly did it lie within the realms wherein all gracious, tender women reign.

Then she changed the subject quite abruptly, thrust it back into those hazy regions of speculation from which Christopher had so hardly and impatiently dragged it the previous night.

"I wonder if your mother were alive, if she would be satisfied with you, Christopher, and if she would still want to make a socialist of you."

"My mother?" he echoed dully.

For a while he struggled with a strange inability to lay hold on the shadowy form he knew so well. He looked round the beautiful room that was but a setting to a lovely woman and then back at her. Why had she spoken of his mother? He again attempted to crystallise the thought of the dearly loved, defeated woman in the presence of her to whom the world denied nothing.

"I can't do it," he said aloud with a quick breath.

"Do what?" she queried swiftly, but got no answer.

"Was my mother a socialist?" he asked presently with difficulty.

"So I have always understood."

"Who told you so?"

"My father. I thought you knew that, Christopher, or I should not have mentioned it. All I know is, she chose to be poor rather than expose you to the dangers of wealth. I know nothing else."

Christopher stood up. "Thank you," he said, "I believe I did know that, but I have never been reminded of it. I do not know her story: I suppose she did not wish me to know it, but I do know whatever she chose, whatever she did, it was chosen and done because it seemed to her the right course and therefore the only one she could take."

Constantia nodded, still gazing at the fire.

"Aymer's training on the top of that," she mused, "I suppose you are accounted for."

He grew red and looked a boy again. "I should have much to account for if I failed them."

"Them?" She swung round.

"Cæsar and my mother."

There was a pause.

"And so you will go to Belgium and think?" she said lightly.

"No, I shall go to Belgium and work."

"You said *think*," she insisted.

"I have thought here. I was not sure when I came, but I am now."

"May I know what you have thought?"

For a moment the strangeness of speaking to her like this held him dumb. How did it happen she should know so much and must know more, she who had been barely a real individual to him before? It bewildered and confused him. He did not understand that the unspoken passionate claim he made on one woman had broken the barriers between him and woman-kind, that because he loved Patricia Connell he could speak to Constantia Wyatt, for they stood together on holy ground.

"You have every right. You helped me after all," he said doubtfully, but smiling "I ought not to have hesitated. Cæsar is waiting for me to make roads, not to take short cuts."

"You think love can better afford to wait than Cæsar?"

"I have my life before me."

"And if you lose her?"

"It is settled," he said simply.

She drew in her breath. By every law of man he was right, and yet all the woman in her cried out against this decision as falseness to some other law imperfectly understood, but clamorous for recognition. Nevertheless how her heart went out to him for the quiet finality of that refusal to yield to a law not of his own making! She was proud he was so much the handiwork of Aymer, while she recognised the very weakness of his strength.

"He will lose her," she mused as she sat alone when he had gone, "and it would break Aymer's heart if he knew, but he won't know. He has succeeded in making a man of him, but, oh, what a nice boy he would have been!"

So Christopher turned his back on the great discovery and went to Belgium. Whereupon Patricia complained bitterly, but her golf improved, and Geoffry Leverson, who knew nothing of road-making, started on a very short cut indeed.

The Roadmaker remained in Belgium longer than he expected and in the laboratory of a great man stumbled on the key of the discovery that in a few years was to make him famous from one end of Europe to the other.

When the apple blossoms were again blushing pink across the land and the blue sky was piled high with dreams of love castles, Christopher remembered the short cut and abruptly announced his intention of returning home. He sent no warning of his coming, but arrived one day at Aston House with his beloved car. It was in his heart to continue his journey straight away, but thinking what pleasure it would give Aymer to watch the practical working of his experiment, he put aside the dictates of his desires and spent the day purchasing materials. Also he called on Constantia and found himself incomprehensibly making excuses for the delay. "I shall go down early to-morrow," he said; "it can make no difference, since they do not know I am in England."

"No, I don't suppose it can," said Constantia thoughtfully.

CHAPTER XVI

Christopher flecked an imaginary speck of dust from the burnished metal of his car. He was all ready to start, but seeing a postman coming up the drive, waited to take down the latest delivery of letters, and as he waited a hansom drove up, and since his car occupied the portico, stopped at the side. A big form emerged with a jovial red face and wide shoulders. It was six years since Christopher had seen the man, but his name and personality and, above all, the antipathy with which he had formerly inspired him flashed with lightning vividness to his mind. Peter Masters glanced at Christopher with a momentary puzzled look and turned to ring the bell.

"If you want to see Mr. Aston, Mr. Masters, he is at Marden, and Aymer also. I'm just going down."

"Ah." The keen eyes searched him up and down. "I've seen you before; can't place you, though; you aren't Nevil's boy."

"No, I'm—" Christopher hardly knew why he changed the form of his answer, or that he had. "I'm the boy Aymer adopted. You saw me about six years ago."

"Oh, I remember. Christopher Aston, they call you. You did not like me. What have you done with that clever head of yours, eh?"

Christopher carefully examined a nut on the car.

"Well, never mind. When will Cousin Charles be back?"

"Not until May if he can help it."

"Not well?"

"Quite well, thank you."

Peter Masters stood biting his lip and considering. The footman brought out some letters which Christopher put in his pocket and then mounted.

"Can I take any message for you?" he asked politely.

"Are you going straight to Marden now?"

"Yes."

"Alone?"

Christopher devoutly hoped he was, but a sudden fear assailed him: he would not make the momentous journey in solitude. He answered somewhat indistinctly.

"You might run me down; I must see Cousin Charles."

"I should warn you it is a new road to me and I've had my car nearly a year; it's due to go wrong somehow, and I drive rather fast."

"I expect you set sufficient value on your own life to insure mine."

"It will be cold. You can't ride in that thin coat."

"You pass the Carlton; I'm staying there. It won't delay us two minutes. What luck."

He walked round and got into the car, oblivious of the trifling fact its owner had neither acquiesced nor expressed an enthusiasm over the luck.

"I hope he is nervous," thought Christopher vindictively, "though there's not much chance of it. He hasn't much hair to stand on end, but I'll do my best to make it."

Peter Masters rolled himself contentedly in the spare rug. "Ready," he said cheerfully.

Christopher, however, made no attempt to start. He beckoned to the footman.

"Fetch me the blue paper-covered book you'll find on the second left-hand shelf of the low book-case in my room, Burton."

He waited immovable while the man went on the errand, being quite determined to start unprompted by Mr. Masters if he started at all. The old butler came out and acknowledged Mr. Masters's presence with a deferential bow. He addressed himself to Christopher.

"Mr. Christopher, will you tell Mr. Aymer we've raised the Raphael in his room, as he said, four inches, but the paper is a little faded and it shows. What will he like us to do?"

Christopher nodded. "All right, I'll tell him. I shall probably be up again next week."

"We shall be glad to see you again, sir."

Burton returned in indecorous hurry with the book. Christopher bade them good-bye in a friendly way and the car glided quietly down the drive out into the busy thoroughfare.

"You are quite at home there," remarked Mr. Masters affably.

"It happens to be my home."

It was a very busy hour and the driver of the car might reasonably be excused if he were silent. At all events if Mr. Masters spoke, Christopher did not hear him. They slipped in and out of the traffic, glided round corners, slid with smooth swiftness along free stretches of road, crept gingerly across a maze of cross-ways and drew up at the Carlton.

Peter Masters, who appreciated the situation and found humour in it, plunged into that Palace of Travellers and reappeared in an incredibly short time, coated for the occasion.

"Now," he said cheerily, "we are ready for the fray—when you are ready, Master Christopher," he added with a twinkle in his eye.

But Christopher's ill-temper had evaporated with the short wait. After all, the man was Aymer's cousin, and he couldn't help being a brute, and if he really wanted to see St. Michael perhaps it was a piece of luck for him that the postman was late. So he laughed and said a little shyly he hoped Mr. Masters would not mind his not talking till they were out of the streets.

"I shall expect conversation with compound interest," returned the other good-humouredly.

He was, however, quite quiet until Christopher turned into a narrow back street.

"That's not your best way," said Peter Masters sharply.

"I'm going to call on a friend," replied the driver without apology.

They threaded their way through a maze of small ill-looking streets, slowly enough, for there were children all over the road; not infrequently a big dray forced them to proceed backwards. Masters noted that Christopher never expected the legitimate traffic should give way to him. They emerged at last on a crowded thoroughfare of South London, where small shops elbowed big ones and windows blazed with preposterous advertisements. There were trams too, and scarcely room for the big car between rail and pavement. Presently they stopped before a prosperous-looking grocery store. A white-aproned man rushed out with undisguised complacency to wait on the fine equipage.

"I want to see Mr. Sartin if he's free," said Christopher, and waited quietly.

In a minute Sam was with them, white-aproned, pencil behind ear. To Masters's amusement his companion greeted the young grocer with the familiarity of long friendship.

"I heard from Jessie the other day," said Christopher when he had explained his appearance; "what about this man Cladsley? Is she going to marry him?"

Sam looked down the street, a little frown on his face.

"Jessie'd no business to write you. Cladsley's all right. Don't you worry about Jessie."

"I'm not worrying," laughed the other, "I only wanted to be sure it was suitable and all that."

"I'll look after Jessie." The words were ungracious, but Sam looked worried and uncertain. "You've done enough for us."

"You old dog in the manger," persisted Christopher good-temperedly, "you'll never let me do anything for Jessie, and, after all, it was she who used to take my part when you fought me, Master Sam, and wouldn't let you bully me."

Sam grinned. "Yes, it was always Jim that was in the right then. Don't you bother. Cladsley's a good sort if she would only make up her mind."

"I gathered his job would be up soon and I thought I might find another for him if it's all straight with them. That's why I came to see you."

Sam appeared still reluctant.

"It's all beastly stuck-up pride on your part," concluded Christopher after more argument. "I expect you'll cut me next; you are getting too prosperous, Mr. Sartin."

But they parted good friends, and the car re-threaded its way through the crowded streets out into a meaner, more deserted neighbourhood, till at length they emerged on a long empty straight road with small yellow brick houses on either side, as yet uninhabited.

"What's the engaging young grocer's name?" asked Masters abruptly.

"Sartin—Sam Sartin."

"Known him long?"

"We were children together."

"Relations, perhaps?"

"No."

"Why did he call you Jim?"

"I used to be Jim."

"James Aston?"

"No."

"What then?"

"I've forgotten," said Christopher very deliberately.

Mr. Masters laughed genially. "I like a good liar. You don't want to tell me anything about yourself. Very likely you are wise, but all the same I am very curious to know all about you—who you are, and how you came to the Astons, and who was your mother, and when and where Aymer met her. You see," he added confidentially, "I used to be about with Aymer a good bit and I thought I knew all—" He stopped abruptly. If he were being purposely tactless he realised he had gone far enough.

"I do not think Aymer ever met my mother. I am certain you haven't. Mr. Aston used to know her, and suggested Aymer's adopting me when he heard I was left stranded in a workhouse. I was just a workhouse boy. Now, are you satisfied as to my private history, sir?"

"No," retorted the inquisitor good-humouredly as ever, "you must have had a father, you know."

"It seems possible. I do not remember him."

He began to resign himself to fate and this Juggernaut of a man who rolled other people's feelings flat with no more compunction than a traction engine.

"Fathers are useful. You may want to remember, some-day."

"I'm quite satisfied at present."

"I'm not suggesting you have anything to complain of. Aymer doesn't do things by halves. Christopher is as much a family name as Aston, for example."

Something in his tone caught Christopher's attention and he looked at him sharply. Peter Masters was gazing straight before him with that same cynical smile on his face it had worn when Christopher was first introduced to him six years ago.

"I wonder why on earth they did that?" ruminated the Juggernaut. "Cousin Charles is capable of any unworldly folly, but Aymer was a man of the world once. It looks like colossal bluff."

And then the meaning of all this swept over Christopher's mind like a wave of fire, scorching his soul, desecrating and humiliating the very mainspring of his life.

Aymer's son! He knew Masters believed it as surely as if he had blurted it out in his own unbearable way, and it was not to save him, it was from no sense of decency Masters had not said it audibly. Christopher longed to fling the unspoken lie back to him, to refuse the collaboration of detail that the passing minutes crowded on his notice. He put on speed; tried to outstrip the evil thought of it, to think only of Cæsar, the dear companion of his days, the steady friend, the unobtrusive mentor and guide. But a thought he could not outstrip slipped into his mind so insidiously and stealthily, he could not tell how or whence it came.

"You only know Cæsar; you never knew Aymer Aston of the silent past."

Faster and faster rushed the car in futile attempt to outpace the whispered treason. The speed indicator stood at 40 and still mounted.

"I should like to remark," said Peter Masters thoughtfully, "that I have not yet made my will and it would cause some inconvenience to a vast number of people to have several millions left masterless."

"It's an open road," returned Christopher, "I know what I'm at. I expect I enjoy life as much as you do."

He slowed down suddenly, however, to about twenty miles an hour to pass an old woman in a donkey cart, and the hateful thought swept on in advance apparently, for he overtook it again when their speed ran up ten points.

Christopher had chosen a rather circuitous route which offered fewer villages than the general high-road. It was a glorious day, the banks were starry with primroses, and all the hedgerows, just bursting into green rosettes, were hunting ground for birds innumerable.

Green emerald grass in water-meadows, fresh green growth on the hillside, and red bud and green promise hung from every tree. The crisp air whispered warnings of frosts still to come, but braced the nerve and gladdened the heart nevertheless, and called imperiously to youth to seek its kingdom. Christopher was at no pains to spare the nerves of the master of millions, and though he invariably crept through villages and towns sedately and drove with an eye for crossroads and distant specks on the white track before him, they swept through the open country with a breathless rush.

How good it would have gone alone, Christopher thought savagely, and resentment rose high in his heart. He was going to meet Patricia for the first time with understanding eyes. In the past months his love had grown with steady insistence until the imperious voice of spring, singing in concord with it, had overridden the decision of his stubborn will, demanding surrender, clamorous for recognition, and now having allowed the claim he was again forced back on the unsolved question of his own history. It was as if some imp of mischief had coupled his love to the Past, and had left him without knowledge to loose the secret knot. The silence became intolerable for fear of the next words that might break it from his companion. It would be better to take control himself—so he slackened speed a little and had the satisfaction of hearing Peter Masters heave a relieved sigh.

"The roads here need re-making," as they proceeded bumpily over a rather bad piece of ground.

"For motors?"

"For everything. A road should be easy going for motors, horses, and foot-passengers. Easy and safe."

"How would you do it?"

"A raised causeway for walkers; a road for carriages, and a track for motors. It only means so many yards more and there is plenty of land. Look at that turf—four yards of it. Might as well be road."

"What are you going to make your roads of?"

Christopher took a deep breath; the pace of the car increased a little.

"That has to be found—will be found. It is a question of time."

"And you mean to find it?"

"A good many people mean to find it."

Masters shook his head.

"It won't pay you so well as iron, Master Christopher. My offer is still open."

Christopher was so surprised that he nearly swerved into an unfenced pond they were passing.

"It was very kind of you to make it again," Christopher managed to stammer out, adding with a bluntness worthy of Masters himself, "I never could understand why you made it at all."

"Neither do I," returned Peter Masters with a laugh, "and I generally know what I'm at. Perhaps I thought it would please Aymer. As I told you just now, we were friends before his accident. I suppose you've heard all about that?"

For a brief moment Christopher felt temptation grip him. He was convinced the man beside him knew the untold story, and at this juncture in his life he would give much to understand all those things he had never questioned or ventured to consider. Then recognising disloyalty in the very thought, he hastened to escape the pitfall. It was no use to take half measures with this man, however, so he lied again boldly.

"Of course I know," and went back again to safer ground. "Whatever your reasons, it was good of you to think of me and kinder still to renew your offer. I expect you will think me a silly fool of a boy to refuse it again."

"Not exactly; but a boy brought up by an Aymer Aston the second."

"That is sufficient luck for one boy to grab out of life."

Peter Masters chuckled. "I take it, young man, you'd rather be fathered by Aymer than by me, eh?"

Christopher muttered a very fervent affirmative between clenched teeth, which did not appear to reach his hearer's ears, for as Masters finished his own sentence he shot a sudden, sharp, puzzled look at Christopher, and his teeth shut together with a click. He spoke no more and when Christopher hazarded a remark he got no answer.

The glory of the day was at its height when Marden came in sight; the whole world seemed to have joined in a peon of thanksgiving which for the moment drowned the unwonted echoes in Christopher's heart that Peter Masters's hard voice had awoken.

Youth was his, Love was his, and Patricia was to be his, and he was going to see her. He covered the distance from the lodge gates to the house in a time that taxed his companion's nerve to the uttermost and bid fair to outpace even the throbbing, rushing pulse of spring that filled the land.

CHAPTER XVII

Patricia was in the orchard, and not only in the orchard, but of it, for she was comfortably perched on a low bough of an ancient hoary apple tree. She had a volume of Robert Bridges's poems in her hand and a thirst was on her to be at the edge of a cliff and look over into blue space below. The secluded orchard with its early crown of pink blushes, the serene shut-in valley screened from cold winds and cradled between the chalky highlands, weighed on her. She looked upwards through the dainty tracery of soft green and pink to the sky above, delicately blue with white clouds racing over it. There was air up there, free and untrammelled. Patricia sighed and then laughed at herself, for it was good, even here in the narrow orchard, life with its coming possibilities, its increasing riches. She was glad to be alone at that moment if only to share a thought with the poet who at this period held sway over her mind.

The previous evening had been one of great moment to her and she was joyfully thankful to find that it obscured and clouded no particle of the daily simple joy of her existence. She had claimed this day to herself, free from all new issues to prove this point, and her heart sang with content for what had been, was, and would be.

The orchard gate clicked, and looking through the intervening boughs and leaflets, she saw Christopher coming across the grass towards her with his even, swinging step.

In her rough grey dress she was as part of the rough tree herself. Her golden head and the delicate lovely colouring of her face rivalled the tree's darling blossoms, so Christopher thought when he reached her. He came straight to her through the maze of old and young trees and had the exquisite joy of seeing her flush with surprise and pleasure at sight of him. Here indeed she felt was the one addition to her day that she needed. She did not descend from her perch, and it was his hand which steadied her there when excitement imperilled her throne.

"To come down on us without warning like this!" she expostulated, smiling down at him. "Why, we might have had no leisure to see you or luncheon to give you! When did you actually come?"

"Half an hour and five minutes ago. I've seen Cæsar and St. Michael, and I've had luncheon."

"And have you come to stay?"

"I don't know yet." He leant his arm on the bough where she sat, which was of exactly convenient height.

"The amount of leisure you seem to have on hand," said Patricia severely, "is outrageous, considering how hard the rest of the family work."

"Especially Nevil," laughed Christopher.

"Especially Nevil. We have not sat down to a meal with him for three weeks. He nearly walked on Max's puppy last week and he has forgotten Charlotte's existence except as a penwiper—she went in to him one morning with a message and came out with an ink smudge on her red dress—she *said* it was his pen—the dress is the same colour as the penwiper, so she may be right. He paid no attention to the message."

"Well, at present, if you take the trouble to go into the Rosery you will find Nevil lying by the fountain catching goldfish with Max. I do not think he remembered I'd been away."

"Oh, I am glad," cried Patricia, clapping her hands; "of course it's very nice of him to be so clever and write so beautifully, but it's much nicer when he's just a dear silly thing—and catches goldfish. But tell me about yourself now. Are you well? And have you been working hard? Why aren't you in Belgium, why have you come, and what are you going to do, and when are you going back?"

"Stop, I can't keep more than five questions in my head at once and I've answered several of yours already. The first is trivial; you have eyes. I have been working as usual; it's no use to explain how, you have no conception of work at all. I am not in Belgium because I am here in a better place. I am going to enjoy myself, I hope, and I shall go away when it pleases me."

"Indeed, Your Highness. You have not explained why you came."

"I think," said Christopher, considering hard and speaking with slow deliberation, "I *think*, only it is so preposterously silly, that I came to see you, or perhaps it was Cæsar or Nevil if it were not Max."

Patricia laughed deliciously and leant forward, making pretence to box his ears. Christopher shook the bough in revenge till she cried pax, and peace supervened.

"Since you have evidently no business of your own to see to," she said severely, "it shall be my business to teach you to appreciate Robert Bridges."

"I don't like his name; who is he?" Christopher grumbled.

"He is a genius and you must sit at his feet and listen."

"Isn't it respectful to stand?"

She regarded him gravely with her head on one side. "True humility sits ill on you, I fear. You may stand if you take off your hat."

He flung it on the grass obediently.

"The Cliff Edge." "The Cliff Edge has a carpet ... of purple, gold, and green."

She read the little poem all through, her sweet, appreciative voice making music of the lines already melodious. Christopher wondered if the writer ever knew how beautiful his words could be made.

"Is that not lovely?" she asked when she finished, leaning forward so that her hand and the book rested for a moment on his arm.

Christopher nodded without moving.

"It makes me thirsty for the sea," she went on, "for sky, for space to move and breathe. Oh, Christopher, things here are either old or small. All the great and beautiful things are old, the glory of it, the house, the life, the very trees, old, old, old. And the rest is small, protected and shut in. I want to feel things that are young and free and great, as the sky and sea and the wind. I am thirsty sometimes to stand on the edge of the cliff and taste the free, free air from off the sea that has no one else's thoughts in it. Do you understand that?—the longing for something that does not belong to any part, to any one?"

"Yes, I understand. I feel it too, sometimes."

"I knew you did. You see, it's because neither of us belong here—to Marden—really. Oh, I don't mean it horridly. It's the dearest place and they are all the dearest people; but the life, the big thought of it all, isn't ours. *Our* people didn't help make it."

Christopher made no answer. He was idly flinging bits of bark into his hat. If he were but certain—oh, if he could but be certain she were right! He looked up at her at last.

There could be no room for the grey shadows of doubt any longer. She *was* right. He felt it as he looked and as the thought she suggested sank deeper into his mind. Was not he truly one with her in it? He, too, had been conscious of a Life and History here at Marden not his own, that exacted no obligations from him, but rather silently insisted on the freedom. Such freedom, mated to hers, was the last great boon he asked of life that had already given him so much. Still he hesitated for very fear of losing the joy of the hour that would be his and hers for eternity when he sealed it with the passionate words in his heart.

"I know just what you mean," he said, "it is no disloyalty to them to feel it—only loyalty to ourselves. As for the sea and all that, I will motor you down to Milford whenever you like."

"Oh, Christopher!" She clasped her hands with joy like a child. "Have you brought the new motor? What is it like?"

"It's a perfect love, Patricia. I drove it down from town to-day. Such a road, stones, ruts—and it behaved like an angel although weighted with an extra sixteen stone of colossal brutality—Peter Masters, Esquire, millionaire."

"Oh, why on earth did you bring him down here?"

"He did not ask permission. He just came—wanted to see St. Michael. Don't let's talk about him. Let's talk about ourselves. We are much more interesting."

"Egoist!"

"Doesn't the plural number cancel the egoism? But I really have something to tell you about myself. Two things, indeed, if you'll kindly listen."

"I will try to be polite. Proceed." She ensconced herself comfortably against the trunk of the tree, folded her hands in her lap and smiled down at him under her half-shut lids. He also moved his position a very little so that he could see her better.

"First, then, Patricia, I have actually done something in Belgium. The roads of which I have dreamed are not quite such fantastic fancies now as they were a year ago."

She sat erect at once, alert and brimming over with interest.

"Oh, Christopher!"

"It is not done yet," he went on slowly, "but it is on the way to be done. It means that all the roads here, and the roads all over the world, will one day be made easy to travel upon. It means that mud, dirt and noise will be evils of the past, and they will be roads that will last down the ages." He stopped with a little catch in his breath and looked at her half ashamed, half pleadingly.

But Patricia was gazing past him through a gap in the trees at a white flinty road that struggled up to the distant downs. "Yes," she said very softly, as if fearing to quench a vision she saw there, "yes, that is a great and a good thing, and like you."

"Thank you," he answered laughing—the spell of their mutual earnestness pressed him too sorely.

"Don't laugh," she returned swiftly with a frown; "it is not the goodness that's like you. It's a sort of strongness about it—something to hold on to for all time." She stopped abruptly, looking at him gravely.

This time he did not laugh, but he put one hand on hers, and his was shaking.

"Christopher," she said coaxingly, "will you really take me down to the sea when I like?"

"Whenever you like."

"Then do it this afternoon. Now, at once," she cried pleadingly, and seeing his face of amazement, added, "you promised, Christopher."

"Of course. I'll do it; but why not to-morrow, when we can have a long day?"

"Because—because to-day is all my own," she said softly, "and to-morrow isn't. Christopher, I did not mean to tell anyone to-day, but I must tell you, I am going to marry Geoffry,"—she flushed rosy red, but he did not see it—"it was last night—he wanted to see Nevil at once, but I wouldn't let him. I wanted this day to myself. It was nice of you to come and make it complete."

His hand still held hers, but it was still and motionless now. She stroked it softly. Christopher drew it gently away.

"You ought to wish me happiness or something, ought you not?" she said.

"I do, Patricia," he said, looking up at her.

He wanted to say more; self-preservation demanded it, and again demanded silence. Their voices seemed to him far away, speaking in some fairy orchard where he was not. He could barely hear them.

"You'll pretend not to know anything about it till to-morrow, won't you?" she pleaded. "Don't spoil my day. It isn't that it won't be perfectly lovely to be engaged, but the past has been, lovely too, and I want to keep it a tiny bit longer. You'll help me, won't you?"

"Yes, I'll help you."

If he could but keep to-day forever shut in his heart with her, though life crumbled to ruins about them! But the invincible hours were ranged against him, and would claim it their own.

"And you'll take me to the sea?"

"Yes, if you come at once."

She descended from her perch with his help. She did not know his hands felt numb and dead as he held and released her.

"You haven't told me the second thing about yourself," she remarked, brushing the bark and lichen from her dress.

"It will keep," he said quietly.

And they went out of the orchard.

CHAPTER XVIII

Whatever may have been the pressing business that caused Peter Masters to seek his cousin's company in so speedy a manner, the immediate necessity of it seemed to have evaporated on the journey. He sat talking of various things to Aymer and Charles Aston, but uttered nothing as to the reason of his visit, and Mr. Aston, with his eye on Aymer, chafed a little and found it hard to maintain his usual serenity. Aymer, on the contrary, seemed more deliberate and placid than usual; there was a slowness in his speech, and an unusual willingness to leave the conversation in his visitor's hands as if he mistrusted his own powers to keep it in desirable channels. He appeared to have suddenly abdicated his position on the objective positive side of life and to have become a mere passive instrument of the hour, subjective and unresisting.

It was his father who was ready, armed against fate, alert, watchful to ward off all that might harm or distress his eldest son. Peter spoke of their exodus from London, their sojourn in the country, told them anecdotes of big deals, and was, in his big, burly, shrewd way, amusing and less ruthlessly tactless than usual. He had long ago given up all hope of interesting Aymer in a financial career, but he nevertheless retained a curiously respectful belief in his cousin's mental powers.

"By the way," he said presently, "I've not bought a car yet. That boy of yours seems to know something about them. Do you think he could be trusted to choose one for me?"

"Perfectly."

Aymer's tone was completely impartial, and Peter ruminated over his next remark a moment.

"You still mean him to stick to his Road Engineering?"

"He is perfectly free to do as he likes."

Charles Aston put in a word.

"He is twenty-two now, and he knows his own mind a good deal better than most boys of that age. He seems bent on carrying out his Road scheme, and there seems no reason why he should not." He pushed over a box of cigars to his visitor.

"No, exactly. No reason at all." Peter selected a cigar carefully. "I expect you find it very interesting watching how he turns out, don't you, Aymer?"

"It is not uninteresting."

"You've not seen Nevil yet," suggested Mr. Aston. "He is just out of a spell of work; come out in the garden and find him while you smoke."

"Well, perhaps we might, if you don't mind being left, Aymer?" Peter's voice was full of kindly interest. To him the great catastrophe was ever a new and awful thing, and Aymer an invalid to be considered and treated with such attention as he knew how.

"Not in the least," said Aymer politely, marvelling how exactly his father had gauged the limits of his endurance. When the heavy curtained door had shut out voices and footsteps and only the stillness of the room was with him the forced passivity slipped from Aymer like a mask, and his was again the face of a fighter, of one still fighting against fearful odds.

He lay with clenched hands and rigid face, and great beads of perspiration stood on his forehead, for that passive indifference towards what had become a matter of life and death to him was the fruit of a victory that had to be won again and again each time his perilous position was assailed by the appearance of Peter Masters.

His very existence had become so bound up in the life of the boy he had taken as his own that the smallest fraying of the cord which bound them together was a thought of new pain. The passionate, fiercely jealous nature that had lain dormant so long had gathered strength from silence and clamoured with imperious insistence on its right, to love, to whole allegiance, to undisputed sway over Christopher.

What right could this man, Christopher's father though he were, in the flesh, show beside his, Aymer Aston's? Every instinct rose in indignant rebellion against the fiat of his own conscience.

For before his deep love was awake to confuse his judgment he had declared that if he might only be permitted to bring Elizabeth Masters's son through the perilous passage of boyhood, he would never stand between Christopher and what, after all, was his right due, and in the eyes of the world, his wonderful fortune. Elizabeth of the brave heart and uncompromising creed had thought otherwise of this fortune, as did Charles Aston and Aymer himself. The first had imperilled her beloved child's bodily welfare to save him from what she thought an evil thing, and the Astons, father and son, had bid defiance to their hitherto straightforward policy and followed expediency instead of open dealing, but there Aymer stopped.

The decision he had made must be adhered to at all costs. It mattered nothing he had not been in a position to count the cost ten years ago. He at least could not discount his own word. If Fate drew Christopher to the side of his unknown father, Aymer must put out no hand to intervene.

But the cost of it—the cost!—He put his shaking hands over his face, trying to consider the position reasonably.

Even if Peter Masters learnt the truth and claimed

Christopher, Christopher was of age and must act for himself, and Aymer could not doubt his action. His misery lay in no suspicion of Christopher's loyal love, but in his own unconquerable, wildly jealous desire to stand alone in the post of honour, of true fatherhood to the son of the woman he had loved to such disastrous end. And behind that lay the bitter, unquenchable resentment that, pretend as he would, Christopher was not his son, not even of unknown parentage, but in actual fact the son of the man who had unknowingly robbed him of love, and whom he had all his life alternately hated and despised.

It was some subtle knowledge of what was passing in that still room that made Charles Aston a shade less kindly, a little more alert than usual to hidden meanings, and it was the sight of Aymer's apparent passivity in the face of all that threatened him, that brought him to the mind to fight every inch of ground before he put into the hands of Peter Masters the tangled clue of the story that he alone knew in all its completeness.

The suspicion that had gripped Peter Masters on the journey down was slowly stiffening into a certainty, but he was still undecided in his mind as to the line of action he would take. If these people with their ultra-heroic code of honour had fooled him, and forestalled him in this matter of his son with deliberate intent to frustrate any advances he might make, it would go hard with them in the end, cousins or no cousins. Such was his first thought; but he had yet to prove they were not simply waiting for a sign to deliver back his son to him, in which case Peter was not unprepared to be grateful, for his heart—and he had one—had gone out to the plucky, determined young man who had lied so bravely. Peter determined, therefore, he would give Charles Aston a chance and see what happened. In a blindly, inarticulate way he felt it was impossible to play with Aymer, he was even conscious it was a matter of great moment to him, though he could not in any manner see why it was so.

"Nevil will survive if we put him off a little longer," said Peter as they crossed the hall, "I want to see you on a private matter, Cousin Charles."

Mr. Aston led the way without a word to his own room. He made no doubt as to what the matter was. Perhaps the shadow of the expected interview had lain too heavily on him of late to leave room for suspicion of other affairs.

It was a long, cheerful room, lined with books, and the furniture was solid and shabby with long service. There was an indefinite atmosphere of peace and repose about it, of leisured days haunted by no grey thoughts, very typical of the owner. The window stood open, though a fire burned clearly on the plain brick hearth, beneath a big hooded chimney-piece.

Mr. Aston indicated a big easy chair to his visitor and seated himself at his writing table, from whence he could see, behind Peter, on the far wall, a portrait of Aymer painted in the pride of his life and youth, so wonderfully like even now in its strong colour and forcible power, and so full of subtle differences and fine distinctions.

"I don't know even if you'll listen to me," began Peter, who knew very well Charles Aston would refuse to listen to no man; "fifteen years ago you told me you'd said your last word on the subject."

"I beg your pardon, Peter, it was you who said the subject was closed between us."

"Ah, yes. So I did. May I reopen it?"

"If it can serve any good purpose, but you know my opinions."

"I thought perhaps they might have altered with the changing years," said Peter blandly.

"Not one bit, I assure you."

"Really. It never strikes you that I was justified in attending to Elizabeth's very plainly expressed wishes, or that it might be a happy thing for the boy that I did so."

"The question between us," said his cousin gently, "was whether you were justified in abandoning them, not whether it was advantageous to them or not."

"I would point out in passing, Cousin Charles, that Elizabeth abandoned me, but we will let that be. My reason for opening the subject at all is not a question of justification." He puffed away slowly at his cigar for a minute and then went on in an even, unemotional voice. "The fact is something rather strange has happened. For twenty years I have believed I knew the exact whereabouts of Elizabeth and my son. I had a good reason for the belief. One man only shared this supposititious knowledge with me." His hearer seemed about to speak, but desisted and looked away from Peter out of the window. Not a movement, a sign, a breath, escaped those hard blue eyes, and Charles Aston knew it. It did not render him nervous or even indignant, but he was a trifle more dignified, more obviously determined to be courteous at any cost.

"That boy and his mother were living at Liverpool," went on Peter calmly. "He was employed in a big shipping firm in a very minor capacity. He was killed in the great explosion in the dock last week."

He spoke as calmly as if he were saying his supposed son had lost his post or had gone for a holiday.

Charles Aston gave a sudden movement and turned a shocked face towards the speaker.

"Terrible!" he said, "I wonder how the shareholders in that company feel? Did you see the verdict?"

Peter waved his hand. "Yes, yes. Juries lose their heads in these cases. But to continue. I went down to Liverpool at once before the funeral, you understand." He paused. "I was naturally much disturbed and horrified, and then—well, the boy wasn't my son, after all."

"Not your son?" echoed Charles Aston slowly.

"No, not my son." There was a tinge of impatience in his voice. "I should not have known, but the mother was there. She went in as I came out."

"His mother was alive?"

"Yes. She was not Elizabeth."

His cousin turned to him, indignation blazing in his eyes. "For twenty years, Peter, you believed you knew your wife's whereabouts, you knew she was in more or less a state of poverty, and you made no attempt to see her face to face? You accepted the story of another with no attempt to personally prove the truth yourself?"

"I had good reason to believe it," returned Peter sulkily. "She would have let me know if she were in want. I had told her she could come back when she had had enough of it."

"And this poor woman, whose son was killed. What of her?"

"I don't know anything about her except she wasn't Elizabeth."

"You had believed her so for twenty years."

"I had made a mistake. She knew nothing about that. I took good care she should not. There was no doubt about her being the boy's mother, and no doubt she was not Elizabeth. She had no claim on me."

"No claim!" Charles Aston stood up and faced him, "not even the claim of the widow—her one son dead. No claim, when for all those years those two items of humanity represented in your perverse mind the two people nearest—I won't say dearest—to you. No claim!" He stopped and walked away to the window.

Peter smiled tolerantly. He enjoyed making this kind, generous man flash out with indignation. It was all very high-flown and impossible, but it suited

Charles Aston. To-day, however, he was too engrossed in his own affairs to get much satisfaction from it.

"Well, well, don't let us argue about it. We don't think alike in these matters. The point I want to consult you about is not my susceptibility to sentiment, but the chances of my picking up a clue twenty years old."

"I should say they were hardly worth considering." He spoke deliberately, turning from the window to resume his place by the table. The fight had begun; they had crossed blades at last.

"There is a very good detective called Chance and a better one called Luck."

"You have secured their services?"

"I am not certain yet. Can you help me?"

He made the appeal with calculated directness, knowing his man and his aversion to evasion, but if he expected him to hesitate he was disappointed.

"No, I can do nothing. I tried for five years to bring you to some sense of your responsibility in this matter. You were not frank with me then, it seems. I can do nothing now."

"And have lost all interest in it, I suppose?"

"No. It is your interest that rises and falls with the occasion, but I decline to have anything to do with it. If—as I do not believe—Elizabeth is still alive she and your son have done without your help for twenty years and can do without it still."

"They have doubtless plenty of friends."

"Let us hope so. What was the name of the Liverpool woman?"

"Priestly. What does it matter? The question is, I must find my son somehow, for I must have an heir."

"Adopt one."

"As did Aymer?" He shot a questioning glance at him. "It's such a risk. I might not be so lucky. Sons like Christopher are not to be had for nothing."

"No, they are not," said Charles Aston drily. "They are the result of years of love and patience, of generous tolerance, of unquenchable courage. They bring days of joy which must be paid for with hours of anxiety and nights of pain. Were you prepared to give your son this, even if you had taken him to you as a boy?"

Peter waved his big hand again. "I quite admit all that is needed to produce men of your pattern, Cousin Charles, and I have the profoundest admiration for the result; but I am not ambitious; I should be content to produce the ordinary successful man."

"I think Christopher will score a success."

"Yes, in spite of you both, by reason of his practical, determined, hard-headed nature which he probably inherits from his father, eh?"

"You are probably right. I am not in a position to say."

"You did not know his parents?"

Charles Aston pushed back his chair and looked beyond Peter to the portrait of Aymer. They must come to close quarters or he would give out, and suddenly it came to him that he must adhere to his universal rule, must give the better side of the man's nature a chance before he openly defied him. The decision was made quite quickly. Peter only recognised a slight pause. "You seem interested in Christopher," Mr. Aston said slowly. "I will tell you what there is to know. About eleven years ago Aymer became possessed of a passionate desire to have a boy to bring up, since he might not have one of his own. In hunting for a suitable one I stumbled on the son of someone I had known who had fallen on very evil days." He stopped a moment. Peter took out another cigar and lit it. "On very evil days," repeated the other. "The boy was left at a country workhouse in this county as it happened. I knew enough of his paternity to know that he was a suitable subject for Aymer to father. I have never regretted what I did. The boy has become the mainspring of Aymer's life; he lives again in him. All that has been denied him, he finds in Christopher's career; all he cannot give the world he has given to this boy, this son of his heart and soul. No father could love more, could suffer more. And Christopher is repaying him. He has known no father but Aymer, no authority but his, no conflicting claim. I pray God daily that neither now nor in the future shall any shadow fall between these two to cancel by one solitary item Christopher's obligation to his adopted father. Perhaps I am selfish over it, but anyway, Aymer is my son, and I understand how it is with him."

There was a silence in the room. Peter puffed vehemently and the clouds of blue-grey smoke circling round him obscured the heavy features from his cousin when his eyes left the picture to look at him.

"Yes, yes, I see. Quite so," said a voice from the smoke at last, and slowly the strong, bland expressionless face emerged clearly from the halo, "but I am no further on my way towards my son. And who's to have the money if I don't find him? Will you?"

"Heaven forbid!—and Nature! Peter, I'm sixty and you are fifty-four."

"Will Nevil's boy?"

"We have enough. We should count it a misfortune. Leave it in charities."

"And suppose he discovers some day who he is, and wanted it?"

"Hardly likely after so long."

"Quite likely. Shall I leave it to Christopher?"

It was the last thrust, and it told. There was quite a long silence. Charles longed passionately to refuse, but even he dared not. The issue was too great. "I cannot dictate to you in the matter," he said at length, "but I do not think Christopher would appreciate it."

"Then I must hope to find a Christopher of my own," returned Peter, rising; "let us meanwhile find Nevil."

The duel was over and apparently the result was as undetermined as ever. The only satisfaction poor Charles Aston derived was from the fact that Peter was unusually gentle and tactful to Aymer that afternoon. He seemed in no hurry to go, urged as excuse he wanted to consult Christopher about a motor, but when they sent to find that young gentleman, they discovered he and Patricia and the motor were missing.

CHAPTER XIX

It seemed to Christopher as he overhauled his long-suffering motor preparatory to the new run, that a great gap of innumerable grey days stretched between him and the moment he brought the car to a standstill before the doors of the house, that had appeared to him to be a Temple of Promise. It was in fact barely an hour and a half and the greater part of that time had been occupied with lunch and a hasty interview with Aymer. That shorter interlude in the orchard just over, had already blotted out a golden landscape with a driving mist that obscured all true proportion of time or space. He longed greatly, with a sense of strange fatigue, to be sitting at Cæsar's side and to find the restless discomfort evaporate as they talked, even as his boyish troubles had melted in that companionship. That must come later: for the present Fate—or Patricia—made a demand on him to which he was bound to answer. Where a weaker nature would have said "impossible," he simply found an ordinary action rendered difficult by his own private view of it, therefore it behooved him to close the shutters on that outlook if he could, and ignore the difficulty.

Renata, who came out with Patricia, protested a little indignantly at the latter's exaction.

"It is so inconsiderate of Patricia, just as you have had such a journey. Why do you give in to her, Christopher?"

"To-day is as good as any day," he answered her, "perhaps the visitor will have gone when we return."

"Oh, I hope so," said Renata fervently, and then blushed at her own inhospitality. "I mean, Cæsar would rather have you to himself, I am sure."

"And I would rather have Cæsar unaccompanied. So there is some use in Patricia's fancy."

"Of course," put in that young lady, "there always is. Please do not waste precious time talking. Tell me where I am to sit, Christopher."

"I'll take every care of her," said Christopher, looking at Renata, "we'll be back in time for dinner. Be kind and get rid of Mr. Masters by then."

"Like a dear little angel," concluded Patricia, kissing her; "think how he bores Nevil, and don't be hospitable."

Christopher settled her in the seat beside him, tucked her in with rugs, put up the front screen and started.

For a few short minutes the joy of having her there beside him, his sole charge for some golden hours to come, his to carry in a mad rush if he would to the ends of the earth, obliterated for a moment the bewildering mist.

He drove for some way in silence. Patricia was too much absorbed in the pleasures of swift motion to talk. Her first words, however, shut down the mists on him again.

"Geoffry must have a car," she declared. "He must get one just like this."

"I thought Geoffry was to be left behind this afternoon?"

"Oh, I suppose he was. I don't believe you are a bit pleased about it really, Christopher."

He clutched at the truth as a plank of safety.

"Well, you can't expect me to be glad to lose your company, can you? I shall never make a golfer now."

She laughed at that and recommended a course at St. Andrew's under a professional, which proposal he treated with scorn, but after a short silence he said in a different voice:

"Don't think I'm not glad at anything that makes you happy, Patricia. Geoffry's a real good sort and—here's a town—you must not speak to the man at the wheel."

Patricia was obedient. She sank into a reverie in which, despite her own determination, Geoffry played a long part. It was characteristic of her exact attitude towards her accepted lover that it was the immediate future in which he figured most clearly. Her thoughts hovered round the pleasant summer to come with the distant excitement of a wedding to crown it. She never considered, or only in the most cursory way, the long years ahead, the daily companionship with the man she had chosen. She was honestly attached to Geoffry. She believed she was in love with him, whereas, as is far more often the case than the young suppose, she was in love with the love that had come to her in the glory of the spring, offered by familiar hands that were dear because of what they held for her.

So they drove through the glowing afternoon, and the line of white road before them appeared to Christopher as a track dividing past and future, the thin edge of the passing minutes. They spoke no more, however, on the forbidden subject. Christopher presently explained to her the visible mechanism of the car and on a stretch of clear road let her put her hands on the wheel beneath his own and feel the joy of fictitious control. Before the sun quenched itself in the sea they stood on the Cliff Edge and looked out across the shining waters into the great space, where a thought-laden air renews itself, reforming, cancelling and creating in the crucible of Life. They clambered down from the lip of the cliff on to a jutting-out shelf of rock, screened with gorse, where the few feet of gravel bank behind them shut out all signs of habitation.

Patricia sat with her hands clasped round her knees drawing slow, deep draughts of the cool air, her eyes on the immense free space, and she spoke not at all with her lips, yet Christopher, lying at her feet, caught her thoughts as they came and went with strange certainty and stranger heartache. He picked a handful of golden gorse petals and pressed the sweet blossoms to his face: ever after their scent was to mean for him that place and rapture of that hour, in which was borne to him the certainty of his right to her, and the knowledge of the surrender he was making in each silent minute. For she was his now, if he told her, if he broke faith, if he claimed the right that was his.

Now in this golden hour he would win if he spoke, sweeping aside the shadowy intervening form of the other with the relentless persistent truth of the faith that was in him, a faith that had no ground in personal vanity or individual pride, but was only the recognition of a great Fact that lay outside and beyond them both, that named Patricia forever his in a world where the Real is disentangled from the Appearance.

Was life to consist, for him, in a relinquishing of his own rights in conformity to the Law of Appearance? Was it but a cowardly fear of convention that held him back from claiming her now on the verge of the world? Or was it a deeper, half-understood trust of the Great Realities of Life, a knowledge that faith, integrity, and honour are no conventions, but belong to Real World of Truth, and that he could snatch no joy of life over their trampled forms? He tried dimly to understand these things, to gauge the nature of the forces that controlled him, but he never doubted what force would claim his obedience. It was already habitual to him by reason of training and instinct to set such Laws of Life as he recognised before his own will. But that will was very clamorous this evening as he pressed the hot yellow whin-flowers to his face drinking their fragrance into his thirsty soul.

When he raised his eyes he looked out at sea and sky and avoided the dear sweet face above him. She still sat smiling out into the serene space, watching as it were the random thoughts of her subconscious self floating in those ethereal realms. It was almost too great a happiness for peace, the fair world, the comprehending companion, who understood without the clumsy medium of words, and the love awaiting her on the morrow. She did not wish for Geoffry's presence now, she was perfectly content that he stood in the beautiful morrow, that he was bringing her a good and precious crown to the golden days of her youth.

She sighed out of pure joy and so broke the spell of the golden and blue-cloaked silence which had reigned. Without moving she gathered a handful of whin blooms and scattered them over the brown head at her feet, a baptism of golden fire. He shook them off and looked up at her, laughing.

"Asleep, I believe, Christopher, you lazy person. What were you dreaming about?"

"Bees, heather and honey," he murmured, surreptitiously gathering up a handful of the golden rain she had tossed him. "Have you had your breath of freedom, Patricia—are you ready for tea and buttered toast?"

"And honey, you provoking materialist," she insisted.

"Honey is stolen property—I always feel a consort of thieves when I eat it."

"Then I'll eat it and you can shut your eyes. Christopher, suppose the car goes wrong on the way home?"

He scoffed at that, but while she ate her honey he made an exhaustive inspection of it.

When the sun dropped out of sight a shivering wind sprang up and the blue sky drew a grey cloak over itself. Christopher wrapped his companion in a fur coat and tucked her in anxiously.

She had become restless and dissatisfied as if the sun had taken her joy to rest with him, or as if the thoughts gathered from space found an unready lodgment in her mind. Christopher made some effort to talk on indifferent subjects, but she answered with strange brevity or not at all, once with such impatience that he glanced quickly at her hands and saw they were hidden by the long sleeves of his big coat she wore.

Presently she said abruptly:

"We ought not to have stayed so long. Why did you go to sleep?"

"I didn't," he retorted, amazed at the accusation.

"Then you ought to have talked."

"I thought we were superior to such conventions."

"That is an excuse for sheer laziness on your part. And even if you are superior," she added, inconsequently, "I am not. What were you thinking about?"

"Shall I tell you of what you were thinking?"

"You can't."

"Out in the great space you saw all the future days weaving for you a dress of blue and gold, of hopes and fulfilment. You saw how they smiled at you, you were glad of the love they bore you, the good they were bringing you. You felt in your own soul how you belonged to them, you were a part of all this dear living world."

"Don't, don't," she cried, half under her breath.

"Isn't it true?" he insisted.

"You have no business, no right to know. Christopher, how dare you." Her face flushed with inward emotion, with some fierce resentment that laid hold of her senses without reason and dragged fear in its wake.

"I'm sorry," he said humbly. "I've often done it before and you never minded."

"It's quite different now. It's unbearable. I don't like it any more, I hate it. Do you hear, Christopher?"

"Yes. It was unpardonable. I am sorry, Patricia, I won't do it again."

"You won't try to understand me like that? Promise," she urged.

"I didn't try then. I only knew. I promise I won't tell you again."

"That's not enough," she persisted, twisting her fingers under cover of the long sleeves. "You mustn't know. You must not be able to do it. I won't bear it. Do you understand?"

"Yes."

"Then promise."

"I've promised all I can. I certainly won't try to know. I can't help it involuntarily."

"You must. I insist—Christopher, quick."

They were running at a great pace along a straight level piece of road with high banks on either side, and by the roadside at regular intervals were piles of broken granite. Christopher's attention was fixed on a distant speck that might be a danger-signal and he did not answer her or notice the nearer signal of danger in her white face.

She was in the grip of her old wild passion again, on fire with her need of assurance, and in a gust of anger she caught at the wheel that seemed to claim his mind. The car swerved violently, jolted up on to the turf, bumped madly along at a dangerous tilt, swerved back into the road two feet clear of a grey pile of stone. Only then did Christopher know her fingers were gripped between his hands and the steel wheel. He brought the car to a standstill and her released hand fell white and numb to her side. She neither spoke nor moved, but gazed before her, oblivious even of her crushed fingers.

There was a running brook the other side of the hedge and a convenient gate. He soaked his handkerchief in it, came back to her and put the numbed hand on the cool linen. His grip had been like iron and the averted disaster so near as to be hardly passed from his senses, yet he felt sick and ashamed at this almost trifling price they had to pay. He felt each bruised finger carefully and bound them up as best he could, and only then did he speak.

"I'm fearfully sorry, Patricia, I didn't know."

She looked vaguely at the white bound hand.

"My fingers? Oh, I'm glad. You shouldn't have tied them up."

He paid no heed, but having examined the car, climbed back to his place.

"We must go on," he remarked, "so it's no use asking you if you are too frightened, Patricia."

"You might put me out on the roadside," she suggested dully.

To that, too, he paid no heed and they started again.

The miles slipped by in unbroken silence. It was not till they were nearly home that Christopher spoke.

"I thought that was all quite gone, Patricia."

"So did I," she returned wearily. "It's ages since I was so stupid. It's generally all right if you are there."

"But I'm not always there anyhow."

"I don't mean there really. I just shut my eyes and pretend you are and hold on. But just now I waited for you to do something. I forgot you were driving."

"You mustn't rely on me to stop you now," he insisted, with new gravity.

"Oh, yes, I do. It's always you if I stop in time; either you actually, or thinking of you. Don't talk about it, Christopher dear, it was too horrible."

She did not explain if she meant the danger or the cause, but he obeyed and said no more. A terrible fear clamoured at his heart. Did Geoffry Leverson know or did he not? and if he knew, would he even understand? He tried to tell himself that if he could manage her, then another, and that her acknowledged lover, could do so too, but he knew this was false reasoning. Such power as he had over her lay in his recognition that the irresistible inheritance was not an integral part of Patricia, but was an exotic growth, foisted upon her by the ill-understood laws of paternity, and finding no natural soil in her pure self—something indeed, of a lower nature, that she must and could override. He could have curbed it in the brief flash just over, he knew, had his attention been free. It had died as it had come and the penalty of the crushed fingers hurt him as unwarrantable, combined with the peril they had run.

It was a fresh addition of cloud to the dimmed day to find Peter Masters had not departed, but was staying the night.

CHAPTER XX

Aymer gazed out of the open window at Christopher and Peter Masters as they walked to and fro on the terrace. He knew the subject they were discussing, and he was already sure how it would end. But what were the real issues involved he could not determine, and he was impotent, by reason of his vow and will, to influence them. He could only lie still and watch, tortured by jealous fear and the physical helplessness that forbade him the one relief of movement for which his soul craved. The patience the long years had schooled him into was slipping away, and the elementary forces of his nature reigned in its stead.

Under the overmastering impulse towards action he made a futile effort to sit up that he might better follow the movements of the two outside. It was a pathetic failure, and he swore fiercely as he fell back and found his father's arms round him.

"Aymer, if you are going to be so childish, I shall tell Christopher not to go."

"No. I'm a fool, but I won't have him know it. He must go if he will."

"There is nothing to fear if he does. What is wrong with you?"

"I want to go back to town, I'm tired of this."

"You are far better here than in town," said his father uneasily.

"I'm well enough anywhere."

"I shall have to tell Christopher not to go."

"No." The tone was sharply negative again, and after a moment's silence Aymer said in a low, grudging voice, "You've always helped before; are you going to desert me now?"

For answer his father got up and pushed the big sliding sofa away from the window.

"Very well, then behave yourself better, Aymer, and don't ford a stream before you come to it. You've got to listen to Penruddock's speech." He folded back the *Times* and began to read.

When Christopher came back a little later he saw no sign of the trouble. Perhaps he was a little too much engrossed in his own perplexities to be as observant as usual.

"Cæsar, do you think it's a shabby thing to stay with a man you don't like?"

"Are you going?"

"I think so. I want to see how he does it."

"Does what?"

"Makes his money. Does it seem shabby to you?"

"You can't know if you like him or not. You know nothing about him."

"I shall be back at the end of the week. You don't mind my going, Cæsar? I'd rather go before I settle down."

"Another week's peace," returned Cæsar, indifferently. "The truth is, you're in a scrape and putting off confession, young man."

Christopher laughed at him.

They were to leave early next morning, so Peter Masters bade Aymer good-bye that night. He apologised clumsily for taking Christopher away so soon after his long absence.

"It's the only free week I've got for months, and I want to study your handiwork, Aymer."

"Christopher has points. I don't know how many score to me," returned his cousin with steadily forced indifference.

"Well, you've taken more trouble over him than most fathers would do."

"Are you an expert?"

Peter laughed grimly and stood looking at Aymer with his chin in his hand, a curiously characteristic attitude of doubt with him.

"You won't be overpleased when he wants to marry, which he is sure to do just when he's become useful to you."

For the first time in his life Peter Masters recognised the harassed soul of a man as it leapt to sight, and saw the shadow of pain conquer a fierce will. The revelation struck him dumb, for incongruously and unreasonably there flashed before his mind a memory of this face with twenty years wiped out. He went slowly away carrying with him a vivid impression and new knowledge.

It was a new experience to him. He knew something of men's minds, but of their emotions and the passions of their souls he was no judge. He puzzled over the meaning of what he had seen as he faced Christopher in the train next day, studying him with a disconcerting gaze. Could Aymer possibly love the boy to the verge of jealousy? It seemed so incredible and absurd. Yet what other interpretation could he place on that look he had surprised? Charles Aston's words, which had not been without effect, paled before this self-revelation. It annoyed him greatly that the disturbing vision should intrude itself between him and the decision he was endeavouring to make, for the better termination of which he was carrying Christopher northward with him.

Christopher, on his part, was chiefly occupied in considering the distracting fact of his own yielding to the wishes of a man he disliked as sincerely as he did Mr. Aston's cousin. Peter Masters was taking him with him in precisely the same manner he had made Christopher convey him to Marden. It was quite useless to pretend he was going of his own will; refusal had, in an unaccountable way, seemed impossible. To save his pride he tried to believe he was influenced by a desire to get away from Marden until the first excitement over Patricia's engagement had died away, yet in his heart he knew that though that and other considerations had joined forces with the millionaire's mandate, yet in any case he would have had to bow to the will of the man who admitted no possibility of refusal. He had been unprepared and unready twice over: in the matter of the journey from London and in the stranger matter of this present journey. Christopher determined the third time he would be on guard, that in all events, reason should have her say in the case.

They were going direct to Stormly, which was midway between Birmingham and the Stormly mines, from which the fortunes of the family had first been dug. Stormly Park was Peter's only permanent residence, though much of his time was spent in hotels and travelling. The house, begun by his father, had expanded with the fortunes of the son. It stood remote from town or village. It was neither a palace nor a glorified villa, but just a substantial house, with an unprepossessing exterior, and all the marvels of modern luxury within. The short private railway by which it was approaching ran through an ugly tract of country terminating beneath a high belt of trees that shut off the western sun and were flanked by granite walls.

On the platform of the minute station two porters in private uniform received them.

"I generally walk up if I'm not in a hurry," said Peter Masters abruptly.

He had not spoken since they left Birmingham, where a packet of letters had been brought him, to which he gave his undivided attention. With a curt nod to the men, with whom he exchanged no word at all, he led the way from the siding across a black, gritty road and unlocking a door in the wall ushered Christopher into Stormly Park.

The belt of trees was planted on a ridge of ground that sloped towards the road and formed a second barrier between the world without and the world within. When they had crossed the ridge and looked down on the Park itself Christopher gave a gasp of astonishment. It stretched out before him in the sunset light a wide expanse of green land, with stately clumps of trees and long vistas of avenues that led nowhere. It was like some jewel in the wide circling belt of trees. It was so strange a contrast to the sordid country without, that the effect was amazing. Christopher looked round involuntarily to see by what passage he had passed from that unpleasing world to this sunkissed land of beauty.

Peter Masters saw the effect produced and his lips twitched with a little smile of pleasure.

"My grandfather planted the place," he said. "He understood those things. I don't. But it's pretty. My mother, Evelyn Aston, you know, used to always travel by night if she could, she disliked the country round so much."

"It is rather a striking contrast," Christopher agreed.

They passed through a clump of chestnuts just breaking into leaf.

"There is coal here," said Peter. "It will all have to go some day. I make no additions now."

They came suddenly on the house, which was built of grey pointed stone, its low-angle slate roof hidden behind a high balustrading. The centre part was evidently the original house and long curved wings had been extended on either side. There was no sign of life about the place, nor did it carry the placid sense of repose that haunts old houses. Stormly Park had an air of waiting; a certain grim expectation lurked behind the over-mantled windows and closed doors. It was as if it watched for the fate foreshadowed in its owner's words. Even the glorious sunlight pouring over it failed to give it a sense of warm living life.

It filled Christopher with curiosity and a desire to explore the grey fastness and trim level lawns beyond. Some living eyes watched, however, for the front door swung open as they approached and two footmen came out. Christopher again noted Peter Masters did not speak to them or appear to notice their presence. On the steps he paused, and stood aside.

"Go in," he said when his visitor hesitated.

Christopher obeyed.

The interior was almost as great a contrast to the exterior as the Park was to the surrounding country. It was rich with colour and warmth and comfort.

They were met by a thin, straightened-looking individual, who murmured a greeting to which Peter Masters paid no attention.

He turned to Christopher.

"This is Mr. Dreket, my secretary. Dreket, show Mr. —" for an imperceptible moment he paused—"Mr. Aston his room and explain the ways of the place to him. I've some letters to see to."

He turned aside down a long corridor. Christopher and the secretary looked at each other.

"I shan't be sorry for a wash and brush up," said Christopher, smiling.

The other gave a little sigh, expressive more of relief than fatigue, and led the way upstairs. As they went up the wide marble steps Mr. Masters reappeared and stood for a moment in the shadow of an arch watching the dark, erect young head till it was out of sight, then he retraced his steps and disappeared in his own room.

Christopher did not see him again till dinner-time. The two dined together at a small table that was an oasis in a desert of space. The room was hung with modern pictures set in unpolished wood panelling. Peter vaguely apologised for them to one accustomed to the company of the masterpieces of the dead.

"I'm no judge. I should be taken in if I bought old ones," he said. "So I buy new, provided they are by possible men. They may be worth something, some day, eh?"

"They are very good to look at now," Christopher answered, a little shyly, looking at a vast sea-scape which seemed to cool the room with a fresh breeze.

"You Astons would have beaten me anyhow," pursued Peter. "I've got nothing old: but the new's the best of its kind."

Christopher found this was true. Everything in the house was modern. There was no reproduction, no imitation. It was all solidly and emphatically modern: glass, china, furniture, books, pictures, the silk hangings, the white statuary in the orangery: all modern. There was nothing poor or mean or artistically bad, but the whole gave an impression of life yet to be lived, an incompleteness that was baffling in its obscurity.

Peter Masters talked much of events, of material things, of himself, but never of mankind in general. He spoke of no friends, or neighbours: he appeared to be served by machines, to stand alone in life, unconscious of his isolation. They played billiards in the evening and the host had an easy victory, and gave Christopher a practical lesson in the one game he had found time to master.

"I've work to do. Breakfast to-morrow at 8 sharp. You are going to Birmingham with me."

No question about it or pretence of asking his visitor's wishes. Christopher did not resent that, but he resented his growing inability to resist. He flung open the windows of his room and looked out. Eastward there was a glow in the sky over the great sleepless city: northward a still nearer glow from a foundry, he thought, but westward the parkland was silvered with moonlight and black with shadows, which under the groups of chestnuts seemed like moving shapes.

He leant out far and the cold night air shivered by. That was familiar and good to feel, but the glare northward caught his eyes again, and held him fascinated. It rose and fell, now blushing softly against a velvet sky, now flaring angrily to heaven. It seemed to quiver with voices that were harsh and threatening. It filled Christopher's heart with unreasonable horror against which he struggled in vain, as with the dim terror of a stranger. At last he closed the window and shut it out.

"I don't like it," said Christopher half aloud. "It's all right, it's only a foundry, but I hate it."

With that he went to bed and in the dark the dance of the fires flickered before his eyes.

The next few days were spent in gathering fresh impressions and disentangling bewildering experiences, and in small encounters with the unanswerable will of his host.

He was taken to the great offices in Birmingham, and the wonderful system by which each vast machine was worked was explained to him. He was even privileged to sit with the great man in the inner sanctum and copy letters for him, though he was summarily turned out to see the sights of the great city when a visitor was announced. He explored the depths of the coal mines and finally spent a long morning at the foundry whose nightly glare still haunted his dreams. It was the latter sight that Peter Masters evidently expected would interest him most, for here were employed the most marvellous and most complicated modern machinery, colossal innovations and ingenious labour-saving inventions in vast orderly buildings; the complex whole obedient to an organisation that left no item of power incomplete or wasted. But Christopher gave but half his mind to all he was shown, the other half was on those still stranger machines, the grimy, brutal-looking workmen toiling in the hot heart of the place, the white-faced stooping forms on the outskirts. They eyed him aslant as they worked, for visitors were rare occurrences. He asked questions concerning them and received vague answers, and a new machine was offered for inspection.

Fulner, the young engineer who had been told off to show him round, understood what was expected of him and did his duty. Masters himself, though he accompanied them, apparently put himself also in Fulner's hands; he took no particular interest in the work, but his eye followed every movement of Christopher's and his ear strained to his questions. Christopher noticed that none but heads of departments paid any attention to the owner's presence, and he would have thought him unknown but for a word or two he caught as he lingered for a last look at a particularly fascinating electric lathe.

"Thinks he's master," grinned one man, with a shrug, towards the retreating form.

"Thinks we're part of his blasted machinery," growled his fellow worker.

Christopher passed on and forgot the lathe.

"Where do these people live?" he asked in the comparative quiet of a store yard.

"In the—the villages round, and as near as they can," said the engineer quietly and looked back. Mr. Masters had gone off to the store-keeper's office and was out of hearing. Fulner looked at Christopher again and apparently came to a decision.

"It is difficult, sometimes, this housing question," he said swiftly, "are you really interested?"

"Yes, I want to know what contrast they get to this. It's overpowering, this place."

"If there was time—" began the other, and stopped, seeing Mr. Masters was approaching. He was followed by a harassed-face sub-manager, who waited uneasily a few yards off.

"Christopher, I shall have to stay here an hour or two. You had better go back. You can catch the 12.40 at the station. Fulner will see you there."

He nodded to the engineer and strode off towards the main offices.

The sub-manager exchanged a look of consternation with Fulner before he followed.

"We'll go this way," said Fulner, leading Christopher to a new corner of the great enclosure, "that is, if you don't mind walking."

He did not speak again until they were outside the high walls that surrounded the works, then he looked quizzically at Christopher.

"You shall see where they live if you wish to," he said, "the contrast is not striking—only there is no organisation outside."

They went down a black cindery road between high walls and presently the guide said quietly, "Are you coming here to us, Mr. Aston?"

"No." Christopher's voice was fervent with thankfulness.

The other looked disappointed and stopped.

"I'm sorry," he said. "We thought you were. There were rumours"—he hesitated, "if you are not coming perhaps it is no good showing you. It makes a difference."

"I want to see where the people live," insisted Christopher, looking him squarely in the face.

The other nodded and they went on and came to a narrow street of mean, two-storied houses, with cracked walls and warped door-posts, blackened with smoke, begrimed with dirt. As much of the spring sunshine as struggled through the haze overshadowing the place served but to emphasise the hideous squalor of it. Children, for the most part sturdy-limbed and well-developed, swarmed in the road, women in a more or less dishevelled condition stared out of open doors at them as they passed.

To the secret surprise of Fulner his companion made no remark, betrayed no sign of disgust or distaste. He looked at it all; his face was grave and impassive and Fulner was again disappointed.

They passed a glaring new public house, the only spot in the neighbourhood where the sun could find anything to reflect his clouded brightness.

"We wanted that corner for a club," said Fulner bitterly, "but the brewer outbid us."

"Who's the landlord?" demanded Christopher sharply.

Fulner paused a moment before he answered.

"You are a cousin of Mr. Masters, aren't you?"

"No relation at all. Is he the landlord?"

"The land here is all his. Not what is on it."

A woman was coming down the road, a woman in a bright green dress with a dirty lace blouse fastened with a gold brooch. She had turquoise earrings in her ears and rings on her fingers.

She stopped Fulner.

"Mr. Fulner," she said in a quavering voice, "they say the master's at the works and that Scott's given Jim away to save his own skin. It isn't true, is it?"

Fulner looked at her with pity. Christopher liked him better than ever.

"I'm afraid it's true, Mrs. Lawrie, but Scott couldn't help himself. Mr. Masters spotted the game when we were in the big engine-room. You go down to the main gate and wait for Jim. Perhaps you'll get him home safe if you take him the short cut, not this way." He nodded his head towards the public house they had passed.

"It's a shame," broke out the woman wildly, but her sentences were overlaid with unwomanly words, "they all does it. I ask now, how's we to get coal at all if we don't get the leavings. Jim only does what they all does. What's 'arf a pail of coal to 'im? I'd like to talk to 'un, I would. Jim will go mad again, and I've three of 'un now to think of, the brats." She flung up her arms with a superbly helpless gesture and stumbled off down the road.

Christopher looked after her with a white face.

"What does it mean?" he asked.

"The men have a way of appropriating the remains of the last measure of coal they put on before going off duty. It's wrong of course: it's been going on for ages. I warned Scott—he's the foreman. They've been complaining about the coal supply at headquarters. Mr. Masters caught Jim Lawrie at it to-day as we left the big engine-room."

"Is it a first offence?"

"There's no first offence here," returned Fulner grimly. "There's one only. There's the club room. We have to pay £20 a year rent for the ground and then to keep it going."

"But surely, Mr. Masters—" began Christopher and stopped.

"Mr. Masters has nothing to do with the place outside the works. It is not part of the System. He pays 6d. a head more than any other employer and that frees him. There's the station."

He paused as if he would leave his companion to make his way on alone. He was obviously dissatisfied and uneasy.

"Won't you come to the station with me?" Christopher asked, and as they walked he began to speak slowly and hesitatingly, as one who must choose from words that were on the verge of overflowing. "I was brought up in Lambeth, Mr. Fulner. I am used to poverty and bad sights. Don't go on thinking I don't care. These people earn fortunes beside those I have known, but in all London I've never seen anything so horrible as this, nothing so hideous, sordid—" he stopped with a gasp, "the women—the children—the lost desire—the ugliness."

They walked on silently. Presently he spoke again.

"You are a plucky man, Mr. Fulner. I couldn't face it."

"I've no choice. I don't know why I showed you it, except I thought you were coming and I wanted your help."

"Are there many who care?"

"No. It's too precarious. Mr. Masters doesn't approve of fools. Mind you, the men have no grievances inside the works. The unions have no chance now. It's fair to remember that."

"Is it the same everywhere?"

"The System's the same. I know nothing about the other works but that. There's the train: we must hurry."

"What do you want for your club?" Christopher asked as he entered his carriage.

"A billiard table, gym fittings, books. We've a license. We sell beer to members," his eyes were eager: the man's heart was in his hopeless self-imposed work.

Christopher nodded. "I shall not forget."

So they parted: each wondering over the other—would have wondered still more if they had known in what relationship they would stand to each other when they next met.

CHAPTER XXI

Christopher stood for a moment inside the great hall at Stormly Park and looked round. It was quite beautiful. Peter Masters, having chosen the best man in England for his purpose, had had the sense to let him alone. There was no discordant note anywhere and Christopher was quite alive to its perfections. But coming straight from Stormly Town the contrast was too glaring and too crude. It was not that Peter Masters was rich and his people were poor. Poverty and riches have run hand in hand down the generations of men, but here, the people were poor in all things, in morals, in desire, in beauty, in all that lifted them in the scale of humanity, in order that he, Peter Masters, should be superfluously rich, outrageously so!

Christopher struggled hard to be just: he knew it was not the superfluous money that was grudged, it was the more precious time and thought saved with a greed that was worse than the hunger of a miser—for no purpose but to add to over-filled stores. He knew all Peter Masters' arguments in defence of his System already: That he compelled no man to serve him, that none did so except on a clear understanding of the terms; that for the hours they toiled for him he paid highly, and his responsibility ceased when those hours were over. If Peter Masters was no philanthropist at least he was no humbug. He said openly he worked his System because it paid him. If he could have made more by being philanthropical he would have been so, but he would not have called it philanthropy: it would have been a financial method.

The grim selfishness of it all crushed Christopher as an intolerable burden that was none of his, and yet, because he was here accepting a part of its results, he could not clear himself of its shadow. So, twenty-two years ago, had his mother thought until the terror of that shadow outweighed all dread of further evil, and she had fled from its shade into a world where sun and shadow were checkered and evil and good a twisted rope by which to hold.

Some dim note from that long struggle and momentous decision had its influence with her son now. Without knowing it he was hastening to the same conclusions she had reached.

He lunched alone and then to escape the persistence of his thoughts decided to explore the west wing of the house which he had hardly entered.

At the end of a long corridor a square of yellow sunlight fell across the purple carpet from an open door and he stopped to look in.

It was a pretty room with three windows opening on to a terrace and a door communicating with a room beyond. The walls were panelled with pale blue silk and the chairs and luxurious couches covered with the same. There were several pictures of great value, on a French writing table lay an open blotter, but the blotting paper was crumbling and dry and the ink in the carved brass inkstand was dry also.

In the middle of the room surrounded by a pile of Holland covers and hangings stood Mrs. Eliot, the housekeeper. Christopher had seen her once or twice and she was the only servant, except the butler, with whom he had heard Peter Masters exchange a word. "Lor', sir, how you made me jump!" she cried at sight of him in the doorway. "It isn't often one hears a footfall down here, they girls keep away or I'd be about 'em as they know very well."

"May I come in?" asked Christopher. "What a pretty room."

The woman glanced round hesitatingly. "Well, now, you're here. Yes. It's pretty enough, sir."

"Are you getting ready for visitors?"

He had no intention of being curious, he was only thankful to find some distraction from his own thoughts, and there seemed no reason why he should not chat to the kindly portly lady in charge.

"No visitors here, sir. We don't have much company. Just a gentleman now and then, as may be yourself."

She pulled a light pair of steps to the window and mounted them cautiously one step at a time, dragging a long Holland curtain in her hand.

"Do you want to hang that up?" asked Christopher, watching her with idle interest. "Do let me do it, Mrs. Eliot, you'll fall off those steps if you go higher. I can't promise to catch you, but I can promise to hang curtains much better than you can." Mrs. Eliot, who was already panting with exertion and the fatigue of stretching up her ample figure to unaccustomed heights, looked down at him doubtfully.

"Whatever would Mr. Masters say, sir?"

"He would be quite pleased his visitor found so harmless an amusement. You come down, Mrs. Eliot. Curtain-hanging is a passion with me, but what a shame to cover up those pretty curtains with dingy Holland!"

"They wouldn't be pretty curtains now, sir," said Mrs. Eliot, descending with elaborate care, "if they hadn't been covered up these twenty years and more."

"What a waste," ejaculated Christopher now on the steps, "isn't the room ever used?"

"Never since Mrs. Masters went out of it. 'Eliot,' says the master—I was first housemaid then—'keep Mrs. Masters' rooms just as they are, ready for use. She will want them again some day.' So I did."

Christopher shifted the steps and hung another curtain.

"I didn't know there had been a Mrs. Masters."

"Most folk have forgotten it, I think, sir."

"This was her boudoir, I suppose."

"Yes. And I think he's never been in here since she went, but once, and that was five years after. The boudoir bell rang and I came, all of a tremble, to hear it for the first time after so long. He was standing as it may be there. 'That cushion's faded, Eliot,' he said, 'get another made like it. You are to replace everything that gets torn or faded or worn without troubling me. Keep the rooms just as they are.' He had a pile of photographs in his hand and a little picture, and he locked them up in that cabinet, and I don't suppose it's been opened since. He never made any fuss about it from the first. No, nor altered his ways either." She drew a cover over a chair and tied the strings viciously. "It's for all the world as if he'd never had a wife at all."

Christopher had hung the three sets of curtains now and he sat on the top step and looked round the room curiously. It was less oppressively modern that the rest of the house and he had an idea the master of Stormly was not responsible for that. He felt a vivid interest in the late Mrs. Masters, Why had she gone and why had neither Aymer nor St. Michael mentioned her existence? He longed to override his own sense of etiquette and question Mrs. Eliot, who continued to ramble on in her own way.

"I takes off the coverings every two months, and brushes it all down myself," she explained, "and I've never had anyone to help me before. If I were to let them girls in they'd break every vase in the place with their frills and their 'didn't see's.'"

"Do those sheets hang over the panels?"

"I couldn't think of troubling you! But if you will, sir, why then, that's the sheet for there. They are all numbered."

Christopher covered up the dainty walls regretfully. Why had she left it? Had she and Peter quarrelled? It seemed to Christopher, in his present mood towards Mr. Masters, they might well have done so.

"Do you remember Mrs. Masters?" he was tempted to ask presently.

"Indeed I do, seeing I was here when he brought her home. Tall, thin, and like a queen the way she walked, a great lady, for all she was simple enough by birth, they say. But she went, and where she went none of us know to this day, and some say the Master doesn't either, but I don't think it myself."

Christopher straightened a pen and ink sketch of a workman on the wall. It was a clever piece of work, life-like and sympathetic.

"She did that," said Mrs. Eliot with a proprietor's pride. "She was considered clever that way, I've been told. That's another of hers on the easel over there."

Christopher examined it and gave a gasp. It was a bold sketch of two men playing cards at a table with a lamp behind them. The expression on the players' faces was defined and forcible, but it was not their artistic merit that startled him, but their identity. One—the tolerant winner—was Peter himself—the other—the easy loser—was Aymer Aston.

So Aymer did know of Mrs. Masters' existence, knew her well enough for her to make this intimate likeness of him.

"Was it done here?" he asked slowly.

"No, she brought it with her. I don't know who the other gentleman is, but it's a beautiful picture of the master, isn't it? so life-like."

"Yes."

He looked again round the room, fighting again with his desire to search for more traces of its late owner, and then grew hot with shame at his curiosity. He left Mrs. Eliot rather abruptly and wandered out of the house, but the unknown mistress of the place haunted him, glided before him across the smooth lawns, he could almost hear the rustle of her dress on the gravel, and then recollected with relief it was only the memory of the old game he used to play at Aston House with his dead mother, transferred by some mental suggestion to Stormly Park. Presently he saw the bulky form of Peter Masters on the steps and joined him reluctantly.

"I want to see you, Christopher," said Peter as he approached. "Come into my room. I shan't be able to go to London this week to buy the car, so you must stay until Monday and go up with me then," he announced, and without waiting for assent or protest plunged into his subject with calculated abruptness.

"This road business of yours, is there money in it?"

"I think so. It is not done yet."

"How long will it take you to perfect it?"

"How can I tell? It may mean weeks, it may mean months."

"What are you going to do when you've found it?"

"Get someone to take it up, I suppose."

Christopher was answering against his will, but the swift sharp questions left him no time to fence.

"I'll take it up now. Fit you up a laboratory and experimenting ground and give you two years to perfect it—and a partnership when it's started."

Christopher looked up with incredulous amazement.

"But it's a purely scientific speculation at present. There are just about half a dozen people on the track. We are all racing each other."

"Well, you've got to win, and I'll back you. You shall have every assistance you want—money shan't count. You can live here and have the North Park for trials, as many men as you want and no interruption."

"But it's impossible. It's not a certainty even."

"No speculation is a certainty. If you bring it off it will mean a fortune, properly managed. I can do that for you far better than Aymer. We should share profits, of course, and I should have to risk money. It's a fancy thing, but it pleases me."

Christopher got up and went to the open window. The tussle between them had come. It would need all his strength to keep himself free from this man's toils. However generous in appearance, Christopher knew they were toils for him, and must be avoided.

"Aymer's done well enough for you so far," pursued Peter Masters from the depths of his chair. "We will grant him all credit, but this is the affair of a business man: it requires capital: it requires business knowledge: and it requires faith. You will have to go to someone if you don't come to me, and I'm making you a better offer than you'll get elsewhere. I'll do more. We'll buy up the other men if they are dangerous. You can have their experience, too. It's only a question of investing enough money."

As he stood there in the window Christopher realised it all: how near his darling project lay to his heart, how great and harassing would be the difficulties of launching it on the world; how sure success would be under this man's guidance, and yet how with all his heart and soul and unreasoning mind he hated the thought of it, and would have found life itself dear at the purchase of his freedom.

His hands shook a little as he turned, but his voice was quiet and steady.

"It is very generous of you, sir, but I could not possibly pledge myself to you or any man."

"I'm asking no pledge. I'm only asking you to complete your own invention, and when it's completed I'll help you to use it."

"I must be free."

"You own you can't use any discovery by yourself, you'd have to go to someone. I come to you. The credit will be yours. I only find the means and share the return—fair interest on capital."

"It's not that."

"Then what? Do you doubt my financial ability or financial soundness?"

The meshes of the net were very narrow. Christopher sat with his head on his hands. He could waste no force in inventing reasons, neither could he explain the intangible truth. It was a fight of wills solely.

"I can't do it," said Christopher doggedly.

"You are only a boy, but I credit you with more common-sense and a better eye for business than many young men double your age. What displeases you in my offer? Where do you want it altered?"

"I don't want it at all, Mr. Masters. I won't accept it. I don't think my reason matters at all. I know I shall never do so well, but I refuse."

"There are others who would take it. Suppose you are forestalled?"

Christopher looked him straight in the eyes.

"It's a fair fight so far."

"A fight is always fair to the winner," returned Masters grimly. There was a silence. The next thrust reached the heart of the matter.

"What is your objection to dealing with me?"

Peter Masters leant forward as he spoke and put a finger on the other's knee; his hard, keen eyes sought the far recesses of his son's mind, but they did not sink deep enough to read his soul. Christopher struggled with the impetuous words, the direct bare truth that sought for utterance. Truth was too pure and subtle a thing to give back here. When he answered it was in his old deliberate manner, as he had answered Fulner—as he would invariably answer when he mistrusted his own judgment.

"If I told you my objections you would not care for them or understand them. You would think them folly. I won't defend them. I won't offer them. It is just impossible, but I thank you."

He rose and Masters did the same with a curious look of admiration and disappointment in his eyes.

"I thought you a better business man, Christopher. Will you refer the matter to your—guardian?"

"No. It is quite my own. Even Aymer can't help me."

Peter's lips straightened ominously.

"You will come to me yet. My terms will not be so good again."

"Then I am at least warned."

"As you will. You are a fool, Christopher, perhaps I am well quit of you."

"I think that is quite likely," returned Christopher gravely, with a faint twinkle of amusement in his eyes. He went away despondently, however, and stopped at the door.

"When would you like me to go?"

"I told you: we go up to London on Monday," said the millionaire sharply. "I engaged you to buy a car and you must buy it."

"I am quite ready to do so."

He left the room with an appalling sense of defeat and humiliation on him. He could hardly credit a victory that left him so bruised and spiritless. It was in his mind to run away and avoid his engagement in London. He might even have done so but for Peter's remark. He walked across the hall with downcast eyes and nearly fell against a tall thin form.

"Nevil!" cried Christopher.

"Yes, Nevil. Christopher, could I be had up for libel if I wrote the life of a railway train?"

CHAPTER XXII

Christopher led the way into the nearest room and turned to Nevil with an anxious face.

"What is wrong? Is it Cæsar?" He stopped abruptly.

"There's nothing wrong. Mayn't anyone leave Marden but you, you young autocrat?"

Nevil deposited his lanky self in a comfortable chair and smiled in his slow way. Then he looked round the room with a critical, disapproving eye.

"Is Peter at home?" he asked, "and do you think he could put me up for a night? I suppose I ought to see him."

Christopher did not offer to move.

"You shan't see him till you tell me what brings you here, Nevil," he said firmly.

The other shook his head. "That's a bad argument, Christopher. However, I'll pretend it's effectual. There's a man at Leamington who has some records he considers priceless, but which I think are frauds. I thought if I came up to-day I could travel down with you to-morrow."

It sounded plausible—too plausible when Christopher considered the difficulty it was to rouse Nevil even to go to London. There might be a man in Leamington, but he didn't believe Nevil had come to see him.

"You are growing very energetic, Nevil," he said slowly, "all this trouble over some fraudulent records."

"They might be genuine, and really important," Nevil suggested cautiously. "At all events I was not returning till Saturday, and Mr. Masters wants me to stay till Monday now, and go to London with him then."

Nevil crossed and uncrossed his long legs, gazing abstractedly at a modern picture of mediæval warfare.

"Those helmets are fifteen years too late for that battle," he volunteered, "and the pikes are German, not French. What a rotten picture. Don't you think you could come back with me? I hate travelling alone. I always believe I shall get mislaid and be taken to the Lost Property Office. Porters are so careless."

He did not look round, but continued to examine the details of the offending picture.

Christopher leant over his chair and put his hands on Nevil's shoulders.

"Nevil, I can't stand any more. Tell me why I am to come back."

The other looked up at him with a rueful little smile, singularly like his father's.

"You were not always so dense, Christopher. I hoped you wouldn't ask questions that are too difficult to answer. To begin with, neither my father nor Aymer know I've come. They think I'm in town. You see, Cæsar misses you, though he wouldn't have you think so for the world, in case it added to your natural conceit, but it makes him—cross, yes, rather particularly cross and that upsets the house. I can't write at all, so I thought you had better come back. The fact is," he added with a burst of confidence, "I've promised an article on the Masterpieces of Freedom for August. I seldom promise, but I like to keep my word if I do, and it's impossible to write now. If you're enjoying yourself it's horribly selfish—but you see the importance of it, don't you?"

"Yes," allowed Christopher with the ghost of a smile, "it's lamentably selfish of you, but I realise the importance. Shall we go by rail to-night?"

"But Leamington?"

"Will the man run away?"

"My father might have been interested to see the papers."

"You dear old fraud," said Christopher with an odd little catch in his voice, "do you suppose St. Michael won't see through you? Is it like you to travel this distance to see doubtful records when you won't go to London to see genuine ones? Why did not St. Michael write to me?"

"Cæsar would not let him."

"He must be ill."

"He is not, on my word, Christopher. He is just worried to the verge of distraction by your being here. It seems ridiculous, but so it is."

"Why didn't you write yourself?"

Nevil considered the question gravely.

"Why didn't I write? Oh, I know. I only thought of it this morning and it seemed quicker to come."

"Or wire?" persisted Christopher.

"It would have cost such a lot to explain," he answered candidly. "I did think of that and started to send one. Then I found I had only twopence in my pocket. If I had sent anyone else to the office everyone would have known I was sending for you and Cæsar would have been more annoyed than ever."

"I quite see. What did Mrs. Aston say?"

"I think she said you'd be sure to come."

Christopher nodded. "Yes, I'll go by mail to-night." Then he shut his teeth sharply and looked out of the window with a frown, thinking of the renewed battle of wills to come, and at last said he would go and find Mr. Masters, since no one appeared to have told him of Nevil's arrival.

He went straight down the corridor to Peter Masters' room. The owner was still seated as he had left him, smoking placidly.

"Changed your mind already?" he asked as his guest entered.

"No, not that, but Nevil Aston has come and I must go back with him by the mail to-night."

"What's up?" The big man sprang to his feet. "Is Aymer ill?"

"No, no. I don't think so. It may be Nevil's fancy. He thinks Aymer wants me back. Of course it sounds absurd, but Nevil, who won't stir beyond the garden on his own account, has come all this way to fetch me to Cæsar."

Peter Masters was half-way to the door and tossed a question over his shoulder curtly.

"Where is he?"

"In the little reception-room."

Christopher followed him down the passage puzzling over this unexpected behaviour.

Nevil was re-exploring the inaccurate picture with patient sorrow and despair. He hardly turned as they entered.

"How do you do, Peter," he said unenthusiastically, "why do you buy pictures like that by men who don't even know the subject they are painting?"

"I'll burn it to-morrow. What's the matter with Aymer, Nevil?"

Nevil looked reproachfully at Christopher.

"Nothing is the matter, as I told Christopher, only I'd a man to see at Leamington and thought I could get a fellow victim here for the journey home."

"I'll meet you in London on Monday," put in the fellow victim quietly to Mr. Masters.

Peter looked from one to the other, lastly he looked long at Christopher and Christopher looked at him. Nothing short of the revelation Peter was as yet unprepared to make would stop Christopher from going to Aymer Aston that night he knew, and if he let the boy go back with the truth untold, it would be forever untold—by *him*. That it *was* the Truth was a conviction now. There was no space left for a shadow of mistrust in his mind.

"If you go by the mail we'd better dine at eight sharp," he said abruptly. "I want to see you, Christopher, before you go, in my room." He turned towards the door, adding as an afterthought, "You must look after Nevil till I am free."

Nevil gave a gentle sigh of satisfaction as the door closed.

Christopher laughed. The relief was so unexpected, so astounding. "We'll have some tea in the orangery," he said after a moment's consideration. "You may not like the statuary, but the orange trees at least offer no anachronisms."

Peter Masters shut the door of his room with a bang and going to an ever-ready tray, helped himself to a whiskey and soda with a free hand. Then he carefully selected a cigar of a brand he kept for the Smoke of Great Decisions, and lit it. All this he did mechanically, by force of habit, but after it was done, habit found no path for itself, for Peter Masters was treading new roads, wandering in unaccustomed regions, and found no solution to his problem in the ancient ways.

Was he, who for thirty-five years of life—from full manhood till now—had never consulted any will or pleasure but his own—was he now going to make a supreme denial to himself for no better reason than the easing of a stricken man's burden?

The man once had been his friend, but the boy was his. And he wanted him. He clenched his fist on the thought. He was perfectly aware of his own will in this matter.

Even from the material or business point of view his need of a son and heir had grown great of late. He had never contemplated the non-existence of one, just as he had never contemplated the non-existence of Elizabeth. He had counted, it is true, on overpowering the alert senses of one who had known the pinch of poverty with superabundant evidence of the fortune that was his. He had noted the havoc wrought to great fortunes by children brought up to regard great wealth as the natural standard of life; he meant to avoid that error, and in the unnatural neglect of the boy he had believed to be his, there was less callous indifference than Charles Aston thought: it was more the outcome of a crooked reasoning which placed the ultimate good of his fortune above the immediate well-being of his child. The terrible event in Liverpool that had shattered his almost childish belief in his wife's existence had also wiped away her fading image from his mind. The whole force of his energetic nature was focussed on the possible personality of his son. This Christopher of Aymer Aston's upbringing, entirely different from all he had purposed to find in his heir, called to him across forgotten waters. His very obstinacy and will power were matters in which Peter rejoiced—they were qualities no Aston had implanted. He was proud of his son and his pride clamoured to possess in entirety what was his by right of man.

What could prevent him? He sat biting his fingertips and frowning into the gathering twilight without—at that persistent vision of Aymer Aston's face.

There were plenty of men in the world who would have shrugged their shoulders over the question of Peter Masters' honesty, some who would have accredited his lightest word and yet would have preferred a legal buffer between them and the bargain he drove: many who considered him a model of financial honesty. It was a matter of the personal standpoint: perhaps none of them would have troubled to measure the millionaire by any measure than their own. Peter's own measure was of primitive simplicity—he never took something for nothing, and if he placed his own value on what he bought and what he paid, he at least believed in his own scale of prices. Had he picked up a banknote in the street he would have lodged it with the police unless he considered the amount only equalised his trouble in stopping to rescue it. Had his son dragged himself up the toilsome ladder to manhood (he ignored the possibility of woman's aid), he would have taken him as he was, good or bad, without compunction, but he recognised that Christopher was not the outcome of his own efforts only, that Aymer having expended the unpriceable capital of time, patience and love, might, with all reason, according to Peter Masters' code of life, look for the full return of sole possession in the result. Was he, then, in the face of his own standard of honest dealing, going to rob Aymer of the fruit of his labours, to take so great a something for nothing?

Let it be to Peter's everlasting credit that he knew his millions to be as inadequate to offer a return as any beggar's pocket. He had no quarrel with himself over his past conduct, he repudiated nothing and regretted nothing, he merely viewed the question from the immediate standpoint of the present. Was he going to violate the one rule of his life or not? He made no pretence about it. If he claimed his son he would claim him entirely. Christopher would refuse, would resist the claim at first—of that Peter was assured. But it would be Aymer himself who would fight with time on his side and insist on Peter's rights, he was equally assured of that. But still Christopher would refuse.

Peter Masters got up and began to walk up and down and parcelled out bribes.

"He shall have the Foundry to play with—a garden city for them if he likes. His own affair run on his own silly lines." So he thought, ready to sweep to oblivion rule and system for the possession of this son of his.

But there remained Aymer.

Whether he gained Christopher in the end or not the very making of the claim would make a break between Aymer and his adopted son,—a gulf over which they would stretch out hands and never meet.

Aymer loved him. Aymer of the maimed life, the shattered hopes, whose destiny filled Peter with sick pity even now, so that he stretched out his great arms and moved sharply with a dumb thankfulness to something that he could move.

He might as well rob a child—or a beggar—better: he could give them a possible equivalent.

He went slowly to the side table and had a second whiskey and soda, mechanically as he had done at first, then he rang the bell.

When Christopher sought him shortly before dinner-time he was told curtly he could go to London at his leisure and purchase a car where and how he liked, so it were a good one.

"I shall want a chauffeur with it," he added, "English, mind. You can charge your expenses with your commission, whatever that is."

Christopher said gravely he would consider the matter.

"You can send me word how Aymer is," concluded Masters shortly. "I suppose he's ill. The whole lot of you spoil him outrageously."

CHAPTER XXIII

Perhaps they did spoil Aymer Aston, these good people, who loved him so greatly, setting so high a store upon his happiness that their own well-being was merged therein.

While it was quite true that neither Nevil nor any other could have worked peacefully in the electrical atmosphere of the house after Christopher left with Peter Masters, it is also true that no temporary personal inconvenience would have driven Nevil to undertake the long and tiresome journey, if his brother's welfare had not been involved.

The need had been great. Aymer's restless misery increased every day of Christopher's absence. He refused to see any of the household but his father and Vespasian, and though at first he made desperate efforts to control himself, in the end he gave up, and long hours of sullen brooding silence were interposed with passionate flashes of temper. It was the old days over again, and all those near him realised to the full how great was the victory that had been won and how terrible life might have been for them all without it. Therefore they were very patient and tolerant, though Mr. Aston began to consider seriously if he would not be justified in breaking his given word to Aymer and summoning Christopher back at once.

He looked very worn and tired when he joined Renata at dinner on the Thursday night.

"Nevil does not mean to be away long, does he?" he inquired anxiously.

"No, I think not. Why, St. Michael? Does Cæsar want him?"

"He asked for him this evening."

"What a pity."

She went on with her soup, with a little rose of colour on her face, thinking of the secret her husband had of course confided to her. Presently observing St. Michael hardly touched his dinner and seemed too weary to talk, she suggested nervously that she should sit with Aymer that evening. He conjured up a kind smile of thanks, but refused in his gentle, courteous way, saying that Aymer seemed disinclined to talk.

When Mr. Aston went back to the West Room a little later, that disinclination seemed to have evaporated. He heard Cæsar's furious voice pouring a cascade of biting words on someone as he opened the door. Vespasian was the unfortunate occasion and the unwilling victim; Vespasian, who was older by twenty years than in the days when he stood unmoved before continuous and worse storms. His usually impassive face was rather red and he now and then uttered a dignified protest and finally bent to pick up the shattered glass that lay between them and was the original cause of the trouble. Aymer, with renewed invective, clutched a book to hurl at the unfortunate man, but before he could fling it, Mr. Aston leant over the head of the sofa and seized his wrists. The left would have been powerless in a child's grasp and the elder man's position made him master of the still strong right arm.

At a faint sign from Mr. Aston, Vespasian vanished.

Aymer made one unavailing attempt to free himself as his father drew his hands up level with his head. He tried not to look at the face leaning over him.

"Aymer," said his father, with great tenderness, "do you remember what I used to do with you when you were a little boy and lost your temper?"

Aymer gave a short, uneasy laugh. "Tie my hands to a chair or a bed head. It was all right then, it is taking a mean advantage now." He ended with a choking laugh again, and Mr. Aston felt his hands tremble under his careful grasp.

"Aymer, my dear old fellow, if you must turn on someone, then turn on me. I understand how it is. Vespasian doesn't. That's not fair. It's the way of a fractious invalid, not of a sane man. Where's your pride?"

Aymer bit his lip. He was helpless and humiliated, but after all it was his father. He looked up at him at last with a crooked smile.

"I've none—in your power like this, sir. Let me go, I'll be a good boy."

They both laughed, and Mr. Aston released him. The colour burned on Aymer's face. Grown man as he was, the sudden subjection to authority so exerted was hard to bear even in the half-joking aspect with which his father covered it.

Mr. Aston knew it. He had deliberately used the very helplessness that was his son's best excuse for his outbreak, to check the same, and however thankful for his success, the means were bitter to him also, only he was not going to let Aymer see it or get off without further word.

"I shall have to send you to school again," he said, picking up the broken glass. "I can't have Nevil's property treated like this. He'll be adding 'breakages' to the weekly bill."

"I'll pay," pleaded Aymer, contritely, "if you won't tell him. Where is he?"

"Gone to London, of all the preposterous things; so Renata says. She expects him back to-morrow, I suppose Bowden will look after him, but I should have wired to them had I known he was going."

He seemed really a little worried, and Aymer laughed.

"What a family, St. Michael! Nevil can look after himself a good deal better than you think. He puts it on to get more attention."

"Do you think he is jealous?"

"Not an ounce of it in him. I have the monopoly of that," he added, with a sharp sigh, and then, without any warning, he caught his father's arm and pulled him near.

"Father," his voice was hoarse and unsteady, "if Peter tells Christopher, what will happen? I can't think it out steadily. I can't face it."

Mr. Aston knelt by him and put his hand on his shoulder, concealing his own distress at this unheard-of breakdown.

"My dear boy, it would not make the slightest difference to Christopher. I'm seriously afraid he'd tell Peter to go to the devil—and he'd come home by the next train. He'd never accept him."

"He'd never forget," persisted Aymer, the sleeping agony of long years shining in his eyes. "It would not be the same, father. He would not be—mine. I could not pretend it if he knew. Peter would be there between us—always as he was—"

He broke off and took up the thread with a still sharper note of pain, "Father, can't you understand. I don't mind a woman. He'll love and marry some day: it's his right. I don't grudge that. But another father—his real one. Oh, My God, mayn't I keep even this for myself?" He hid his face on the cushions, all the wild jealousy of his nature struggling with his pride.

His father put his arm round him, hardly able to credit the meaning of the crisis. Was that white scar on his son's forehead no memorial to a dead jealousy, but only an expression of a slumbering passion?

"Aymer, old fellow, listen. Peter isn't going to tell, I feel sure of it. And it would make no difference. You must allow I know something of men. I give you my word of honour, Aymer, I know it would make no difference to Christopher. You wrong him. You will always be first with him."

"It's not Christopher," returned Aymer, lifting hard, haggard eyes to his father, "it's myself. Twice in my life I've wanted something—someone for myself alone. Elizabeth—and now Christopher! It's I who can't share."

"Jealousy, cruel as the grave." Involuntarily the words escaped Mr. Aston.

"More cruel."

He dropped his head again. St. Michael continued to kneel by him in silence. The elementary forces of nature are hard matters with which to deal. Silence, sympathy, and the loan of mental strength were all he could offer.

It came to his mind in the quiet stillness how in just such a crisis as this, when he was not at hand to help the same cruel passion had wrought the irrevocable havoc with his son's life. He looked at the dark head pressed on the pillows and remembered his young wife's half-laughing pride in her first-born's copper coloured aureole of hair. He recollected the day he had first held him in his arms, himself but just arrived at man's estate, and this helpless little baby given into his power and keeping. He had done his best: God knows how humbly he confessed that more than truthful Truth, yet even all his love had failed to save that little red-haired baby from this … jealousy, cruel as the grave! Perhaps he had been too young a father to deal with it at first. Was it his failure or were there greater forces behind—the forces of ages of other failures for which poor Aymer paid....

Aymer moved till his head rested against his father's arm, like a tired child. Presently he looked up rather shamefacedly.

"It's over. What a fool I've been. Don't tell Christopher, father."

A faint reflection of what Aymer considered his own terrible monopoly, caught poor St. Michael for a fleeting moment, a jealous pang that his son's first thought must go to the boy. He realised suddenly he was tired out and old, and got to his feet stiffly.

Aymer gave him a quick, penetrating glance.

"Send Vespasian back, father," he said abruptly, "and you go to bed. What a selfish brute I've been." And when Mr. Aston had bidden him good-night he added in the indifferent tone in which he veiled any great effort, "If Peter should want Christopher to stay longer, you might tell him to come back—it doesn't pay to be so proud—and I'll apologise to Vespasian."

"He's worth it," said Mr. Aston with a smile, "he and I are getting old, Aymer."

"Negatived by a large majority, sir," he answered quickly.

It was not of Christopher he thought in the silent hours of the night, and Mr. Aston's brief jealousy would have found no food on which to thrive had it survived its momentary existence.

When Mr. Aston came down in the morning the first sight that met his astonished eyes was Christopher, seated at the breakfast table and attacking that meal with liberal energy. He sprang up as Mr. Aston entered.

"My dear boy, I thought you were not coming till to-morrow at the earliest."

"Will it be inconvenient?" asked Christopher, with demure gravity. "I'm sorry, but I was so bored."

He stumbled a little over the prevarication. St. Michael was not Peter Masters, even excuses found no easy flow in his presence.

"I'm delighted," said Mr. Aston, and looked it.

He had breakfasted in his room, so he sat down by Christopher and tried to find out the reason of the opportune return.

"Your letters did not sound at all bored."

"I only realised it yesterday evening," returned Christopher, with great gravity, "so we—that is I—came down by the mail last night—and Nevil...."

"Nevil?"

"Yes, I picked him up, you know. He was seeing a man in Leamington."

Christopher carved ham carefully, and avoided Mr. Aston's eye, smiling to himself over his promise to Nevil not to betray him.

"Nevil went to London. How did—" Mr. Aston stopped suddenly, "Christopher."

"Yes, St. Michael."

"You are not to lie to me whatever you do to others. Tell me what it means."

Christopher regarded him doubtfully and then laughed outright.

"Nevil did not like travelling alone. He thought he would get lost, so he asked me to look after him."

"He went from London to Leamington to get a companion to travel home with?"

"Exactly. Isn't it like him, St. Michael?"

They again looked steadily at each other.

"And being a bit weary of fighting for the right of individual existence," went on Christopher, "I agreed to bring him home. Mr. Masters has been most kind, but he does like his own way."

"And what about you?"

"Oh, I like mine, too. That's why it was so boring. How's Cæsar?"

"He will be pleased to see you. Where is Nevil?"

"Gone to bed, I expect. How he hates travelling."

"Yes."

"He hates explanations still more, please St. Michael."

"He should have prepared a more plausible story."

"He thinks it quite credible. He expected me to believe—about the man in Leamington."

"And did you?"

"Well, do you?"

They both laughed and Christopher looked at the clock.

"Do you think Vespasian will let me take in Cæsar's breakfast?"

"He would be delighted, I'm sure. Cæsar won't believe in Leamington either, Christopher."

"But he will easily believe I was bored—which is true. I don't think he is as fond of Mr. Masters as he pretends to be."

Whether Aymer believed or not, he asked no questions. He only remarked that Peter was far more likely to have been bored and Christopher had no eye to his own advantage. To which Christopher replied flippantly that it was a question of "vantage out," and he was not going to imperil his game with a rash service.

After that he sat on the foot of the bed and talked frankly of his visit, and minute by minute the jealous fire in Aymer's heart died down to extinction.

Presently, however, he said abruptly and rather reproachfully: "You never told me Mr. Masters had married."

For a confused second the room and the occupants were lost in a fiery mist and only Christopher's voice lived in the chaos. Then Aymer found himself struggling to maintain hold of something in the mental turmoil, he did not know what at first: then that it was his own voice. It amazed him to hear it quite; steady and cool.

"Why should she interest you? Did Peter tell you?"

"No. Never mentioned it. One day I found Mrs. Eliot, the housekeeper, in a room, a sort of boudoir, playing about with holland covers, and I helped her. What was she like?"

"Mrs. Eliot?"

"No, you old stupid. Mrs. Peter Masters. I know you knew her, because there's a pen-and-ink sketch of you and Mr. Masters playing cards in the room."

"Oh, is there."

"Is she dead?"

"Yes."

"What was she like—to marry Mr. Masters?"

"Like? Like other women," returned Aymer, shortly.

Christopher looked at him sharply and realised he had committed an indiscretion—that this was a subject that might not be handled even with a velvet glove.

"Explicit," he retorted lightly. "However, that's not important. Now for something of real moment."

He plunged into an account of Peter's final offer to him, and his own refusal.

"Why on earth did you refuse? Wasn't it good enough?" demanded Aymer curtly.

"No, not with P. M. attached. Might as well take lodgings in Wormwood Scrubs—quite as much liberty. But, anyhow, Cæsar, you see now what you have got to do."

"Get you apartments in Wormwood Scrubs?"

"No. Do be serious. Give me a laboratory here and some experimental ground. Do, there's a dear good Cæsar." In reminiscence of old days he pretended to rub his head against Cæsar's arm.

"Ah, you invented Peter's offer to wheedle me into this. I suppose."

"Exactly. Seriously, Cæsar, if you would, it would be excellent. I've been thinking it out, I could work here safely. No one to crib my ideas. But I must have trial ground."

"That's Nevil's affair."

"Well, I undertake to manage Nevil if you are afraid," said Christopher, with an air of desperate resolve.

"I thought you didn't like Marden," persisted Cæsar, fighting in an unreasoning way, against his own desires, "and this engaged couple will wander round and get in the way."

He looked Christopher straight in the face with scrutinising eyes, but he never flinched.

"I'll put up a notice, 'Trespassers will be blown up.'"

"Well, you'd better talk to St. Michael, but remember, I can't buy up the other fellows. You'd better have taken Peter's offer."

"I'd much rather bore you than Mr. Masters."

"I'm not complaining."

That was the nearest approach he made to expressing to Christopher his deep, quiet content at the arrangement that astute young man had so skilfully suggested. St. Michael said a little more and Christopher knew without words that he had pleased them both.

CHAPTER XXIV

It took very little time for Christopher to establish himself in the desired manner. Indeed, before another week had passed the suggestion was an accomplished fact. After that his actual presence in the house might almost have been forgotten except by Cæsar. Mr. Masters' half serious threat was like a spur to a willing steed. He spoke little of what he was doing, but the experimental ground was criss-crossed with strange-coloured roads, and the little band of men who worked for him, with the kindly indulgence of the "young master's whim," began to talk less of the fad and to nurse a bewildered wonder at the said young master's strict rule and elaborate care over little points that slow minds barely saw at all.

As for the engaged couple, Christopher rarely met them. He did not intentionally avoid either Patricia or Geoffry, singly or collectively, but he was not sorry their preoccupation and his separated them. He did not lose his sense of possessorship of Patricia: in his innermost mind she was still his, and Geoffry was but the owner of an outside visible Patricia that was but one expression of the woman who stood crowned and waiting in his heart.

There was no question of the wedding, or if there were between themselves, Geoffry was not allowed to voice it. Patricia was enjoying life and in no hurry to forego or shorten the pleasant days of her engagement.

Towards the end of September Christopher began to relax his long hours of work and the tense look on his face gave way.

"I shall know in about a fortnight if it's coming out all right," he said to Cæsar abruptly one day, "and it's a fortnight in which I can do nothing but wait."

"Go and play," said Cæsar, watching him anxiously, "you concentrate too much. You'll be getting nervous."

Christopher laughed and gripped Cæsar's hand in his firm, steady grasp.

"Never better in my life," he said. "Concentration is an excellent thing. I'm beginning to appreciate Nevil."

He spent the next five days in true Nevil fashion, however, following the whim of the moment, and "lazing" as thoroughly as he had worked. Geoffry and Patricia claimed his attendance, or Patricia did and Geoffry made no protest. They were supremely happy days. The three talked of nothing in particular, just the easy surface aspect of the world and the moment's sunshine, and Geoffry was secretly surprised to find his pleasure so little diminished by the third presence.

Then one day that wore no different outer aspect to its fellows in their livery of autumn sunshine, the three walked over the wooded ridge to the open downland where the brown windswept turf was interspaced with stretches of stubble and blue-green "roots," where a haze of shimmering light hung over copse and field, and beyond the undulating near country a line of hills purple and grey melted into the sky-line.

They had discussed hotly a disputed point as they mounted from the valley and came out on this good land of promise in a sudden silence. Patricia seated herself on the soft turf at the edge of a little chalk pit and sat in her accustomed attitude with her hands folded, looking straight before her, and the two men sat on either side of her. And over all three a sense of the smallness of the matter over which they had differed drifted in varied manners.

Geoffry realised how little he really cared about it. Christopher was amused at their futile efforts to solve a problem of which they knew nothing, but Patricia was angry, first that she had been betrayed into expressing concern in something of which she was really ignorant, and secondly that neither Christopher nor Geoffry had agreed with her. The matter of the discussion—it arose from the subject of village charities—became of no importance, but the sense of irritation remained with her, and she was unaccountably cross with Christopher. Geoffry's point of view she could ignore, but Christopher's worried her.

Geoffry dismissed the whole thing most easily; he did not trouble about Christopher's view, and he thought Patricia's a little queer, but then to him Patricia's views were not Patricia herself. He made the common mistake of divorcing that particular aspect of his lady love with which he was best acquainted from the multitudinous prisms of her womanhood. He would have allowed vaguely that she had "moods," that these overshadowed occasionally the sunny, beautiful girl he loved, but no conception of her as a whole had entered his mind. He was in love with one prism of a complex whole, or rather with one colour of the rainbow itself.

This particular truth with regard to Geoffry's estimate of Patricia impressed itself on Christopher with disagreeable persistency during the walk, and renewed that nearly forgotten fear that had come to him during the ride from Milton in the spring.

So presently he found himself watching her inner attitude towards her accepted lover in the forbidden way, without sufficient knowledge of what he was actually doing to stop it. Perhaps some subtle appreciation of this in the subconscious realm, roused a like uneasiness and dissatisfaction in Patricia herself.

At all events Christopher soon found grounds for no immediate fear and left the future to itself.

"Shall we go on?" he suggested, marking how her hands grew white as she pressed them together.

She negatived the proposal, imperiously saying they had only just got there and she wanted to rest.

"You are getting lazy, Patricia," said her lover gravely. "I warn you, it's the one unpardonable sin in my eyes."

"You mistake restlessness for energy," she retorted quickly. "I'm never lazy. Ask Christopher."

Geoffry did no such thing. He continued to fling stones at a mark on the lower lip of the chalk pit.

"It's fairly hard to distinguish, anyhow," said Christopher, thoughtfully. "There are people who call Nevil lazy, whereas he isn't. He only takes all his leisure in one draught."

"Oh, I don't know. It's simple enough, isn't it? I never feel lazy so long as I'm doing something—moving about."

Geoffry jumped down into the little white pit as he spoke, as if to demonstrate his remark. Patricia looked scornful.

"So long as your are restless, you mean," she said.

"Well, you must teach me better if you can. I say, Patricia, do you always turn reproof on the reprover's head?"

He leant against the bank looking up at her, smiling in his easy, good-tempered way. He wished vaguely the line of frown on her pretty forehead would go. He wondered if she had a headache.

He ventured to put his hand over hers when he was sure Christopher was not looking. She neither answered the caress nor resented it.

Presently he began to explore the hollow, poking into all the rabbit-holes with his stick.

Christopher sat silent, which was a mistake, for it left her irritation but one object on which to expend itself, and after all it was Geoffry who should have tried to please her by sitting still.

Suddenly a frightened rabbit burst out of a disturbed hole, and Geoffry, with a shout of delight, in pure instinct flung a stone. By a strange, unhappy fluke, expected least of all by himself, the stone hit the poor little terrified thing and it rolled over dead. He picked it up by its ears and called to them triumphantly to witness his luck, with boyish delight in the unexpected, though the chances were he would never have flung the stone at all had he dreamt of destroying it.

A second flint whizzed through the air, grazing the side of his head. He dropped the rabbit and stood staring blankly at the two on the bank.

Patricia's white, furious face blazed on him. Christopher was grasping her hands, his face hardly less white.

"Are you hurt?" he called over his shoulder.

"No," the other stammered out, unaware of the blood streaming down the side of his head, and then dabbed his handkerchief on it. "It's only a scratch. What's happened?"

"Patricia mistook you for a rabbit, I think," returned Christopher grimly and added to her in a low voice, "Do you know you struck him, Patricia?"

She gave a shiver and put her hands to her face. Even then he did not leave go of her wrists.

"A happy fluke you didn't aim so well as I did," called Geoffry, unsteadily coming towards them.

"Don't come," said Christopher sharply. "Wait a moment. Patricia," he tried to pull her hands from her face: her golden head dropped against his shoulder and he put his arms round her.

"What is the matter with Patricia. Is she ill?" asked Geoffry at his shoulder, his voice altered and strained.

"It's all right now. Sorry I wasn't quicker, Geoffry. Don't touch her yet."

But Geoffry was hard pressed already not to thrust the other aside, and he laid his hand on the girl's arm. Christopher never offered to move.

"Patricia, what's the matter. You haven't really hurt me, you know. What on earth were you doing?"

But she gave no sign she heard him. Only her hands clung close to Christopher and she trembled a little.

"She is ill," cried Geoffry quickly. "Put her down, Christopher, she's faint."

"No, she is not," returned the other through clenched teeth, "she will be all right directly, if you'll give her time. For heaven's sake go away, man. Don't let her see you like that. Don't you know your head is cut."

Geoffry put up his hand mechanically, and found plentiful evidence of this truth, but he was still bewildered as to what had actually happened, and he was aching with desire to take her from Christopher's hold.

"It was just an accident," he protested. "She didn't mean to hit me, of course. Let her lie down."

"She did mean to hit you, just at the moment," returned the other, very quietly, "haven't you been told. Oh, do go away, there's a good fellow. I'll explain presently."

He was sick with dread lest Patricia should give way to one of her terrible paroxysms of sorrow before them both. She was trembling all over and he did not know how much self-control she had gained. Then suddenly he understood what was the real trouble with poor Geoffry.

"Don't mind my holding her, Geoffry," he went on swiftly, "I've seen her like this before and understand, and I can always stop her, but she mustn't see you like that first."

Geoffry stood biting his lip and then turned abruptly on his heel and left them—and for all his relief at his departure, Christopher felt a faint glow of contempt at his obedience.

"Is he gone?" Patricia lifted her white face and black-rimmed eyes to his.

"Yes, dear."

"Did I hurt him?"

"Not seriously. Sorry I was not quicker, Patricia."

"I did not even know myself," she answered, wearily. "Christopher, why was I born? Why didn't someone let me die?"

He gave her a little shake. "Don't talk like a baby. But, Patricia, how is it Geoffry doesn't know?"

She looked round with languid interest.

"Why did he go?"

"I sent him away."

"He went?"

"What else could he do?"

She made no further remark, but sat clasping and unclasping her nervous hands, as powerless against the desperate languor assailing her as she had been against the gust of passion.

Across the wide, smiling land westward a closed shadow, sharp of outline and rapid of flight, drove across the stubble field, sank in an intervening valley, and skimmed again over the close green turf to their feet as it touched the edge of the chalk pit. She shivered a little.

"Take me home, Christopher."

He helped her up and with steady hands assisted her to smooth her hair and put on her hat, and then they turned and walked back along the path they had come. Christopher was greatly troubled. It seemed to him incredible that Geoffry had been left in ignorance of this cruel inheritance. He tried to gauge the effect of it on his apparently unsuspecting mind and was uneasy and dissatisfied over the result.

"Someone must explain to Geoffry," he said presently; "will you like him to come over to-night and tell him yourself, Patricia?"

"I don't want to see him." There was a deep note of fatigue in her voice, also a new accent of indifference. Her mind was in no way occupied with her lover's attitude towards the unhappy episode.

"Someone's got to see him and explain. It's only fair," persisted Christopher resolutely.

"What is there to explain. What does it matter?"

"He thinks it was an accident."

She walked on a little quicker.

"Patricia, you must tell him."

Then she turned and faced him, and her pallor was burnt out with red.

"Christopher, I will not see him. I can't. What's the use? What can he do?"

"He must learn how to help you, learn how to stop it," he said doggedly.

She gave a curious, choking laugh. "Geoffry stop it? Don't be absurd, Christopher. You know he'd make me ten times worse if he tried. Anyhow, I'm not going to marry him."

"Patricia!"

"Don't, don't. I can't bear anything now. But I won't marry him, or anyone. It's not safe."

She went on down the path swiftly, without looking back, hardly conscious of the tears falling from her brimming eyes. Christopher followed her silently, furious with himself because of some unreasoning exultation in his heart, some clamorous sense of kinship with the golden land and laden earth that had been absent as they came, but it died when, presently emerging from the wood on to the park land facing Marden, she turned to him again regardless of her tears.

"He won't want to marry me now, anyhow," she said wistfully, with a child's appealing look of distress.

A great pity welled up in his heart and drowned the last thought of self, carrying visions of the cruel isolation this grim inheritage might entail on her, and he had hard work to refrain from taking her in his arms then and there to hold for ever shielded from the relentless pressure of her life. The temptation was more subtle and harder to withstand than on the sunny, gorse-covered cliff at Milton, for it was her need and her pain that cried for help and love, and she who suffered because he withstood. He could in no wise see what course he was to take beyond the minute, but he knew quite clearly what course he must not take, and such surety was the reward he won from that other fight.

He answered her appeal now with quite other words than those she perhaps sought, and it was the hardest pang of all to know it and recognise the vague discomfort in her eyes.

"You mustn't be unfair to Geoffry, Patricia. You haven't any right to say that. He will want to do his best for you when he understands."

"He went away."

"I sent him. I—I was afraid you were going to cry."

Had he done wrong? He cast his thoughts back rapidly. He knew he could not have borne that they two should witness one of her wild fits of repentance and misery. It would have been unbearably unfit. He could not have left her to Geoffry, and yet it had been Geoffry's right. He walked on by her side wondering where he had blundered.

"You would not have gone, Christopher, no matter who said so." Her directness was dangerous. She was then going to allow herself no illusions of any kind, not even concerning the man she loved, and Christopher became suddenly aware he was very young: that they were all three very young, and had no previous experience to guide them in this difficult pass, but must gain it for themselves, gain it perhaps at greater cost than he could willingly contemplate.

"It is no question of me, whatever," he said slowly. "I've been used to you and I understand. I don't know how it would be if I had not known, neither do you, but it's clear, you or Nevil must explain the matter to Geoffry at once."

"You can do it."

"It's not my place."

"You were there."

"That was mere chance."

She slipped her arm through his in the old way.

"Dear Christopher, I love Nevil, and he's awfully good, but you are like my own brother. Please pretend you are really. If I had a brother, he would see Geoffry for me."

"But Nevil might not like it."

It was a difficult pass, for how could he explain to her it was of Geoffry he was thinking, not of Nevil. His evasion at least raised a little smile.

"Nevil! An explanation taken off his hands!" She spread her own abroad in mock amazement.

"Tell him yourself, Patricia."

"Christopher!"

He looked straight ahead, a certain rigidness in the outline of his face betokening a decision at variance with his will.

"What am I to tell him?"

"What you like."

"I shall not tell him the silly thing you said just now, you know."

"What thing?"

"About not marrying."

"It doesn't matter," she said indifferently, "he won't marry me if he thinks I tried to hit him."

Christopher closed his mind and reason to so illogical a conclusion, but he disputed the point no more, and it was not till he left her and turned to face instantly the task she had laid upon him, that he realised how overwhelmingly difficult it was.

CHAPTER XXV

"I suppose no one realised you did not know all about it as you'd known them all so long."

Christopher concluded his simple and direct account with these words, and waited vainly for a reply from his hearer, who stood by the window with his back to him.

"It's so nearly a thing of the past, too, that it hardly seemed worth mentioning," he went on presently, an uneasy wonder at the silence growing on him.

At length Geoffry spoke, in a thick, slow way, like a man groping in darkness.

"You mean she did throw that stone deliberately, meaning to hit me?"

He had no sight at present for the wider issues that beset them or for Patricia's story: his attention was concentrated on the incident immediately affecting him and he could see it in no light but that of dull horror.

"Deliberately tried to do it?" he repeated, turning to Christopher.

"There wasn't anything deliberate about it. She just flung the stone at you precisely as you flung one at the rabbit. Sort of blind instinct. She does not know now she really hurt you."

He glanced at the crossing strips of plaster with which the other's head was adorned on the right side.

"It's horrible," muttered Geoffry, "I can't understand it."

"It's simple enough." There was growing impatience in Christopher's voice. "She inherits this ghastly temper as I've told you. It's like a sudden gust of wind if she's not warned. It takes her off her feet, as it were, but she's nearly learnt to stand firm. She has a wretched time after."

"It's madness."

"It's nothing of the kind. She wasn't taught to control it as a child. They just treated it as something she couldn't help."

"By heavens, are you going to make out she can help it, and that that makes it better?"

Christopher faced him with amazed indignation. Geoffry's whole attitude and reception of his story seemed to him incredibly one-sided.

"Of course it's better. A hundred times better. Do you mean you'd rather have her the victim of a real madness she could not control? Think what you are saying, man."

"To me, it's fairly unbearable if it's something she can help and doesn't."

Exasperation nearly choked the other. To have to defend Patricia at all was almost a desecration in his eyes, but he was her ambassador and he stuck to his orders.

"She does help it. She's nearly mastered it now."

Geoffry put his hand to his injured head and gave a short laugh.

Christopher got up abruptly.

"What am I to tell her, then?" he demanded shortly.

The real tenor of the discussion seemed to break suddenly upon Geoffry and he was cruelly alive to his own inability to meet it. He spoke hurriedly and almost pleadingly.

"Don't go yet. I've got to think this out. Can't you help me?"

"What's there to think about? I've told you. I can tell you how to help her if you like."

"I've got to think of a jolly sight more than you seem to imagine," returned the sorely beset young man irritably, but unable to keep a touch of conscious superiority out of his voice, "a jolly sight more, if I marry her."

"If you marry her?" Christopher turned on him with blazing eyes.

"I'm not saying I shan't—but it's a pretty bad pass for us both. I know how she feels. Marriage isn't just a question of pleasing oneself, you see. I must think it out for both of us."

Christopher began to speak and desisted. The other went on in an aggrieved tone.

"I ought to have been told. Heredity of that sort isn't a thing to be played with, you know. Anything might happen. Why wasn't I told?" He walked to and fro, and stopped by Christopher again.

"I wouldn't mind a bit," he burst out, "if it were just a bad joke, if she flung at me in fun and didn't expect to hit."

"She has a good aim as a rule," put in Christopher, too blind with fury now to realise the other's unhinged condition, but Geoffry went on unheeding.

"But to do it in a rage, and for nothing. Just a cold-blooded attack and no warning. I can't get over it. Anything might happen."

His first indignant pang that Christopher had been sent on this awkward errand had died out in the stress of the moment: he was ready to appeal for sympathy, for help, or even bare comprehension in the impossible situation in which he found himself, but Christopher had nothing to bestow on him but blind, furious resentment. He longed to be quit of his service and free to give way to his own wrath.

"There was plenty of warning for anyone with eyes and sense to use them, and there was nothing cold-blooded about it whatever, as I've told you fifty times. If you choose to make a mountain out of a molehill you must, but I'll not help you. I would have done my best for both of you if you'd taken it decently."

"You? What concern is it of yours?" retorted the other, stung back to his original jealousy.

"It's my concern so far as Patricia chooses it to be," he answered curtly. "I'm going now. You'd better write to her yourself, when you've decided if the risk is worth taking or not."

"It's my risk at least, not yours—yet awhile," was the unguarded reply.

The young men faced each other for a moment with passions at the point of explosion. It was Christopher who recollected his position of ambassador first and turned abruptly to the door. In the hall he narrowly escaped encounter with Mrs. Leverson, Geoffry's large and ample mother, but slipped out of a garden door on hearing the rustle of her dress. In the open air he breathed freely again and hastened to regain his motor, which he had left near the gates. Once outside Logan Park he turned the car northward along a fairly deserted high-road and drove at full pressure, until the hot passion of his heart cooled and his pulse fell into beat with the throb of the engine, and he found himself near Basingstoke. Then he turned homeward, driving with greater caution and was able to face matters in a logically sane manner.

"They won't marry and it's a blessed thing for both of them," was the burden of his thoughts, though it mitigated not one bit his indignant attitude towards Geoffry. Presently he turned to his own interest in the matter.

His first idea was that he was free to claim her who was his own at once, without loss of time, but that impulse died down before a better appreciation of facts. Patricia must be left free in mind to regain possession of every faculty, that was but common fairness: also he was by no means certain at this time what response she would make to his claim, and if it should be a negative his position at Marden would be difficult, and there was Aymer to consider. Quite slowly, and with no appreciable connection with the chief subject a recollection of that first journey with Peter Masters from London came to the surface of his mind, and written large across, in Peter's own handwriting, were the words, "Aymer's son."

He had put that idea deliberately behind his back, hidden it in the deepest recess of his mind, with a strange content and a germ of pride unconfessed and unacknowledged to himself. It remained a secret feeling that touched at no point his steady faith and devotion to his dead mother.

But Peter's suggestion had utterly quenched his original intention of asking Mr. Aston or Cæsar of his own origin, as he had intended to do at the time of his return from Belgium. The actual possibility or impossibility of the idea counted nothing so long as the faintest shadow of it lurked there in the background. If it were a fact, it was their secret, deliberately withheld; if it were not, he must be the last to give it life.

The incalculable power of suggestion had done its work and the suggested lie, taking root, had grown at the pace of all ill weeds and obscured his usually clear visions of essentials. The more he questioned the possible fact the denser seemed the screen between him and Patricia, until he called himself a fool to have dreamed she was ever his to claim at all.

It was in this wholly unsatisfactory mood he was called upon, on his return, to face Patricia and give his own account of the interview.

Patricia was lying in wait for him at the door of her own sanctum, which he had to pass on his way to his room. He would have gladly deferred the interview, but she summoned him imperiously.

"There's a good hour till dinner, Christopher, and I must know what he said. How long you've been!"

He followed her in and closed the door behind him. The little white-panelled room was so perfect an expression of its owner that at all times Christopher felt a still wonder fall on him to find himself within its confines. It was singularly uncrowded and free, and the monotonous note of light colour was broken by splashes of brightness that were as an embroidery to the plain setting.

Patricia turned to him with questioning eyes and no words, and the difficulty of his task made him a little curt and direct in speech, for otherwise how could he avoid voicing the tenderness that flowed to her.

"I told him about it and he seemed surprised he hadn't been told before, and he hadn't really taken in what happened this afternoon at all. I expect he'll write to you."

A faint ghost of a smile touched her white face.

"You are not really telling me what I want to know, Christopher."

"There's nothing else. He hadn't got the real focus of the thing when I left."

"I understand."

She turned away and leant her arm on the mantelpiece, wondering in a half-comprehensive way why the stinging sense of humiliation and helpless shame seemed so much less since Christopher had come. What had been well-nigh unbearable was now but a monotonous burden that wearied but did not crush her: she feared it no longer. He stood looking at her a moment, gathering as it were into himself all he could of the bitterness that he knew she carried at her heart, and then turned away to the window, realising the greatness of her trouble and yearning to do that very thing which unconsciously by mere action of his receptive sympathy he had done already.

Presently she came to him and put her hand on his arm.

"You'll understand, anyhow, Christopher," she said with a little sigh.

"We shall all do that here."

"But Geoffry won't."

"I suppose he can't."

She recognised the hard note in his voice at once, and seating herself on the window-seat set to work to fathom it.

"It will help me if you can tell me exactly how he took it, Christopher. Was he angry, or sorry, or horrified or what?"

He had to consider a moment what, out of fairness to Geoffry, he must withhold, and choose what he considered the most pardonable aspect.

"I think he was frightened, Patricia, not at you, so much as at some silly ideas he's got hold of about heredity. Not his own: just half-digested ideas, and he probably finds it pretty difficult to listen to them at all. He just thinks he ought to, I suppose."

Again the faint little smile in her face.

"You are a dear, Christopher, when you try to whitewash things. Listen to me. Whatever Geoffry said or does or writes, I've decided I will not marry him. I've written to say so and posted it before you came in, so he should know that nothing he had said or done influenced me in the slightest."

Christopher gave a sigh of relief and she went on in the same deliberate way.

"And I shall never marry at all. I can't face it again. I'll tell Renata about Geoffry, and may I also tell her you will explain to the others if she can't satisfy them?"

"I will do anything you wish." Then he suddenly claimed for himself a little latitude and spoke from his heart.

"Patricia, dear, I'm glad you've done it. It's the best and right thing, however hard, and if I could manage to take all the bother of it for you I would. Honestly, Geoffry wouldn't have been able to help you, I fear. But as to never marrying, you must not say that or make rash vows, and you must never, never let yourself think it isn't safe to marry, or that sort of nonsense. It's in your own hands. We are always strong enough for our own job, so Cæsar says. Shall I find Renata and ask her to come to you?"

They stood facing each other, an arm's length separating them, and she looked at him across the little space with so great gratitude and affection in her eyes that he felt humbled at the little he offered from so great a store at his heart.

"Christopher, how do girls manage who haven't a brother like you? I've been fretting because I was all alone and no one to stand by me—will you forgive me that, dear?"

Her eyes were brimming with tears. She laid her hand on his arm again and drew nearer. Her entire ignorance of their true relationship to each other left her a child appealing for some outward sign of the one dear bond she knew between them.

Christopher recognised it and put his arm round her and she kissed him. "I'll never forget again that I've got you," she whispered, "such a dear good brother."

He neither acquiesced nor dissented that point, but very gravely and quietly he kissed her too, and she thought the bond of fraternity between then was sealed.

CHAPTER XXVI

Matters were made as easy for Patricia as the united efforts of those who loved her could compass. Geoffry, in his gratitude for her decisive action, which lifted the onus of a broken engagement from his shoulders, found a substantial ground for his belief that they had sacrificed themselves on the altar of duty. Mrs. Leverson sighed profoundly with unconscious satisfaction over the highly heroic behaviour of them both and yielded easily to Geoffry's desire to travel. They eventually sold Logan Park, which they had purchased about ten years previously, and passed out of the ken of the lives that were so nearly linked with theirs.

Life renewed its wonted routine at Marden except that Christopher was often absent for weeks together. The final experiments hung fire and he had to seek new material and fresh inspiration further afield, but never for long. The end of a set term would see him back by Aymer's side sharing his hopes and disappointments impartially, always declaring that nowhere could he work with better success than at Marden Court. He was five years older than his natural age in development and resource, and the dogged obstinacy that was so direct a heritage from his father, stood him in good stead in his stiff fight with the difficulties that stood between him and his goal. Peter Masters made no sign and no greater success seemed to crown the other workers' endeavours, but there was always the secret pressure of unknown competition at work and it told on Christopher. He became more silent and so absorbed in his task as to lose touch of outside matters altogether. It was this absorption in his ambition that made the daily intercourse with Patricia possible at all. Unsuspected by her, his love, lying in abeyance, was but awaiting the growth in her of an answering harmony that must come to completion before he could make his full demand of it.

One day in March, when the land was swept with cold winds and beaten with rain, Christopher came out of the little wooden building, where he worked, and stood bareheaded a moment in the driving rain. First he looked towards the house and then turning sharply towards the left made his way once more to the edge of the last of the experimental tracks that threaded that distant corner of the park like the lines of a spider's web.

He stood looking down at the firm grey surface from which the pouring rain ran off to the side channels as cleanly as from polished marble. He walked a few yards down its elastic, easy-treading surface, ruminating over the "weight and edge" tests that had been applied, and on the durability trials from the little machine that had run for so many long days and nights over a similar surface within the wooden shanty.

It was morning now. His men, whose numbers had increased each month, had gone to breakfast, and he was alone with his finished work.

The strain and absorption of the long months was over. He had at last conquered the material difficulties that had been ranged against him. The dream of the boy had become a tangible reality, ready by reason of its material existence to claim its own place in the physical world. This unnamed substance whose composition had awaited in Nature's laboratory the intelligent mingling of a master hand, would add to the store of the world's riches and the world's ease, and was his gift to his generation.

As he stood looking down at the completed roadway, the Roadmaker suddenly remembered his own slight years and the inconceivable fraction of time he had laboured for so wide a result, and there swept up to him across the level way a new knowledge of his relationship to all the past—that he was but the servant of those who had preceded him and had but brought into the light of day a simple secret matured long ago in the patient earth.

It is in this spirit of true humility and in the recognition of their actual place in the world that all Great Discoverers find their highest joy. It is the joy of service that is theirs, the loftiest ambition that can fire the heart of man, making him accept with thankfulness his part as a tool to the great artifices and filling him with love and reverence for the work he has been used to complete. As Christopher stood bareheaded in the rain that windy March morning, his heart swept clear for the time of all personal pride or self-gratification, he offered himself in unconscious surrender again to the Power that had used him, craving only to be used, divining clearly that achievement is but the starting post to new endeavour.

At last he turned away, locked up the hut and went down towards the house, and at the entrance of the little plantation between park and garden he met Patricia.

They exchanged no greeting but a smile, and as he stood on the slope above her, looking at her, he was aware of a great sense of peace and rest, and on a sudden, her understanding leapt to meet his.

"It is done—you have finished it?" she cried, and her hands went out to him.

"Yes," he said, quietly, freeing himself from the strange inward pressure by the touch of that outward union. "This piece of work is done, Patricia. The thing is there—my Road stuff. It's all right. It will stand whatever it is asked to stand. It is ready to use if anyone will use it."

"Oh, I'm glad—so glad!" she cried. "Christopher, it is just the best thing in the world to know you have succeeded."

Her complete sympathy and generous joy seemed to open his mind to the outward expression of the speaker, which of late, since the breaking of her engagement with Geoffry, he had tried hard not to observe.

It seemed to him her face had lost a little of its childish roundness, that there was something accentuated about her that was nameless and yet expected. Also for the first time in his life he was conscious that her presence by his side was helpful. He had been unaware till she came that he needed any aid in what, to him, was a great moment in his life, but he knew it was restful and good to walk by her, a strange relief to tell her how the last difficulties that had arisen on the heels of each other had finally been met: how strong had been his temptation to give his discovery to the world before the tedious tests had gone to the uttermost limits experimental trials could reach.

"It's so simple really," he said, "just a question of proportions once the material is there. I felt anyone might hit on it any day, and yet it would have been such a sickening thing to have someone else planting an improvement on the top of it within a few months. It may need it now, but at least it would mean the test of years, and not immediate improvement. Do you happen to know if Cæsar had a good night or not?"

"You've got to have some breakfast yourself first. I don't believe you remember you never came in to dinner last night at all."

"Didn't I? Breakfast must wait till I've seen Cæsar anyhow. He must know before anyone else, and you'll never be able to hold your tongue through breakfast, you know."

"But I'm first, after all." She tilted her chin a little with a complacent nod at him.

He stopped with a puzzled expression.

"So you are. It never struck me—but—but," he hesitated, unable to read his own hazy idea, and concluded, "but, you are only a girl, so it doesn't matter."

The look in his eyes atoned for the "only," and she bore no resentment, for she had met his look and read there the thought he could not decipher, and it sunk deep into her heart, with illuminating power.

At the garden door, where the paths branched, she stood aside.

"Go and tell Aymer and get your breakfast."

"You are not going to stay out in this rain?"

"You know I love rain, and I've had breakfast."

Before he could stop her she had turned and disappeared up the winding path that led out eventually on to the open down.

Christopher looked after her a moment doubtfully, but her strange fondness for walking in the rain was well known and he had no reason or right to stop her. So he went indoors to Cæsar. But Patricia walked on with rapid steps, never pausing till she was well outside the confines of the park amongst the red ploughed fields and bare downs. The rain swept in her face and the wind rushed by her as she walked with lifted head and exultant heart, hearing the whole chorus of creation around her, conscious only of the uplifting joy of the great light that had broken in on her. At last she stopped by a gate that led into a field of newly-turned earth—downland just broken by the plough, lying bare and open to the breath of heaven, and beyond, the swelling line of downs was blurred with misty rain and merged into the driving grey clouds above. Behind her in an oak tree a robin was singing with passionate intensity. She drew a deep breath and then held out her arms to the world.

"I understand, I understand," she whispered. "Love and Christopher. Love and Christopher, there is nothing else in the whole world."

She had accepted the revelation without fear, without question, without distrust. She gave no thought at all at present as to Christopher's attitude to her, as to whether he had anything to give in return for her great gift of herself. She gave herself to Love first, to him after, if such were Love's will. But it made no difference whether he knew or not, she was his, and the recognition drowned all lesser emotion in the great depth of its joy. She wasted no time in lamenting her blindness or the interlude with another lesser love: it troubled her not at all, for by such steps had she climbed to this unexpected summit. Just at present the glory of that was all-satisfying, so much more than she had ever looked for or imagined possible, that to demand the uttermost crown of his returning love was in these first moments too great a consummation to be borne.

She stood there with her hands clasped and the only words she found were, "Christopher and Love," and again, "Love and Christopher," as if they were the alphabet of a new language.

Quite slowly the physical horizon crept up to this plane of exultant joy and claimed her, but even as she recognised the claim she knew the familiar world would bear for her a new aspect, and found no resentment, only a quiet relief as it closed her in. The languor and fatigue of the backward journey did not distress her, every step of the way she was studying the news.

Every blade of grass and every twig spoke of this new language to her, proclaiming a kinship that made her rich in sympathy and comprehension of all humble lovely things.

She was seized with fear when she reached home that she would encounter Christopher in the hall before she was prepared to accept him as the most unchanged point of her altered world. Instead she met Constantia Wyatt, who was at Marden with her family for Easter, just coming down, who asked her if she had been having a shower bath.

Now Constantia felt a proprietary right over Patricia by reason of her knowledge of Christopher's sentiments, and her own prophetic instincts. She had most carefully refrained from interference in their affairs, however, and accepted the post of lookeron with praiseworthy consistency. But she looked on with very wide-opened eyes, and this morning when Patricia answered with almost emphatic offhandedness that she had only been for a solitary walk in the rain, she could not refrain from remarking that she appeared to have gathered something more than raindrops and an appetite on her walk, and only laughed when Patricia, betraying no further curiosity, hurried on.

"Something has happened," she thought to herself. "Patricia's eyes did not look like that last night. She is grown up."

But her rare discretion kept her silent, and when later on she was confronted with the news of Christopher's victory she guessed one-half of the secret of Patricia's shining eyes.

Patricia exchanged her dripping garments for dry ones and curled herself up on the sofa in her own room before the fire, with full determination to fathom her growing unwillingness to meet Christopher, and to accommodate herself to the new existence, but the gentle languor of mental emotion and physical effort took the caressing warmth of the fire to their aid and cradled her to sleep instead, till the balance of nature was restored.

It was in this manner that Patricia and Christopher arrived at the same cross roads of their lives, where the devious tracks might merge into one another, or, being thrust asunder again by some hedge of convention, continue by a lonely, painful and circuitous route towards the destined goal.

The matter lay in Patricia's hands, little as either she or Christopher suspected it, and poor Patricia was hampered by a power of tradition and a lack of complete faith of Christopher's view of her inherited trouble.

Ever since the broken engagement with Geoffry, she had bent in spirit before her own weakness, withstanding it well, and yet a prey to that humiliation of mind that accepts the imperfect as a penalty, instead of claiming the perfect as a birthright. Having given in to this attitude, she now, as a natural consequence, could but see the view offered from that comparatively lowly altitude, and that shut her in with the belief her duty lay in renouncing marriage, and also, more limiting still in its effect, the idea that Christopher also held this view in his secret heart.

She wasted no time in the consideration as to whether he loved her or not: she was sure of that much crown to her own life; but slowly the false conviction thrust itself upon her that had he thought otherwise the long, empty months that had passed would not have been possible. She was too young a woman to balance correctly the power of strenuous occupation on a man as weighed against the emotion to which a woman will yield her whole being without a struggle. Looking back on the long days that had elapsed since the affair by the little chalk pit on the downs, it seemed to her clear that Christopher had avoided her, and there was sufficient truth in this to make it a dangerous lever when handled in connection with the fear of her mind.

It was, therefore, by a quite natural following-out of the mental process that she ultimately arrived at the conclusion it was her duty to assist Christopher to renounce herself, and for that purpose, that she might less hamper his life, she must leave Marden Court.

The decision was not arrived at all at once. The day wore on and the natural order of things had brought her and Christopher face to face at a moment when she had forgotten there was any difficulty about it. Cæsar had issued invitations to a family tea in his room in honour of Christopher's achievement, as was a time-honoured custom when any of the members of the family distinguished themselves in work or play. Christopher served tea, as it was Cæsar's party, and it was not until he gave Patricia her cup that he recollected she had not crossed his path since that morning in the rain.

"Where have you hidden yourself?" he demanded severely.

"You said I could not hold my tongue, so I determined I'd prove you false," was her flippant rejoinder.

"At the cost of self-immolation. I think it proves my point."

"I appeal to Cæsar." She got up and took a chair close to the sofa.

"Cæsar, I wish you'd keep that boy of yours in order. He is always so convinced he is in the right that he is unbearable."

"Allow him latitude to-day. He'll meet opposition enough when he tries to foist this putty-clay of his on the world. By the way, what are you going to call it, Christopher?"

Everyone stopped talking and regarded the Discoverer with critical anxiety. He looked slightly embarrassed and offered no suggestion, and it was Constantia who insisted airily that they should all propose names and he should choose from the offered selection.

Christopher was made to take a chair in the midst of the circle and to demonstrate in plain terms the actual substances of which the "Road-stuff," as he inelegantly termed it, was made.

The younger members of the family called pathetically for some short, ready name that would not tax pen or tongue. After a long silence Nevil, modestly suggested "Hippopodharmataconitenbadistium."

This raised a storm of protests, while Constantia's own "Roadhesion" received hardly better support.

Cæsar flung out "Christite" without concern, and demanded Patricia's contribution.

"Aymerite," she ventured.

Christopher's glances wandered from one to the other. She was seated on his own particular chair close to Cæsar, in whose company she felt a strange comfort and protection, a security against her own heart that could not yet be trusted to shield the secret of her love.

Mr. Aston was called on in his turn and he looked at Christopher with a smile.

"I think we are all wasting our time and wits," he said placidly. "Christopher has his own name ready and your suggestions are superfluous."

They clamoured for confirmation of this and Christopher had to admit it was true.

"I call it Patrimondi," he said slowly, his eyes on Patricia, "because it will conquer the country and the world in time."

Which explanation was accepted more readily by the younger members of the party than by the elder.

But "Patrimondi" it remained, and if he chose to perpetuate the claims of the future rather than the past in this business of nomenclature, it was surely his own affair. Patricia, at all events, made no objection. She had recovered her equilibrium to find the relationship between them was so old that it called for nothing but mute acceptance on her part: the only thing that was new was her recognition of the barrier between them, whose imaginary shadow lay so cold across her heart.

Constantia offered a refuge. Her watching eyes divined something of Patricia's unrest. She visited her that night at the period of hair-brushing and found her dreaming before a dying fire.

"You get up too early," Constantia remonstrated, "it's a pernicious habit. If you would come and stay with me in London, I would teach you to keep rational hours."

"Would you have me, really?" cried Patricia, sitting bolt upright, with every sense alert to seize so good an opportunity of escape.

"Why, yes. I've been wanting to have you a long time. You had better come back to town with me to-morrow."

"I'd like it better than anything in the world," asserted Patricia, fervently and truthfully.

"I wonder if people ever grow up at all here," Constantia said, smiling, "you are all so preposterously young, you know."

"You were brought up here yourself."

Constantia laughed outright. "But I have been educated since I married: that is when most people's education does begin. We are only preparing for it before."

"And if one never marries, one remains uneducated, I suppose."

Constantia kissed her. "Your education is not likely to be neglected, my dear. Go to bed now, we will settle with Renata to-morrow."

CHAPTER XXVII

It is one thing to produce, and another to launch the production on an unwilling world. Christopher soon found he had but exchanged an arduous engrossing task for a sordid uphill struggle. Yet if his mind sometimes flew back to Peter Masters' offer, it was never with any desire to open negotiations with him, nor did he ever remind Aymer of the possibility. They fought together against the difficulties that beset the great venture and their comradeship reduced the irritating trivialities of the first start to bearable limits.

Since the day when he received Peter Masters' curt acknowledgment of satisfaction with the selected car, neither Christopher nor the Astons had heard one word from the millionaire. His restored interest in the family appeared to have evaporated as rapidly as it had risen, and peace fell on Aymer's troubled mind. He flung himself heart and soul into the business of launching Christopher's discovery, and verified his cousin's old opinion of his business qualities. The initial difficulties of obtaining the patent being overcome and a small, private company formed, they started a factory for the manufacture of Patrimondi within five miles of Marden, and a decently capable staff was secured to meet the slow, but steadily increasing, demands for the new material.

After some months of uphill work they suddenly received an order for laying the roadways and a special motor track at an International Exhibition. From this plane Patrimondi leapt into fame. Within three months of the opening of the Exhibition the little factory had doubled its staff and even then could not produce enough to meet the demand. With the mounting strain Christopher began to prove of what metal he was made. He stuck to the work with steady persistence, meeting success as he had met difficulties, counting each but expected incidents in a life's work. This level-headedness enabled him to bear a physical strain that would have broken down the nerve of any man more subject to outward conditions. A large proportion of extra work was entailed on him by the starting point of Patrimondi being so distant from London, but he resisted all suggestions to move it nearer town, or make his own headquarters there, or take any step that would serve to separate Aymer from easy contact with the work that made so great a difference in his monotonous life.

Since the last appearance of Peter Masters, Aymer had seemed to lose something of his old independent spirit of resistance. The mine of strength within himself, which his father had developed, was nearing exhaustion, and he lived more and more by force of his interest in outward things, and the active part he played in Christopher's life. But this diminution of his inward strength made the question of any move too serious to be contemplated, although they still vaguely spoke of a time when they would return to London. Mr. Aston knew that he himself could not face the old strenuous life again.

He had dropped out of the line of workers too early, and though seventy years found him still a man of active habits and vigour of mind, he was too conscious of his divorce from the past to endure meeting it daily face to face.

The fortunes of Patrimondi continued to leap forward by untraceable impulses. They were able to choose their work now, and Christopher gave the preference first to roads whose construction was under his own direction from the very foundation, and secondly to such work as least separated him from Cæsar, but this last fact he was careful to conceal even from Mr. Aston's watchful eyes.

In the world of workers he became known as the "Roadmaker," and fabulous stories of his origin and fortune were circulated. Unknown to himself or to those nearest to him, men high up in the financial world kept their eye on the young man—made no prophecies—said nothing—but were careful for reasons best known to themselves to help rather than oppose him when he happened to cross their path. But the greatest of all their race, Peter Masters himself, made no sign at all. No fabulous fortune was, however, gathered in. "Patrimondi" paid well, but the working expenses were great. Christopher made big returns to the men, not in wages only, but in every condition of their work. Those in power under him soon learnt it was better to forget the momentary interests of the company than the living interests of the workmen, but in return for his care Christopher did insist on, and get from his men, an amount of work that made other employers open their eyes with envious wonder.

All this time Patricia held her place in his life. It would have been hard to trace her actual influence on his daily actions, but it was there, preserving his finer instincts under the load of material cares, linking him indissolubly to that world of high Realities which is every man's true inheritance. Yet he made no attempt to claim her and at times wondered at his own procrastination. The idea implanted by Peter Masters bore strange fruit, for even an unconsciously harboured lie must needs hamper the life behind which it finds shelter. He could make no advance towards Patricia while that invidious doubt of his parentage existed, and he lacked the remorseless courage of Mr. Aston to inflict pain for however justifiable a cause on Cæsar. Also perhaps his pride had a word to say. If there was a secret, it was theirs, and they had not chosen to divulge it to him. Again, he had fathomed something of the depth of the jealous love bestowed on him, and his own affection and gratitude would have their say. All and each of these reasons arrayed themselves against his love. When he tried to face it first one and then the other weighed heaviest, till at length he called time to his side and flung himself into his work the harder to leave that ally free scope. All of which meant that he was yet but a worshipper at Love's throne, and failed to recognise that his place was on it.

Christopher was in France when he saw the notice of Peter Masters' death in the papers, and he was more staggered by it than he cared to admit to himself. The millionaire had been knocked down at a busy crossing with no more ceremony than would have served for his poorest workman. He had been carried to the nearest hospital and died there almost directly, alone, as he had lived. There was the usual hasty account of his life, but by some magic that had perhaps root in Peter's own will, no mention was made of his marriage.

Christopher wrote home on the subject this-wise:

"It seems to me the more terrible since I think he was a man who never believed any such mischance could dare to happen to him. He always gave me the impression of one who read his own mortality for immortality, and was prepared to rule Time as arbitrarily as he ruled men. It does not look to an outsider as if he had gained any particular happiness from his fortune, but happiness is a word everyone spells in their own way.... I shall be back at the end of the week, for I find Marcel quite capable of finishing this piece of work...."

Such was the epitaph pronounced over Peter Masters by his own son, and Aymer, reading, sank beneath the dead weight of responsibility that was his. The outcome of neutrality can be as great a force as that of action, and to assume the right to stand aside is to play as decisive a part as the fiercest champion. Nevertheless he held to that neutral attitude through the pangs of self-reproach.

There was no will, Mr. Aston told him, when he returned from the plain business-like affair of the funeral.

The news, incredible as it was, was yet a respite to Aymer.

He did not trouble to conceal it.

"But I am certain Saunderson knows something. Do not count on it, Aymer."

"I count every chance in my favour," returned Aymer deliberately. "I discount even your belief that Peter knew, since he said nothing."

Mr. Aston looked at him sadly. He had no such hope, nor was he even certain he was justified in seconding Cæsar's wish that the fortune should pass

Christopher by. The nearer the great thing came to them the more difficult was it to ignore the vastness of the interests involved, and the greater the responsibility of those who stood motionless between Christopher and it. Yet Mr. Aston knew as well as Aymer that neither of them would move from their position, and if they had acted wrongly in following the wishes of the dead woman in preference to the material instincts of the living man, they must accept the result, and Christopher must accept it, too.

But he felt keenly Aymer's failure to present an unbiassed face to the turn of circumstances.

"How long will it be before Saunderson acts if he has any clue to go on?" Aymer asked wearily after a long silence.

"He would act immediately, but whether that would land him on the right line would depend on the strength of the clue. Aymer, my dear fellow, try and put the matter from you. You are not going to act yourself."

"No, but I'm no hand at waiting."

That was true, and as usual the days of suspense told heavily on Aymer. Christopher's return was an immense relief. He had had a heavy spell of work and travelling, and allowed himself a few days' holiday. It happened that Patricia was also at Marden. She spent so large a percentage of her time with Constantia now that her presence in the house that had been her home more resembled a visit than Christopher's comings and goings. No one had mentioned the fact that she was there to him, and he found her in the drawing-room before dinner kneeling by the fire and coaxing it into a cheery blaze.

"You are a regular truant, Patricia," he complained after their greeting.

"Constantia maintains I am at school with her and calls me truant when I run down here for a few days."

"Are you at school? What does she teach you?"

"Subjects too deep for mere man," she retorted lightly. She continued to kneel with her back to him and the light touched her wonderful hair, that still seemed too heavy a crown for the proud little head. It was like molten gold. Christopher felt a new heartache for the days when he could touch it without fear in the blind bravery of boyhood. He wanted to see her face which she so persistently turned from him.

"I am not sure it is a suitable school for you."

"Since when have you become responsible for my education, sir? Would you prefer my going to school with Charlotte? You are confounding me with Patrimondi. You will end by rolling me out flat on a high-road one day."

She was talking arrant nonsense in self-defence, for every fibre of her being was quivering at his presence. The old hushed cry awoke in her heart "Christopher and Love—Love and Christopher." If she looked at him he must see it, her eyes must needs betray the pitiful whisper but for the clamour of foolish words. Where was Renata? Why were they all so late to-night of all nights? Yet she had hurried her dressing—chosen her gown even, on the chance of this interview that outmatched her schooled frivolity. The need to see her face and her eyes again pressed on the man—became imperative—as something of great moment, strangely difficult to achieve.

At last he abruptly spoke her name.

"Patricia."

She involuntarily turned to him and found what had appeared so hard was quite easy, for she discerned some unusual trouble in his mind, and was woman enough for the mothering instinct to sweep up over the personal love.

"What is it, Christopher?"

He had wit enough to keep his advantage, for there was something to read on the upturned face that must not be deciphered in haste.

"I am seriously worried, Patricia. You might assist instead of hindering me."

"Well, what is it?"

"What is Constantia teaching you?"

"Me again," she returned with a show of indignation, "why on earth should that worry you?"

"I don't like new facets to familiar diamonds," he grumbled obscurely, "you are getting too old. Patricia."

"You are losing your manners." But even under the banter the colour died from her face and her hand fell listlessly to her side.

"I won't allow you to be older than I am."

She was saved further embarrassment by Renata's entrance, but all dinner time she was conscious of his silent "awareness" of her and was troubled by it, and it was a new and unpleasing sensation to be troubled by any attitude of Christopher's. Then his scrutiny stopped abruptly as if she were suddenly placed outside his range of vision, and that attitude suited her mind as poorly as the other.

She hardly knew if it were by her own will or Christopher's that she sat with him and Aymer that evening. She was quite powerless to resist the request that might have been a command, and there is some pain in life that we cling to, dreading its loss more acutely than its presence.

Mr. Aston was away, a rare occurrence now, and the three sat talking before the fire, till the dear familiar intercourse and the peace put to sleep the dull ache in Patricia's heart. They talked—or rather the men talked—of Christopher's latest experiences abroad. He had been to the scene of a vast tunnelling operation in which his part was to come later.

"They suggest we should take over their men's shanties as they stand."

"Will you?" demanded Cæsar. These things were in Christopher's hands.

"They might serve as material," he answered drily. "Two of their overseers and twenty men asked for berths with me. They are mostly Italians. If we keep them to make our encampment, I shall have to go myself. It is rather odd how these men pick things up. I heard—" he broke off abruptly.

"We didn't," remarked Cæsar suggestively after a minute.

"It was not much, but it is funny how a nick-name travels. There were about five hundred men there still, and I heard one say as I passed, 'Ecco il 'Roadmaker.'"

He was evidently boyishly pleased at the recognition, though he did not conclude the sentence. The man had saluted him as he added to his comrade, "C'é un maestro d'uomini, non di brutti."

Patricia gave Cæsar a quick look and caught his answer. It was as if some sudden bond of sympathy were tied between them.

Cæsar continued skilfully to ply Christopher with questions and extracted the information that the Patrimondi Company was much disliked by the big manufacturing powers.

"They say we spoil our men, and their own grumble. They sent me a deputation to ask us to cancel the Sunday holiday, which they never grant on contract work, and they feared the result of our example."

"And you politely agreed?" suggested Cæsar, watching Patricia.

"I told them to—" again he stopped and laughed; "well, Patricia, I told them such was the time-honoured custom of my country and regretted my inability to consider their request."

"I expect they only get into mischief on Sunday."

Cæsar flung out this with assumed contempt, but it brought no quick retort. Christopher answered slowly, with his eyes on the fire.

"We plan excursions for them when there is anything to see or amusements of some kind. They are like children. If they are not amused they must needs make mischief."

His voice was rather grave and Aymer knew there must have been difficulties here of which he did not mean to speak openly.

"It is deplorable if our Roadmaker is going about destroying other people's comfortable paths. Don't you agree with me, Patricia?"

She flushed up quickly, grasping his meaning at once.

"Not if their paths encroach on weaker people's rights. I think it's just what is wanted." Then because Cæsar laughed, she realised he was only drawing her, and flung him an appealing glance.

"But we mustn't encourage him openly, Patricia, or he'll leave us no old tracks at all."

"I'm only the humble instrument of a company," protested Christopher. "I merely carry out the regulations of my superiors."

"Who are entirely at your mercy, you should add."

Christopher disdained to reply to so obvious a fallacy. Presently, when he had gone to fetch some drawings to show them, Cæsar said quizzically.

"Has he obliterated any of your pet footpaths, Patricia?"

She shook her head.

"The Company has great confidence in him," he announced gravely.

She looked straight at him. There was a kind intelligence in his eyes, and he held out his hand to her. "Present company not excepted. But we must not spoil him, Patricia."

And she understood that her secret was Aymer's and it lent her a sense of security and rest to know it, so that when she went to bed she reproached herself for her former childish moods. "I should be glad his strength of purpose and commonsense are so great," she told herself, forgetting love and commonsense were ever ill neighbours. "I am never going to marry, and it would be difficult to say no to him. To-night was just one of the best of times that can be for us."

That unwise thought aroused the dull throbbing ache in her heart again and the reasonable salve she offered it had no effect. She slept with it, woke with it, and knew it for the close companion of many days.

But Christopher's last thought was, "I am not going to do without her any longer, if I am to meet her any more in this way. I should have read her soul again to-night if I had not remembered in time."

Aymer Aston lay awake wondering what was the matter between the two that they did not guess their palpable secret. He was the richer for another day's respite and every day was a tide carrying him to the shore of safety.

CHAPTER XXVIII

A chilly, rainy mist shrouded the country and blotted out the familiar beauty. Not a day for walking, but Christopher had chosen to tramp to a far-off corner of the estate on some pretence of business and had come back through the wet, dripping woods, burr-covered and muddy. He was met in the hall by a message that Mr. Aymer wanted him at once, so without waiting to change he strode away, whistling, to the West Room and came to a standstill on the threshold, finding Aymer had visitors with him.

There were two gentlemen, one was Mr. Shakleton, the son and successor of the old solicitor who had played his part in the finding of Christopher, the other was a stout, complacent man with gold-rimmed glasses and scanty sandy hair, and all three of the occupants of the room looked towards the door as if waiting for and expecting him. A glance at Cæsar's face brought Christopher swiftly to his side and established instantly a sense of antagonism with the visitors.

"You want me, Cæsar?"

"Yes. We want you. Mr. Shakleton you know. This is Mr. Saunderson."

Both men stood up and to Christopher's amazement bowed profoundly.

"I am very honoured to meet you," said Mr. Saunderson suavely. "I hope it will be the commencement of a long and fruitful acquaintance."

Christopher felt rather at a loss to know if the man meant to be impertinent or was merely being silly. He looked at Cæsar with the hostile impatience he felt only too apparent. The hostility but not the impatience deepened as he noticed the drawn beaten look on Aymer's face. Also he was uncomfortably conscious of the three pairs of eyes watching him with rapt attention. The mild Mr. Shakleton, however, seemed entirely obscured by the expansive personality of the bigger man.

"Confound him," thought Christopher, "has he never seen burrs on a wet coat before or is my tie up?"

"Christopher," said Aymer, at last, "come and sit by me, will you. I think I should like to tell you myself." He looked at Mr. Saunderson as if waiting permission.

"Of course, of course, Mr. Aston. I quite understand. It is not the sort of news we tell people every day."

Christopher sat on the edge of the sofa with his eyes fixed on Cæsar.

"Are you sure it won't keep," he asked abruptly, "you look rather tired for business, Cæsar."

"It won't keep. It concerns Peter Masters. Mr. Saunderson says public rumour has underestimated his fortune rather than exaggerated it. He was worth nearly three millions."

"Three millions six hundred and forty-one thousand." Mr. Saunderson rolled it out in sonorous tones after a little smack of his lips that set Christopher's teeth on edge.

"It seems, Christopher," Aymer went on, with an abruptness that did not accord with his opening words, "that it's yours. You are his heir."

He made not the smallest movement or sign by which the two strangers could gather one passing glimpse of the agony it cost him to say it, for their attention was fixed on the younger man. But Christopher saw nothing else and had thought for nothing but how soonest to quench that fierce pain.

The preposterous catastrophe was evidently true, but surely his own will and wishes were of some account. He put his hand on Aymer, searching for words which would not form into sense.

"Take your time, take your time, young man," broke in Mr. Saunderson's resonant voice. "It's not the sort of event a man can be hurried over. You will grasp it more clearly in a few minutes."

Christopher turned and looked at him.

"I believe I quite grasp the matter," he said coolly. "Mr. Masters has, with no doubt the kindest meaning in the world, left his fortune to me. It's unfortunate that I don't happen to want all this money. I couldn't possibly do with it."

Mr. Saunderson leant back in his chair with a tolerant smile as if this were just what he would expect to hear after the shock, but Aymer bit his lip as if face to face with some inevitable ill.

Christopher leant towards him.

"You are worrying about it, Cæsar. There can't be any need to say any more now. Of course it's out of the question my accepting it. They can't make me a millionaire against my wishes, I suppose. Anyhow it's a preposterous will."

"There is no will," began Cæsar and then looked at the big lawyer, "tell him," he added shortly. Mr. Saunderson cleared his throat.

"That is so. There is no will and the fortune naturally goes to the next of kin."

"Very well, then," returned Christopher, with blunt relief. "I believe he told me once he had a son somewhere. You had better find him. I don't want to deprive him of his luck."

Again the embarrassing silence. Then the big lawyer got up and bowed solemnly to Christopher.

"We have found him. Allow me to be the first to congratulate you, Mr. Masters."

Christopher wheeled round on him like a man struck.

"No!" he cried with passionate emphasis. "Cæsar, it's not true. Tell them so."

But Cæsar lay very still and looked past them all, staring blankly at the opposite wall. It seemed to Christopher the watching eyes of the others imprisoned him, held him in subjection. He got up.

"Let me out," he muttered between his teeth, though none impeded him. He walked across the room to the fireplace and stood with his back to them, his hand mechanically altering the order of a procession of black elephants that stood there.

Aymer broke the silence, speaking with clear evenness.

"Shakleton, will you take Mr. Saunderson into the library. You will find my brother there, probably."

"Certainly, Mr. Aston. Shall I leave these?" He indicate the papers on the table before him.

"Yes. Leave them where they are."

Mr. Saunderson rose. "You must not be alarmed, my dear sir," he said in a forced whisper, with a glance towards Christopher, "such news often takes a man off his feet for a while. He'll soon appreciate it."

"No doubt. Order anything you like, Shakleton."

They were alone at last, yet Christopher did not move.

"Christopher, come to me," called Aymer quietly.

At that he turned and walked mechanically to the sofa, seating himself, again with his elbows on his knees, and his eyes absently fixed on the carpet.

"Did you know this before, Cæsar?"

Aymer's face twitched. "Yes, always."

"Did—he—know?"

"Yes, apparently."

"You did not tell him?"

"No."

Christopher looked up sharply and met his eyes, and again he forgot his own intimate trouble before the greater one.

"Thanks, Cæsar," he said, dragging up a smile, "it would have been far harder at your hand."

Then suddenly he sunk on his knees by Aymer's side, and hid his head against the arm that had sheltered him as a child.

"They can't make me take it," he whispered, "even if I am his son. But Cæsar, Cæsar, why didn't you tell me before?"

"I hoped you would never know. Did you never have any suspicion yourself?"

"Never. It was the last thing I should have imagined."

"You have never asked me anything. You must sometimes have wondered about yourself."

"I was quite content." Christopher spoke with shut teeth. Under no provocation must Cæsar know the falsehood that had lain so long in his mind. He saw it in its full proportion now, and hated himself for his blindness in harbouring so ugly a thought.

"We were never certain how much Peter knew and I've never known for the past three years whether he meant to claim you or not."

"If you'd only told me, Cæsar!"

"It was my one hope you should not know."

"I don't think I've earned that," he said reproachfully.

"It was myself, not you, I thought of. You've got to know the whole thing now. Go and sit there in your old place and don't look at me till I've finished."

So Aymer at last reached the moment when he must break the seals of silence—that expected moment that had hung over him like some shadowy fate as a foretaste of judgment, when he must retrace the painful footsteps of his life across the black gulf from which he had climbed. But as he turned his face to the darkness, there was light also on the other side, and he forgot he had feared.

"Peter and I were friends, as you know. He was five years my senior, but it did not make much difference. He was a worker, just as I was a player. He had tremendous capabilities and he put all his big brain into his work and when he wanted change he came to me. I represented to him the reverse side of his strenuous life and he was oddly fond of me. Before he was thirty he had well started his fortune as he raced to wealth. I raced to ruin and found every inch of the road made easy for me. Peter came into conflict with the socialistic party. There was a certain James Hibbault, who was a great power, and Peter, who was not so heavy a power in those days, employed the wisdom of the serpent to crush him. He came up to London and offered me a chance of new amusement in abetting his plans. The Hibbaults were middle class people without middle class virtues. They lived a scrambling, noisy life propagating their crude ideas and sowing broadcast the seeds of a greater power than they knew. They were, however, a real force to be reckoned with, they and their party, because of certain truths hidden in their wildest creeds— truths which did not suit Peter's creed in the least. He made their acquaintance, and he introduced me to them. They were sufficiently new to amuse me, but I should have probably have tired of them soon had it not been for your mother."

He paused a moment. "Do you remember her, Christopher?"

Christopher nodded.

"Elizabeth Hibbault," went on Aymer slowly, "was extraordinarily beautiful, with the beauty of grace rather than of feature. She was as distinct from the rest of her clamorous family as a pearl from pebbles. She was an enthusiast, a dreamer, passionately sincere, passionately pitiful. She recognised truth as a water diviner finds water. She was brought up in a labyrinth of theories, creeds of equality, in hatred for the rich, and out of all the jargon she gathered some eternal truths which she made her own. She did not live with her people: she had rooms of her own and she was a black-and-white artist. But she was often at the Hibbaults. Peter probably knew her accustomed days. She used to speak of her faiths. It was like one note of gold in the discordant babble. Men came and listened to her and she never knew it was not for her words but for her magnetic wonderful unknown self that they came. She might, and probably did, impress men who were dreamers or fanatics already, but those to whom all her beliefs were childish nonsense went just the same, Peter and I with them."

He stopped a moment and shot a glance at Christopher, who never moved.

"I lost my interest in Peter's schemes and he ceased to explain them to me, but I still visited Elizabeth at her own rooms when I was allowed. She was very anxious to convert Peter and myself, more especially Peter. I was not in love with her, Christopher, yet, but she fascinated me. I speculated as to how it would be with her if all the fire and devotion she brought to a mere Cause were turned into a more personal direction. She paid more attention to Peter than to myself, and she evidently considered him a more desirable convert. One evening we went together to call on her and they fell into the usual line of discussion, he answering her in a tolerant amused way as if she were a precocious child. I stayed behind when he left and she walked up and down in restless agitation, half forgetful of me. 'The personality of the man!' she cried fiercely, 'he is too strong, he is ruthless! One cannot escape him. I cannot get him out of my head.' I told her she had much better tackle me. She told me plainly that I was a negative force in the world and my cousin an active. That was enough for me. I thought she despised me and I vowed she should recognise my possibilities as well as Peter's. If any man were to turn the passionate stream of her nature back on herself, or to love—to see the woman rise above the fanatic—it should be I, not Peter. But I said nothing of this to him. I do not think he ever knew it at all. It began in pique on my side, then jealousy, lastly passion. Christopher, if I had loved her from the first beginning of things I should not be ashamed to meet your eyes now. Don't look round yet. I laid deliberate siege to her heart and found she possessed my mind night and day. Soon it was not Peter who was my rival, but her own soul. I was confident I should win, though Peter, it was clear, was also wooing her persistently. He at least meant her well, Christopher. He loved her in his uncomprehending way, wanting her for the woman she was *not*—except in his mind. And I—I wanted her for the outward woman she was."

He paused long enough for his listener to face clearly the portrait of the worn, broken woman he remembered, the outward woman that bore no likeness to the clear knowledge of the inner soul.

Aymer continued:

"At last I felt it was time to end it. Peter had been in town some time then. I knew the senior Hibbault and he were coming to some understanding, but I guessed nothing of the nature of it. She never mentioned him to me at this time. She stood, poor girl, between the two of us like a trapped creature, and because she feared herself and neither of us, she overstepped one snare to fall into the other. Christopher, I don't know what was in my mind when I went to her that last evening: I had not seen her for some days, but when I stood before her I knew suddenly I loved her, and then, like a flash, I saw it was neither Peter nor her that stood between us, but my own evil self. I told her all—that she was the victor and I the conquered. I was proud of my new humbleness. For once I recognised myself and my true place in the order of the world. But she knew me better than I guessed, and she was afraid to tell me the truth. She put me off with gentle words, terrified lest I should guess before I left her—Don't turn away, Christopher—At last she owned she had written me a letter and I should find it when I got back. Her attitude maddened me. The better self, if it ever existed, got stamped out. I told her nothing should come between us, that nothing short of death should keep me from her, while I could move hand or foot."

The white scar on Aymer's forehead was very plain and his face had grown thin and sharp. Christopher for the first time looked up at him and away again.

"I went home at last, Christopher, wild to get this mysterious letter to which she would refer me. I went back and took seven devils with me—my passion and love fighting for possession. Nevil and I had a room of our own on the ground floor. I think they use it for storing papers in now."

Christopher gave a slight movement: he knew that well.

"I went straight in, knowing any letter for me would be taken there. Nevil was going upstairs as I crossed the hall and he called to me across the banisters that Wayband had sent back my revolver and he had opened it. Revolver shooting was a passion just then and I was accounted a crack shot. I answered him savagely and went on. The letter lay on the table. She had been married to Peter two days before at a Registrar's office. I felt I must have known it from eternity, but it caught me on the crest of my fury, it overwhelmed me in a torrent of mad shame and wild jealousy. I had failed—had been beaten at my own game—beaten and fooled by some God who had used my passion for his own ends. Those short minutes of purer love burnt my soul like fire till I raged at my folly. Christopher, I'd give all I have left to say I was mad. I wasn't. I knew what I was doing. The revolver lay there on the table and an open box of cartridges by it. It was the coward's way out of the agony, and I took it. I shot myself—the crack shot of Waybands Club missed his own life by a hair's-breadth."

Even then, after the long years, Christopher caught an echo of bitterness in the voice. He dully wondered at his own inability to move or speak or send out a thought of consolation to the man who had suffered so fiercely.

Aymer gave a little gasp and was still a moment Then he went on:

"That's all my story, Christopher. Now comes your mother's part of it. The first result of her marriage was that the Hibbaults' name ceased to be a power for the Socialist party—became less than a power. James Hibbault severed his connection with them entirely. I think Peter gave him a place at one of his big affairs. He had bought them out, and for a time the party fell into disrepute. But Elizabeth, whom he had married, he had not bought. I think she believed she had and could influence him, that she could sway him without loss of her own being. I know she clung to her true personality with passionate strength. I had failed to break it down, but I think Peter failed here also. When she heard of her father's and brother's betrayal of their party—it was nothing else—she was nearly crazy with grief. It was some time before Peter could get her to acknowledge their marriage at all, and she never, I believe, spoke of her people again. But at last he got her to Stormly. I know very little of what happened there. I believe he was willing she should play Lady Bountiful to his people if it pleased her—even made her a big allowance for the purpose. But she went amongst them and she would have none of it. She would make no compromise with what she regarded as wholly evil. She found Peter had only played with her regarding her creed—that he never had the least intention of altering his plan of life to suit it. She hated it all a hundredfold more than you did, Christopher, and the thought of bringing a child into an atmosphere that was rank poison to her, became a nightmare. Perhaps she was not wholly accountable then—there was no woman to stand by her or counsel patience. Anyhow, about six weeks before you were born, we believe she just disappeared. No one knows how Peter really felt about it. In the face of the world he shrugged his shoulders and went on with his life as if wife and expected child had never been. We suppose he tried to find her at first, but he always declared there was no need—she would come back when she had had enough of the world. Eventually a letter reached him saying you had come into the world and that, rather than put you under the power of your father and all he stood for, she would bring you up among the people she loved and pitied. My father tried all he could to make Peter seriously seek for his wife. We know now he had some false clue and that he believed she and you were living in Liverpool. But either from pride or indifference he would never see for himself these two whose fortunes he watched so closely. Saunderson tells me it was the younger Hibbault who supplied him with the false clue and found it to his advantage to keep up the fraud. They can't trace either Hibbault now. They seem to have emigrated. My father once visited Peter, before Elizabeth left him. There was some dispute at the works and a certain foreman named Felton protested against his orders. My father heard the interview between them, and the man made a strong appeal to him. He did his best as go-between and failed. Peter did not quarrel about it. He was just immovable in his heavy way, but your mother was greatly troubled over the whole business and was generously good to Felton and his wife in the face of Peter's direct commands. Ten years afterwards this man, tramping from Portsmouth to London in search of work, met your mother again. He was evidently a man of strong memory, and he knew her."

Christopher nodded. He remembered the little narrow paths in the tiny garden, the smell of the box edging, a pink cabbage rose that fell when the man's sleeve brushed against it. The man and his mother had talked long and the old woman had asked him if he knew the man. The next day they were on the road again and he had felt a resentment towards this man as the cause. All these recollections crowded themselves into his mind.

"Felton seems to have been a man with some strength of character. He had easily promised your mother not to betray her existence to her husband, but the memory of her face and some uneasy sense of unfitness troubled him, I suppose. He remembered Mr. Aston, who had spoken for him, and that he was something to do with these people. He turned up here one day and Nevil had the sense to send him direct to us in London. It was just at the time when I was wanting to adopt a child. I had stopped cursing fate and myself, and I wanted something of my own almost as fiercely as I wanted my freedom."

There was another long pause. This time Christopher put out his hand and laid it on Aymer's.

"There isn't any more. We followed up the clue and found you. My father made another appeal to Peter on behalf of his unknown son, and Peter declared the subject was not discussable: so I kept you. I vowed I'd never stand between your own father and you, but also that I'd never put out a hand to bring you together. That visit you paid him, Christopher, was the blackest time I've had since the day I realised what I'd done. I thought I had got over my jealousy, and I had not."

Christopher leant over him and gripped his hands.

"Cæsar," he said in a breathless low voice, looking him straight in the eyes. "Cæsar, there was no need of that then—there never has been, nor could be. I have no father at all if it be not you."

CHAPTER XXIX

"It does not seem to me a very great thing to ask in the face of things."

Mr. Saunderson dangled his eyeglasses and regarded Christopher with a dubious air.

"I want three days to consider the matter," continued Christopher impatiently. "Where is the difficulty? You don't seem to remember you are asking me to give up my chosen life and work and take on a job that I loathe."

If Mr. Saunderson's face had been capable of expressing more than displeasure, it would have done so, but he was of no plastic build, mind or body, and "displeasure" was the nearest he could get to active anger.

"You have a singular way of regarding what most men would think overpowering good luck, Mr. Masters."

Christopher turned sharply.

"You at least cannot compel me to take that name. It has never been mine and never will be."

"Gently, gently, young man. I am willing to make every allowance for your perturbation, but really, in speaking of my late client ..." he stopped with a shake of the head.

"I was speaking of a name, not of him, Mr. Saunderson. However, I apologise. Once more, will you let the whole matter stand still for three days. I don't mean to accept the thing, you know, but I can't argue it out now. I will meet you in town on Wednesday."

"If you insist, there is nothing more to be said of course," returned Mr. Saunderson, huffily. "As to your refusing your own rights, that will be less simple than you imagine, but I shall hope you will soon view the matter in another light."

"There was no provision made in case the inheritor should refuse or not be available?"

Christopher confronted him suddenly with the question, and the poor man, who was as completely off his balance by Christopher's incomprehensible reception of his tidings, as that young man himself, was evidently confused.

"There were no instructions at all beyond the memorandum stating his wife and child were last heard of in Whitmansworth Union."

"But in the former will, which you say was destroyed?"

"I am not at liberty to divulge anything that might be contained in that document."

"There is nothing to prevent your acting on such instructions at your own prompting," Christopher insisted bluntly.

Mr. Saunderson looked at him critically. "That is an ingenious suggestion Mr. ..." he paused.

"Aston," said Christopher. "It's the name those who have treated me as a son gave me, and I see no obligation to change it."

The lawyer rose.

"Then we are to defer further discussion till Wednesday?"

"Until Wednesday. In town, not here."

He left with Mr. Shakleton in his wake, and Christopher was at last alone and free to weigh if he would the weight of this stupendous burden, which he resolutely decided was not his to bear. He stood looking out of the window at the still driving mist and had to drag his thoughts back from the external aspect of things to the inner matters he must face. But there was no lucidity in his mind, nothing was clear to him but his fierce resentment against the dead man, and a passionate pity for a faded woman.

"It was the beauty of grace rather than feature...." He was stung with intolerable shame for the manhood he must share with one who had wrought such havoc in the woman he was most bound to protect from herself, as well as from the world. The risks and chances of those early days flickered before him. He had been abandoned to such for some vague ultimate good to the colossal idea of fortune which neither he nor its late possessor could spend. Was he more bound to take it and its cares to himself than its author was bound to care for his own flesh and blood? Anger clouded his reason and he knew it. Yet if he could not think coherently on the matter, of what use were the three days of grace he had claimed? He could not endure company at present, and the four walls of his room were as a prison. At last he sent a hasty message to the motor house, tossed a few necessaries into a bag and wrote a note to Cæsar. "Dear Cæsar, I've got to make up my mind about this and I must do it alone, so to come to some decision I'm going off in the car. I'll be back when I've got the thing straight in my mind. Tell St. Michael and Nevil about it, but if you can help it don't let anyone else know.— Christopher Aston."

He drove slowly down the drive, out into the highroad and, turning westward, sped away into the misty distance.

A great stillness fell on Aymer when Christopher left him. He had lived so long under the shadowy fear of the thing that had now happened, that it was hard to credit the fear had passed in fulfilment. He had been forced back to face the past, and, behold, the terror of it was gone. He could only measure the full value of the effort he had made by the languor and listlessness that now wrapped him round, as a child who had overtaxed his strength and must needs rest. A hazy doubt crept into his mind as to what it was he had so dreaded—the resuscitation of the past, or Christopher's reception of it. In either case the fear had faded as some phantom form that melted in daylight.

He stumbled on one thought with vague wonder. No barrier had been raised between him and his adopted son: instead he found the only barrier had been erected by his own lack of strength to face that truth until the inexorable hand of God forced him to the issue.

As to the future he recognised that might be left to Christopher, whose whole life, since Aymer took him, had been a preparation for this situation. His long struggle to keep a grip on life was ebbing fast, it was good to leave decisions in another's hands, to rest, and accept.

When Mr. Aston returned Cæsar gave him Christopher's note with a brief remark.

"Saunderson has been."

The note, short as it was, told the rest. Mr. Aston looked anxiously at his son, but Aymer met his eyes with a quiet smile.

"I'm glad you were away, St. Michael. You've had enough to contend with, and there was no need. There is nothing for either of us to do. It's Christopher's affair."

Mr. Aston looked at the note again and reread the signature, then he gave it back, satisfied.

"What will happen if he won't accept it?" he questioned thoughtfully.

"It is for him to decide." Aymer's tone was earnestly emphatic. "Father, we've done our part. We can't alter it if we would. Leave him free."

"It is the crown of your success that you can do so, my dear old fellow."

"The coronation has not taken place yet," returned Cæsar, with a touch of dry humour that reassured his father more than any words that all was well with his son.

Meanwhile, hour after hour, Christopher's car raced over the white roads. The twinkling lights in the villages through which he sped grew fewer and at last ceased. A more solid blackness was the only inkling of dwellings on either hand. Once the low, vibrating hum of the car seemed to bring a light to a high window, but it fell back into the dark before he had caught more than a faint glimmer on the blind.

He met nothing: the road for all he knew was utterly empty of life. In the silent, motionless darkness it was like a path into illimitable space. He knew every mile of it, yet in the night the miles stretched out and raced with him.

It was far from village or town when at last Christopher wrenched his mind from the mechanical power that held it prisoner, and realised that town or no town, bed or no bed, he must stop. He brought the car to a standstill under the lea of a low ridge of downs, at a point where an old chalk pit reared its white face, glimmering faintly in the darkness. He hazarded a fair guess as to his whereabouts. Whitmansworth must be fifteen or twenty miles ahead. It was nearly midnight now. He would get no lodging even if he went on. He backed the car off the road into the circle of the chalk pit, made as comfortable a resting place as he could with rugs and cushions between the motor and the white wall, and extinguished the lamps. The cool, still night had him to herself, and cradled him to sleep as a mother her child, under the folds of her dark mantle.

He woke when the first fingers of dawn busied themselves with the hem of that dusky cloak, and sound as faint and tremulous as the light itself whispered across the earth. He watched a while to see the dim shapes reform under the glowing light, and the clouds that still curtained the sky, take on themselves a sombre grey uniform. But directly the line of white road took distinctness Christopher struck camp, and boldly raced to meet the full day. An early shepherd paused to watch him pass, returning impassively to work as he disappeared. Two or three labouring men also stared; one even commented to a fellow worker that "these yere motors take no more heed o' decent hours than o' natural distances. Five in the mornin' weren't part o' the gentry's day when I were a boy," he grumbled, "and five miles were five miles, no more nor less. 'Tisn't more nor a mile now."

At wayside farms life was in full swing. Dumbly impatient cows listened for the clatter of milk-pails, and solemn cart horses trudged to the upland fields. Presently he passed through a town where his own Patrimondi made pleasant, easy going. The town servants were cleaning the smooth, elastic surface with big jets of water. Christopher went slowly by with an eye on his handiwork. He fancied he saw a small defect at a turn and stopped to examine it. An indignant worker told him brusquely he needn't try to pick holes in their roads because there weren't any, and Christopher returned meekly he thought they looked good, but fancied the mark he examined was a flaw.

"It ain't any business of yours, anyway," was the angry retort, "the men who laid this knew what they was a-doin'."

Another man had joined him who had worked on the new road when Christopher was to and fro there, and recognised him. He plucked the other by the sleeve.

"Shut up, you fool," he growled, though not so low but Christopher heard him. "It's the Roadmaker himself. Mornin', sir."

Christopher gave him a few words of recognition and went on.

The slate roofs of Whitmansworth came into sight as the church clock struck six. He could see the white Union House high on the hill to the left, but he had no mind to halt there. He stopped the car at the gate of the town cemetery. It was not a beautiful place. Just a little square field with an avenue of young trees and an orderly row of green mounds and haphazard monuments, but in one corner amongst a row of unmarked graves was a white cross. "In remembrance of my mother," was the sole inscription it bore. Christopher stood and looked at it gravely. The thought of another grave amongst the family tombs in the trim churchyard at Stormly crossed his mind. It was better here in the little, plain unpretentious cemetery amongst the very poor whose sorrows she had made her own. She would sleep more quietly so.

But he found no message from her here, nor had he expected it. Her actual presence had not consecrated the spot for him, and he was impatient to gain the road made sacred by reason of the tired, failing footsteps that made their last effort there: the Via Dolorosa of his mother's life.

He passed the milestone where he had waited for his fortune fifteen years ago, and saw it in his mind's eye hastening towards him from the east in the person of Charles Aston. That was the *true* Fortune,—this spurious thing they were trying to harness to his back was evil to the core. Had not that been the very meaning of those painful steps that had struggled away from it along this very road—the meaning of the lonely grave amongst the broken-down poor of Whitmansworth Union?

He stopped the car near a little bridge where a thin brooklet made a noisy chatter, and sat still, his chin on his hand, thinking deeply.

This was the spot for which he had raced all these hours, for here he and she had rested that terrible night to gather strength for the last mile that lay between the woman and rest.

"It's better to be tired and hungry oneself, Jim, than to make other people so. Don't forget that."

"I am not really tired," the child maintained stoutly, "but it's going to rain again. Can't you come on?"

"Presently."

"You think it is the right road?"

"I don't know, Jim. I was sure of it at first, but I'm sure of nothing now."

The words and scene were as clear to him as the day they happened. He saw in it now a deeper significance, a possible meaning that was the last note of tragedy to his mother's story. For that note is reached only when the faith in which we have lived, acted and endured, fails us. That is the bitterness and foretaste of death. Then only can the shadow of it fall on us, and in great mercy gather us into its shade.

The Right Road! There was no doubt or shadow for Christopher yet. He had taken the first step on the Road he had chosen, and he would not look back. He would not stultify his mother's sacrifice. Such faint echoes as he heard calling him back were temptations to which he must turn a deaf ear. He would go forward on his chosen path, and Peter Masters' millions must look after themselves.

That was the final decision. Yet he sat there, still figuring the persons of the woman and the child trudging down the road towards him, and as he gazed, without conscious effort, the forms changed. The boy grew to manhood: the woman took to herself youth, youth with a crown of golden hair and the form of Patricia.

A throb of exultation leapt through him. Here were the real riches and fulness of life within his grasp and he, in blunt stupidity, had not chosen to see, had set material good and vague uncertainties before his own incomparable gain and happiness. Whatever had held him back before, the clouded life or personal ambition, or Cæsar's need, it was swept away now like some low-lying mist before the wind, and left the clear vision, the man and the woman together on the long, smooth Road he would lay for her tender feet.

There should be no more delay than the needed time to race from here to her. Twenty-five miles of country that his car was eager to devour. He slipped away swiftly from the past as he had done before on this very road—to a new future.

CHAPTER XXX

Patricia sat by the fire in her little sitting-room seeking for a plausible excuse to return to Constantia as soon as might be. The grey weather, the strange sense of impending events weighed on her, she knew. She was in the mood when the old evil might flash up again, and for this reason she kept away from her sister a while, hoping to nurse herself into a better mind before evening. Christopher had gone again in his usual abrupt way. Presumably Cæsar understood, but she found herself wishing she also held his confidence. She was hungry for a repetition of that first evening as a starved child is hungry for a crust, when the better things seem as far away as heaven. She must go back to Constantia when she could frame a suitable reason for her capricious movements. She was much safer there, beside the considerate friend, who kept the surface of life in a pleasant ripple, and never seemed to look into the depths or ask her what she found there to trouble her, as dear little sympathetic Renata did occasionally. Yet how could she go if Christopher were really coming back to-day, as St. Michael said, and the future held any possibility of another golden hour? The force of her deep love turned back on herself, broke through spirit and heart and let loose in her mind strange imaginings, alternate glimpses of a heaven or hell that had no relationship with tradition. She put her hands over her face and kept quite still in the grip of a sudden agony that made her physically cold and faint and exhausted. It would pass as it had passed before, yet was she forever to be at the mercy of this torturing realisation of empty years and eternal loss? Did Christopher love her or not? The assured "yes" and the positive "no" were as two shuttlecocks tossed over her strained mind by the breath of circumstance. Her own erroneous idea that her still unconquered passion kept them apart was breeding morbid misery for her, as all false beliefs must do. She had kept herself under control to-day by dint of isolation, and the inadequacy of that course filled her with self-contempt. In her solitary fight against the life forces within and without, she was getting worsted. She knew she resisted the invasion of their hours of depression with less courage than of old. It did not seem to matter so greatly if there were nothing to be won from life, and she was very tired. It had been a mistake to come to Marden at all, there was too much time to think there. She returned to that fact eventually. The afternoon wore on and she fell into a lethargy with no desire to escape it, and did not hear Christopher's motor arrive.

Christopher for once paused in the hall, instead of going straight to Aymer's room, as was the invariable rule, after even a day's absence.

"Where is Mrs. Aston?" he asked the footman, who replied vaguely, when Renata herself appeared. But it was not Renata that Christopher wanted.

"Where is Patricia?" he questioned with more truth.

"Upstairs in her room, I think. She seems rather worried and tired, Christopher. Do you want her?"

There was a note of anxiety in Renata's gentle voice. She was always nervous and anxious if she fancied Patricia was worried, struggling to stand between her and the petty annoyances which were supposed to be so irresistibly maddening to a true Connell.

"Yes, I want her." He smiled as he said it. "But I'll go to her. Don't trouble."

He went upstairs two steps at a time, and along the familiar corridor, and outside the door paused for the first moment since he had seen his vision on the highroad.

The corridor was already dark, but when he entered in obedience to her languid "Come in," the fire light made a rosy glow and filled the quiet space with tremulous light.

Patricia sat facing the fire, with her back to the door. He could see her golden head over the back of the chair, and his heart beat quickly.

"May I come and talk to you, Patricia?"

For the moment she did not answer or move. She was almost in doubt if she could accept his presence just now, until he was actually standing on the rug before her, looking down at her with keen, searching eyes, before which all her wild thoughts sunk back into oblivion, and a sense of quiet content and security stole over her.

"What have you been doing?" he demanded. "You look very tired."

"The result of laziness," she rejoined, and then was angry with herself for allowing an opening for mere trivialities.

"No, that's not true, Christopher. It's a bad day with me. I'm afraid to face anyone, even my own maid."

With no one else in the world could she have owned so much, and the keen pleasure of exercising her right to open dealing with him, outweighed the humiliation of her avowal.

Christopher seemed intent on his own affairs, however, for he asked her abruptly if St. Michael or Cæsar had told her the news.

"What news?"

"Something rather disconcerting has happened to me," he said slowly, "but I'll tell you that presently. The most important thing now is that I want to get married."

All the cold waters of the world closed over her head for a moment. It was as if he had wrenched a plank from one drowning. She answered him, however, in a low, mechanical voice:

"Soon, Christopher?"

"That will be for her to say, if she will have me at all."

"You have not asked her yet?"

"I am asking her."

She looked up at him, puzzled and incredulous of the apparent meaning. Then suddenly he was on his knees by her side, with his strong arms round her.

"My dear, my dear, surely you must know. Is there need for any words between us? I've known so long all you must mean to me. Listen, Patricia, you will have to forgive me a great thing. I've let outside considerations, absurd ambitions, and the shadow of a lie, stand between us. I've waited when I should have spoken. You *will* forgive me that, my dear one, will you not? I'm not humble a bit in asking. I am so proud of the one great thing, that *I* can give you, Love,—can hold you and wrap you in it, so that nothing can hurt you any more. You understand, you recognise my right, Patricia?"

She could say nothing, understand nothing, but the great peace of perfect security. She let him hold her still, with her head against his shoulder and his dear face near, so near she seemed to lose sense of her own identity. All the answer to her life's riddle lay there, behind the love that emptied her soul of need. Out of the blissful unspeakable light some words vibrated into new meaning.

"There shall be no more sea."

It meant this then, this experience that was theirs. For him and her there was no more tempest, no more restless craving or peril, all had passed with the old incompleteness.

Still, she had not spoken audibly to him nor had he pressed her to do so. Words were too imperfect a medium. But presently, when all had been said in the silence that could be said, he touched her hair with caressing hand and reminded her:

"You have never answered me, sweet."

She put her hand on his as it held her and whispered, "Have I not, Christopher?"

And then he kissed her.

Afterwards as they sat watching the red fire, it seemed to her there was no problem in all the world he could not solve, no struggle in which he would not prove victor, nor any knowledge too deep to reach. In the illumination of their great love the gates of life became visible and open, never to be quite closed again.

She spoke at last slowly and quietly.

"Christopher, I am not going to ask you if you are afraid or have counted the risk you run, I being what I am. I know what you would say and I love you so well that now at this moment I have no fear either. But it will come nevertheless. Others will point out to you that it is a mad thing to do, and I shall say it too. It is then you must hold me, Christopher, against my will and against myself. For this is my clear sane hour, when I really know, and I know it means my salvation. Only when that certainty slips from me you must keep and save me yourself, dearest."

He held her hands against him and looked down into her eyes. "As I would keep and save myself, beloved."

She smiled a little, understanding to the finest shade his meaning, and then a quiver of weakness touched her.

"I should die if you let me slip, Christopher."

"You are going to live," he said firmly, and kissed her again.

CHAPTER XXXI

Christopher entirely forgot to tell Patricia of his fortune or parentage. He remembered that little omission as he went down to dinner and looked back to see if she were visible, but she was not in sight, and as he was already late he had to go in without her.

She came down still later, looking so beautiful with such a touch of warm colour in her face, and so sweet a light of wonder in her eyes that even Nevil regarded her with speculative interest.

Aymer had long given up dining with them, and no one spoke of the lawyers' visit or of Christopher's rapid flittings, or indeed of any of the subjects on which their minds were really intent. But there seemed a tacit understanding amongst them that dinner must not be a long affair and was a prelude to something yet to happen.

They went out together and Christopher delayed Patricia in the hall.

"I must see Nevil and Cæsar and tell them at once," he said hurriedly, "then I want you, my dearest. I've news for you, which I forgot just now. You must know it, though it makes no difference to us."

Nevil came out at that moment and she slipped away after Renata with curiosity wide awake.

"Am I to congratulate you as a millionaire or commiserate with you as a bearer of burdens, old fellow?" asked Nevil, flinging himself into a big chair.

"You will congratulate me, I hope, but not about that confounded money though. Nevil, you are Patricia's guardian. Will you and Renata give her to me?"

He spoke abruptly and without any preamble, gripping the back of a chair in his hands. A sudden doubt as to the family acceptance of what was an unquestionable matter in his eyes suddenly assailed him.

"You want to marry Patricia?"

Christopher nodded. "You can hardly urge we have not had time to know our own minds," he said, smiling a little.

"No," Nevil admitted, and then added rather distractedly, "What ought I to urge, though, Christopher? Of course it's the greatest possible thing that could happen to Patricia, but for you?"

"I'm appealing to Patricia's guardian, who has only her interests to consider. I'll look after my own. However," he went on hastily, "it's only fair to tell you, Nevil, I don't mean to take either the fortune or the name. So long as you'll lend me your own I'll stick to it. Failing that, my mother's will serve me."

Nevil made no comment beyond a nod. The younger man waited with what patience he could command.

"Does it seriously affect the matter?" he asked at last, "my refusing the beastly money?"

Nevil got up slowly and shook himself.

"It affects Patricia's guardians not one bit. It's not as if it were that, or nothing."

"No, I've enough. Of course if I hadn't I might feel differently about it. I can keep her in comfort, Nevil."

Nevil got up deliberately and altered the position of a bronze on the high mantelshelf.

"It's not Patricia I'm thinking about," he said in his slow way, "but hang it all, you belong to us, Christopher. We must think of you! Have you counted the risks?"

"I probably understand them better than anyone."

"Then I dismiss further responsibility. I'm really more pleased than I can say, Christopher. Poor little Patricia! What fortune for her!"

"You clearly understand there won't be any fortune?" persisted the other bluntly.

"Oh, Peter's fortune? Of course not. Where's the obligation? I'll go and tell Renata."

He strolled off and Christopher hurried to the West Room, where he found Aymer and Mr. Aston waiting expectantly. Christopher came to a standstill by the fireplace and to his amazement found his hands shaking. He had never imagined there would be any difficulty in this interview, yet he found himself unaccountably at a loss before these two men. The absurdly inadequate idea that they might consider it unjustifiable greed in him to grasp so great a prize as Patricia Connell when they had already given him so much assailed him.

Both men were aware of his unusual embarrassment and neither of them made the slightest attempt to help him out, for Mr. Aston had a very fair idea of what had happened, and had conveyed his suspicions to Aymer. They both found a certain amusing fascination in seeing how he would deal with the situation, and it was a situation so pleasing to them both that they failed to realise it might present real difficulties to him.

He faced them suddenly, and plunged into the matter in his usual direct way.

"Cæsar and St. Michael, I've something to tell you both. I am not sure if it will be news to you or not, but Patricia has said she will marry me."

He came to an abrupt stop, and turned away again towards the fire.

"It's very good news," said Mr. Aston quietly, "if in no way surprising."

"You don't think I'm asking too much when I've had so much given me? I feel abominably greedy."

"You might think of me in the matter," protested Aymer, plaintively. "What on earth does it matter if you are greedy so long as you provide me with a real interest in life. I began to think you meant to defraud me of my clear rights."

A very grateful Christopher crossed the room and took his usual seat on the sofa.

"I've been a blind idiot," he admitted, "or rather an idle one. I've known for years it must be Patricia, and left it at that."

"Why?" demanded Aymer.

But that he could not or would not tell them.

Mr. Aston then suggested Christopher should explain what he meant to do concerning his inheritance.

"Which you have treated so far with scandalous disrespect," put in Aymer.

"I can't touch it. It would be treason to—to my mother. And I don't want it. I hate it, the way it's done, the caring for it."

There was something so foreign to Christopher's usual finality of statement in this, that the two older men looked at each other with sudden apprehension and then avoided the other's eye. For in their secret hearts they both knew that Christopher must presently arrive at the unconfessed certainty that had come to them, that this was not a matter in which he was free to act as he would. The call had come for him to take up a burden he disliked and sooner or later he would hear the voice and recognise the authority to which he had been taught to bow his own will. Yet both of them, without consultation or any word, knew it was not for them to interpret the call for him. Their work was over now. If they had taught him to set no value on the prizes of the world and to regard the means as of equal importance to the end, they had also taught him that duty may come in many disguises, but once recognised, her sway must be absolute. Christopher would discover her in time, but they must hold their peace lest conflicting motives should hamper his surrender to her call.

"I'm going to meet Mr. Saunderson in town to-morrow," Christopher went on, "I am not quite clear yet how it's to be worked. I am only clear I won't touch money of that sort. It costs too much. I feel pretty certain Mr. Saunderson *has* instructions what to do, if I refuse it."

He looked at Mr. Aston with an unusual desire for confirmation of his hope and his decision. A strong inclination to appeal for such support pressed him sorely. But he knew it was only confirmation of his own determination he sought, and his ingrained independence of mind shrank from such a proceeding.

"If you know what you want to do and what you ought to do, why appeal to me?" Cæsar had repeatedly told the small boy he was fitting out for life: yet who so kind or patient when the decision still hung in the balance and uncertainty held the scales? There was no uncertainty now, Christopher told himself, and allowed none either to himself or to them. One concession only did he permit himself. He turned to Mr. Aston a little shyly.

"Would you go with me, St. Michael? I am afraid of Mr. Saunderson's wrath if I am unprotected."

Mr. Aston gravely expressed his willingness to hold his hand and see him through. After which Christopher went out to fetch Patricia. He found her sitting on the floor at Renata's feet, the latter fussing over her with matronly joy and sisterly love, and talking inconsequently between times of Charlotte, with what would appear to an outsider irrelevance of the first order.

"Charlotte will be a most desirable bridesmaid," Christopher remarked after he had listened a moment, whereupon Renata became greatly confused and Patricia laughed without any embarrassment whatever.

"Charlotte has not yet had time to signify her approval," she said. "I rely on her judgment to a great extent, you know. If she offers any objection we shall have to reconsider it."

"I'm not afraid. Charlotte has always approved of me," asserted Christopher cheerfully.

"Of course Charlotte will be pleased," put in that young lady's mother, quite seriously. "What nonsense you are talking, Patricia."

She got up and offered a transparent excuse to slip away and leave the lovers alone.

Patricia, still kneeling by the fire, leant her head against Christopher.

"I used to try and make up my mind you would marry Charlotte when she grew up," she said dreamily.

"How ingenious of you. Unfortunately, it was my mind, not yours, that was concerned, and that had been made up when Charlotte was in pinafores. Now come and talk business, dear."

So at last he told her the news he had been so tardy in delivering, told her the whole story very simply and as impersonally as he could, but Patricia's heart brimmed over with pity for him. She divined more clearly than the men the strength of his hatred for the burden with which he was threatened, and the burden of past memories in which that hatred had its root. In the fulness of her love she set herself the future task of rooting out the resentment for another's sorrows, which she knew must be as poison to his generous soul. At length Christopher, having read in her love the confirmation for which he so childishly longed, took her away to be introduced to Cæsar in her new character as his promised wife. She waited for no such introduction whatever, but seated herself on the big hassock by the sofa that was still Christopher's privileged seat and leant her head against the edge of Cæsar's cushions, but she failed to find anything to say and Christopher was so occupied in watching her as to forget to speak.

"It's taken him a long time to recognise his own privilege, hasn't it, Patricia?" said Cæsar, gently putting his hand on hers. "I was getting impatient with him. It was time he grew up."

"You aren't disappointed then?" she asked with a little flush of confusion. "Mrs. Sartin will be. She always expects him to marry a duchess at least. She is so insufferably proud of him."

"She does not know him so well as we do, that's why."

"I'll not stay here to be discussed," remarked Christopher decidedly, "you can pull my character to pieces when I'm away. When did you last see Mrs. Sartin, Patricia?"

"Last Thursday. She comes to tea every week with Maria."

Maria was Mrs. Sartin's second daughter, midway between Sam and Jim, and was just installed as second lady's-maid to Mrs. Wyatt.

"Is Sam more reconciled to her going out?"

"Not a bit. You know he wanted to send her to a Young Ladies' Academy in Battersea. I know he'd have done it but for Martha, who has more sense in her fingers than he has in his whole head."

"Hadn't Maria anything to say in the matter?" This from Cæsar.

"No one has much to say when Sam and his mother dispute," said Christopher, shaking his head. "Sam would be a tyrant, Cæsar, if he could. He always wants to push people on in his own way."

"Sam is not singular," put in Mr. Aston, in his meditative way, "character is all more or less a question of degree. There are the same fundamental instincts in all of us. Some get developed at the expense of others, that's all."

"There but for the grace of God goes ..." said Patricia, laughing.

Christopher felt in his pocket and produced a coin.

"Apropos of which, Cæsar," he said with a flicker of a smile, "I found this, the other day rummaging in an old box."

He tossed it dexterously to Cæsar. It was a sovereign with a hole in it and the broken link of a chain therein. Cæsar looked at it and then slipped it in his own pocket.

"It's mine, at all events," he said shortly, "and we are all talking nonsense, especially Christopher."

But Christopher shook his head.

"Mayn't I understand all this?" demanded Patricia.

"No," returned Cæsar, before Christopher could speak. "It's not worth it. John Bunyan was a fool."

"Not at all, but the other man might have retorted, 'there with the grace of God goes I.'"

This was from Mr. Aston, and Christopher gave him a quick look of comprehension.

"The Court is with you, sir," said Aymer languidly. "Let us discuss wedding presents."

CHAPTER XXXII

At eleven o'clock on Wednesday, Mr. Aston and Christopher were ushered into Mr. Saunderson's office by a discreetly interested clerk. The bland and smiling lawyer advanced to meet them with that respect and courtesy he felt due to the vast fortune they represented. His table was covered with orderly rows of papers, and the door of the safe, labeled P. Masters, Esq., stood open.

"Punctuality is the essence of good business," said Mr. Saunderson, with effusive approval as he indicated two lordly armchairs placed ready for his visitors. Mr. Aston and Christopher had both a dim, unreasonable consciousness of dental trouble and exchanged glances of mutual encouragement.

Mr. Saunderson blinked at them genially behind his gold-rimmed glasses and spoke of the weather, which was bad, dilated on the state of the streets, lamented the slowness of the L. C. C. to enforce the use of Patrimondi beyond the limits of Westminster, and as the futile little remarks trickled on they carried with them his complacent smile, for in every quiet response he read Christopher Masters' fatal determination, and prepared himself for battle. It was Christopher, however, who flung down the gauntlet. He answered the question anent the use of Patrimondi in the metropolis, and then said directly:

"Mr. Saunderson, I've considered the matter of this fortune you tell me I've inherited, and I do not feel under any obligation to accept it or its responsibilities. It's only fair to let you know this at once."

Mr. Saunderson leant back in his chair and rubbed his chin, and his eyes wandered from one to the other of his visitors thoughtfully.

"The matter is far too complicated to be disposed of so lightly, I fear," he remarked, shaking his head. "Let me place the details of the thing before you and as a business man you can then judge for yourself."

He had at least no fault to find with the grave attention they paid him, indeed, the entirely unemotional attitude of the younger man was to the lawyer's mind the most alarming symptom he had noted. Still he could not allow to himself that his task presented more than surmountable difficulties, for Mr. Saunderson had no real knowledge of the forces at work against him, of the silent, desperate woman who had given her life for her faith, who had once been beautiful, and whose worn body slept in the little dull cemetery at Whitmansworth.

"I believe you are acquainted with the great premises known as Princes Buildings," began Mr. Saunderson, "that simplifies my task. For the whole affair is so amazingly managed that I can offer you no precedent with which to compare it. There are seven floors in that building, and on each floor the affairs of the six great concerns in which Mr. Masters was interested, are conducted. Such an arrangement was only carried out at enormous expense and trouble. I may tell you, however, that the condition of Mr. Masters' interesting himself in either of the companies, was their domicile beneath this one roof. Now in five of these big concerns he occupied merely the place of a director, with no more official power than any other director might have. Yet in every case, I think I may say, no decision of any importance would have been taken by the company in opposition to his advice, and he was the financial backbone of each. On the two top floors of these great premises we have a rather different state of things. For here are the offices of the three smaller companies which were directly under the control of Mr. Masters, and which are the original source of his fortune. I allude to the Steel Axle Company, the Stormly Mine and the Stormly Foundry Companies. These affairs he continued to keep under his own eye, never relaxing his attention, or the excellent system he had established, under which the whole great affair worked with such marvellous smoothness and success. I beg your pardon, did you say anything?"

Christopher shook his head. Mr. Saunderson resumed.

"You will understand Mr. Masters' wealth was directly drawn from these companies, bringing him an income of roughly £130,000 a year. The administration of this income, of which he spent about one-fourth on himself, was the occupation of the offices on the top floor of Princes Buildings. A certain proportion of income was regularly reinvested in concerns in which Mr. Masters took no active part, and was accumulative. It is this reserve fund which has brought the actual fortune to such high figures as I have quoted you, nearly £4,000,000. A great deal of money also has been devoted to the purchase of freehold property. You would be surprised how great an area of Birmingham itself belongs to Mr. Masters."

Christopher gave an involuntary movement of dissent, and the lawyer hurried on.

"Not perhaps districts that it would be interesting to visit now, but which will undoubtedly be of vast interest to your heirs. They represent enormous capital and of course will eventually be a source of colossal wealth.

"Now, so perfect is the machinery and system under which all these giant concerns are worked, that they will run without difficulty on their present lines until you have mastered the working thoroughly, and are able, if you should wish it, to make your own plans for future greatness. I say this, because it seems to me you are inclined to overrate the difficulties of your position. I do not say, mind you, matters could go on indefinitely as they are, but you are a young man of intellect and capacity, you have only to step into the place of one who has set everything in order for you, and before two years are up you will have the details of the system by heart, and will, I am convinced, be recognised as an able successor to your father."

Christopher's mouth straightened ominously. It was an unlucky slip on Mr. Saunderson's part, but he was oblivious to it. He was indeed incapable of appreciating the sentiment towards his late client, which was playing so large a part against him in this tussle of wills.

Christopher heard in every word that was spoken the imperious Will that would force him to compass its ends, even from the land of Death. It was not wholly the unsought responsibility, the burden of the wealth, the memory of his mother that buttressed his determination to refuse this stupendous thing, it was also his fierce, vehement desire to escape the enforced compliance with that still living Will-power. Peter Masters' unwritten and unspoken word was, that he, Christopher, should succeed him. He had left him no directions, no choice, no request, he had relied on the Greatness of the Thing which Christopher loathed with his whole soul, he had claimed him for this bondage with an unuttered surety that was maddening. Minute by minute Christopher felt his former quiet determination rise to passionate resistance and denial of the right of that Dominant Will to drag his life into the vortex it had made.

Quite suddenly Mr. Saunderson was aware of the strength of the antagonism that confronted him. Unable to trace the reason of it, he blundered on hopelessly.

"Mr. Masters was, I should say, quite aware of your natural ability. He has had more regard for your fortunes than you probably suspect. I have letters of his to various men concerning the starting of this ingenious invention of yours, Patrimondi." He bustled over some papers on the table as if searching, and did not see Christopher's sudden backward movement: but Mr. Aston bent forward and put his hand as if accidentally on Christopher's shoulder as he spoke:

"Never mind them, now, Mr. Saunderson. Mr. Masters was, we know, naturally interested in that affair, but to continue your account, what will happen if Mr. Aston refuses to accept his position? Let us suppose for a moment there had been no clue left. What would you have done?"

Mr. Saunderson brought the tips of his red, podgy fingers together with great exactness.

"That is a supposition I should be sorry to entertain, sir," he said deliberately.

"I am afraid you must entertain it," put in Christopher, suddenly, his resolution to escape urging him to curt methods.

The light eyes of the lawyer rested on him with something very like apprehension in them.

"In the case of there being no direct heir the money would go to the nearest of kin."

"We will pass that over," Mr. Aston said quietly. "I am the nearest relative Peter had, after Christopher, and I decline it at all costs."

"Unclaimed and unowned money would fall to the Crown, I suppose. It is impossible to imagine it."

"The Crown would see no difficulty in that, I expect," put in Christopher. "How could you stop the Thing going on, that's what I want to know?"

"You could give the money to Charities and shut down the works and leave thousands to starve."

Christopher moved impatiently.

"The money invested in each company could be divided amongst the shareholders, I suppose, or in the case of the Stormly Mines amongst the work-people."

"If you want to ruin them."

"Mr. Saunderson, I am not going to accept this fortune. I don't like the way it was made, I don't want it, I won't work for it."

"Why should you work for it, after all? You can go on with your own life and delegate your powers to another or others, and let all continue as it is. The income would be at your disposal to save or spend. You need never enter Princes Buildings if that is what troubles you. You can spend the money in philanthropy, or gamble it away at Monte Carlo, or leave it to accumulate for your heirs. If you'll do that I'll undertake to find suitable men to carry on the affairs."

Christopher's face flushed angrily, but he made an effort to control himself, however, and answered quietly.

"I cannot take money I've not earned, Mr. Saunderson."

Mr. Saunderson made a gesture of despair.

"All you have to do," went on Christopher, watching him closely, "is to act as if that clue had never fallen into your hands or as if when you followed it up you found I was dead. Do you mean to say Mr. Masters did not provide for that contingency?"

"As I have told you before, Mr. Masters provided for no such contingency," snapped the lawyer; "he never entertained such a preposterous idea as your refusing."

"To conform to his will," concluded Christopher drily.

The three men were silent a while, each struggling to see some way out of the impasse into which they had arrived.

"You say the various companies are entirely distinct from each other?" queried Mr. Aston thoughtfully, more for the sake of starting a line of inquiry than because he saw any open door of escape.

"Entirely unconnected, but Mr. Masters, or his successor, holds the ends of the various threads, so to speak. Apart from him each affair has a multitude of masters and no head. If the money left in each company were divided as a bonus—a preposterous suggestion to my mind—they would each be free and would presumably find a head for themselves."

"Then you had better work out some such scheme, and once free of the source of the money we can deal with what's left at leisure. The Crown will make no difficulties over its share and we can set the London hospitals on their feet or establish a Home for Lost Cats." He got up and walked across the big room to the window, looking moodily into the street.

Mr. Saunderson looked genuinely pained and cast appealing glances at Mr. Aston, who only shook his head.

"It is a matter for Christopher to decide for himself, Mr. Saunderson. I cannot and may not influence him either way."

"There is not the smallest doubt of his parentage," said the lawyer in a low voice, "one can hear his father in every sentence."

"It is unwise to remind him of it."

The other looked astonished. "Indeed, you surprise me. Yet he is really deeply indebted to his father for the success of his own invention."

"Still more unwise to insist on that. You must remember he had a mother as well as a father."

Mr. Saunderson opened his mouth to say something and closed it again. Presently he opened a folded paper and, having perused it, laid it back in a drawer. Christopher rejoined them.

"Mr. Saunderson," he said frankly, "I fear I've spoken in an unseemly manner, and I beg your pardon. I can quite understand I must seem little short of a madman to you, but I've perhaps better reasons for my refusal than you think. Put it, if you will, that I feel too young, too inexperienced to deal with this fortune as Mr. Masters meant it to be dealt with, and on those grounds I ask you to devise some scheme for breaking it up without letting the workers suffer. I'll subscribe to any feasible plan you suggest. Will you undertake this for me?"

"It will take time." Mr. Saunderson regarded him watchfully, as he spoke, "a great deal of time."

"How long do you ask?"

"Two years."

"Then in two years' time, Mr. Saunderson, send me your scheme, and I'll be your debtor for life."

Mr. Saunderson smiled faintly.

But on that understanding they ultimately parted.

"My own belief is," said Mr. Aston when he was giving an account of the interview to Aymer, "that Mr. Saunderson means to do nothing at all and is only giving Christopher time. Also, though he persistently denies it, I believe he *has* instructions behind him. We know Peter had an immense belief in Time and never hurried his schemes."

Aymer moved restlessly.

"And you share his belief?"

"I believe in the long run Christopher will do the thing he is meant to do and neither you nor I, old fellow, can say what that is. You have taught him to follow the highest Road he can, see, and I tell you again, as I have before, you must leave it at that."

CHAPTER XXXIII

Thus by tacit consent did the whole question of Peter Masters' Fortune and the Refusal slip into the background of the lives of those mostly concerned, and only for Christopher did that background colour all the present and alter the perspective of his outlook.

He told Aymer plainly that it was a bitter thought to him to be indebted to Peter Masters for even a share of the Patrimondi success.

"According to Saunderson he must have subsidised the Exhibition people," he said moodily.

"It was a very excellent advertisement."

"It meant he had his own way and left me indebted to him when I had refused his help."

"Good heavens, what a mercy you two were not flung together earlier in life!"

Christopher faced him abruptly.

"Am I so like him then?"

"Absurdly so. Your own way and no one else to interfere."

Christopher was silent for a while, but presently he said in a low voice, "That's not quite true, Cæsar, is it? You can interfere as much as you like."

"I'd be sorry to try."

Again Christopher was silent, but his face softened. He thought of how the personality and jealous love of this man to whom he owed so much had stood between him and Patricia and how he felt no shadow of resentment at it.

"I think I shall adopt Max when he leaves school," remarked Cæsar languidly, "he'll let me manage him in my own way till he is an octogenarian."

"Cæsar, you have no discrimination at all. Once you wanted to adopt Sam, now Max. Both as pliable as elastic, and as unmalleable."

"I've a great affection for Max."

"So have I. Is Nevil going to give him to Patrimondi?"

"No, to me."

"Honestly?"

Aymer nodded. "He'll have to manage the estate some day, not so far off, either."

Christopher patted the sofa rug absently.

"When he's at Cambridge he'll have to spend the Long Vacation learning from his ancient uncle."

Christopher gave an involuntary sigh.

"Jealous again?" demanded Aymer quizzically, but he put his hand on Christopher's and they both smiled.

Patricia and Christopher were married at Christmas, Charlotte having given her consent with the remark, it was better than having a horrid stranger in the family anyway.

They established themselves in a house on the verge of the sea, within easy motor or train distance of Marden and the Patrimondi works. It was a relief to all to find how easily Cæsar appeared to take the new separation, but the quiet peace and unspoken happiness of the united lives seemed to include him in its all-embracing results. There could be no room for jealousy in a love that usurped no rights, but only filled its own place.

The days of doubt which Patricia had feared came and passed in the autumn weeks preceding the marriage, and Christopher had kept his word and held her firmly against the weak terrors that assailed her. Once they were married, however, she seemed to pass out of the shadow of the fear, and to break from the bondage of her race. In some wonderful way her husband's clear, perpetual vision of her as separate from the tyranny of heredity, did actually free her. She too saw herself free, and in so seeing, the fetters were loosed. If it were a miracle, as little Renata sometimes thought, it was only one in so far as the Love which can inspire such faith and vision is yet but a strange unknown power with us, to which nature seldom rises, and can rarely hold when grasped.

But these two held it, rising with each other's efforts, sinking with each other's daily failures; their lives so intricately woven together that they needed no outward semblance of interests or visible companionship to bring the knowledge of their Love to their hearts.

Christopher continued his work, journeying far and wide. Sometimes she accompanied him actually, sometimes she remained in their home on the cliff edge, alone but not solitary, looking with joy for his return, but free from aching need. Quite slowly the Woman learnt to recognise her unseen, unreckoned sway over the Man, to discover how he could only rise to the full height of his manhood by strength of the inspiring love she brought him. She was pressed by an uncomprehending world to fill her leisure hours with many occupations, useful and useless, but she resisted steadily. She took life as it came to her, day by day, wasting no strength, but refusing no task, shirking no responsibility, drinking in every joy, and holding always faithfully in her heart his true image as he had held hers, knowing that when perchance the outward man blurred that image for a moment it was but the outward casing; the inner soul remained true to the likeness in which it was created.

As the months slipped by Christopher saw that his work continued to grow, that the good roads of which he had dreamed stretched far and wide across the country, and he knew he had won for himself a place in the history of men. Moreover, he loved his work.

It was a never-ceasing pleasure, and when it ended came the greater, deeper joy of his undivided love. If the aim of man is happiness, he had achieved that end as far as any human being might do so.

Yet all the while a black thread wove itself into the warp of his existence. He tried not to see it, for recognition of it would cancel that white web of life that grew daily beneath his hand. Still it was there, and the white web became uneven and knotted. He was restless, even irritable, the white turned to grey, yet still he resisted the unknown forces that pressed him onward to the dissolution of this present beautiful life. And Patricia herself, with her unbroken faith in his readiness to follow the highest when he saw it, fought with the silent Powers till at length that silence was broken by a cry so imperious that even his dogged will could refuse sight and hearing no longer.

CHAPTER XXXIV

As Christopher was preparing to leave the works one Saturday afternoon he was told that a man had just arrived from Birmingham who refused to give his name, but who asked for him. Christopher hung for a moment on the step of his car and then descending again went straight to the room where his unknown visitor was waiting. He proved to be a spare, stooping man, with lips so thin and white as to be almost invisible. His eyes, which he hardly raised from the floor, were bright with the fire of fever, and his shaking hands, one of which held a cap, concealing the other, were narrow, and the knuckles stood out with cruel prominence.

"What do you want with me?" Christopher demanded shortly.

The man looked at him sideways and did not move, but he spoke in an uncertain, quavering voice.

"You are Masters' son, ar'n't you?"

Christopher turned on him with fierce amazement, and checked himself.

"Answer my question, if you have anything to say to me, and leave my private affairs alone," he said sternly.

"There you are," grinned the man, the thin mouth widening to a distorted semblance of a smile, "seems to me, seems to my mates 'tain't such a private affair, neither, leastways we pay for it."

Christopher's instinct to turn the man out struggled with his curiosity to know what it all meant. He stood still, therefore, with his eyes fixed on the weirdly displeasing face and neglected to look at the twitching hands.

"It were bad enough when Masters were alive, curse him, with his 'system' and his 'single chance,' and his sticking to his word, but we knew where we was then. Now, none of us knows. Here's one turned off cos he broke some rule he'd never heard of; another for telling a foreman what he thought of him; my mate's chucked out for fighting—*outside the Mill Gate*, look you—What concern be it of yours what we do outside? It's a blessed show you do for us outside, isn't it? I tell you it don't concern you anyhow, you lazy bloodsucker—and look at me—I've worked for your father fifteen year, and you turn me off—you and your precious heads of departments,—because I was a day behind with my job. Well, what if I was? Hadn't I a wife what was dying with her sixth baby, and not a decent soul to come to her? We've been respectable people, we have, till we came to live in the blooming gaudy houses at Carson."

"That's the Steel Axle Company's works, isn't it?" put in Christopher quietly. He had not moved; he was intent on picking up the clue to the mad indictment that lay in the seething flow of words.

"Yah. Don't know your own purse-strings," spluttered the denouncer, growing incoherent with rising fury; "sit at home with your little play-box of a works down here, with fancy hutches for your rabbits of workmen, clubs, toys, kitchen ranges, hot and cold laid on. Oh, I've seen it all. Who pays for it, that's what I want to know? who pays for your blooming model works and houses?"

"I pay for it," said Christopher still quietly, "or rather the company does. It comes out of working expenses."

The man gave an angry snarl of disbelief. "You pays, does you? I tell you it's we who pays. You take our money and spend it on this toy of yours here. I'll—"

Christopher put up his hand. "You are utterly mistaken," he said, "I have no more to do with the late Peter Masters' works or his money than the men in the yards out there."

The black ignorance, the fierce words interlarded with unwritable terms, the mad personal attack, filled him with a shame and pity that drowned all indignation. There had been injustice and wrong somewhere that had whipped this poor mind to frenzy, to an incoherent claim to rights he could not define.

"Why do you come to me?"

The man gave almost a scream of rage.

"Come to you? Ain't you his son? Don't it all belong to you, whether you takes it or whether you don't? Are you going to skulk behind them heads in Birmingham and leave us at their mercy, let 'em grind us to powder for their own profit and no one to say them yea or nay? There was a rumour of that got about, how you was going to shunt us on to them, you skulking blackguard. I wouldn't believe it. I told 'em as how Masters' son, if he had one, wouldn't be a damned scoundrel like that. He'd see to his own rights."

What was that in the shaking hands beneath the cap? Christopher's eyes, still on the tragically foul face, never dropped to catch the metallic gleam; his whole mind lay in dragging out the truth entangled in the wild words. The voice quivered more and more as if under spur of some mental effort that urged the speaker to a climax he could not reach but on the current of the crazy syllables.

"So it ain't no concern of yours if we lives or dies, if we work or be turned off without so much as a word to carry us on again? 'Tain't nothing to you we've got fifty masters instead of one, so long as you gets your money. I tell you I won't serve fifty of 'em. One as we could reckon on was bad enough, but fifty of 'em to battle flesh and blood and make their own food out of us, and no one what we can call to account as it were, I tell 'ee we won't have it. I won't serve 'em." The poor wretch had forgotten he was already dismissed from such service. "If you won't be their master, then by God, you shan't be master anywhere else."

His hand with the revolver he had clutched under cover of his cap flew up. The report was followed by a splitting of glass and a cry without.

For a brief second that was like a day of eternity, Christopher and the man continued to face each other; the swaying blue-grey barrel of the smoking weapon acted like a magnetic point on which their numbed minds met and mingled in confusion, with that independence of time we ascribe to dreams. For the echo of the report had not died from the room when those outside rushed in. The would-be assassin instantly crumpled up on the floor, a mere heap of grimy clothes, unconscious even of his failure.

The men clamoured round Christopher with white faces and persistent inquiries as to whether he were hurt.

He reassured them of that as soon as it appeared to him his voice could sound across the deafening echo of the shot.

"Not hurt in the least," he said dully, looking down at the huddled form. "Is he dead?"

They straightened out the poor creature they would gladly have lynched, and one of them shook his head.

"A fit, I think. Let him be."

A new-comer rushed in with horror-stricken face, and stopped his tongue at sight of Christopher.

"How's it outside?" whispered one to him.

"Dead." The word was hardly breathed, but Christopher spun round on his heel.

"Who's dead?"

They looked at him uneasily, and at one another.

He moved to the door mechanically, when an old man, a north-countryman and a Methodist preacher of some note, laid his hand on his arm.

"Don't 'ee take on, lad. 'Tis the Lord's will which life He'll take home to him. Maybe He's got bigger work for you than for the little 'un."

"Who is it?" His dry lips hardly framed the words.

"It's Ann Barty's little chap as was passing. We thought 'twere but the glass."

"Better a boy than a man," muttered another.

Christopher paid no heed. He went out with the old Methodist beside him. A group of men stood round something under the window which one of them had covered with a coat. They made way for the master, and not one of them, fathers and sons as they were, but felt a throb of thankfulness the small life had been taken in preference to his. But Christopher knelt down and raised the coat.

"One shall be taken, the other left."

It was old Choris who said it. A little murmur of assent went up from the circle, bareheaded now, like Christopher. He looked up with fierce, unspoken dissent to their meek acceptance of this cruel thing, and then replacing the coat very gently, stood up.

"Has anyone gone to Ann Barty?" he asked quietly.

Someone had gone, it appeared. Someone else had gone for a doctor. Christopher ordered them to carry the little form into the waiting-room, where it was laid on the table. Someone fetched a flag from the office and laid it over the boy.

Without direct orders all work in the mill had ceased, little knots of men had gathered in the yard and there was a half-suppressed unanimous murmur from two hundred throats when a group of men came out of the room with the shattered window, carrying the still conscious form of the author of the outrage. It rose and fell and rose again threateningly. Christopher came out of the waiting-room and at sight of him it fell again.

"They must go back to work," he said to the head foreman, who waited uneasily. "They can do nothing, and if we stop work there will be trouble."

"Where are you going, sir?"

The foreman ventured this much on sheer necessity.

"To Ann Barty."

"What shall I say to them?" Again he eyed the men uneasily.

"Tell them I wish it," returned Christopher simply. "It's only an hour to closing time, but it will steady them down."

He went back to the motor car he had been on the point of entering not fifteen minutes ago, and they made a lane for him to pass through, following him with their eyes till the gate closed behind him. The foreman stood on the steps of the office and gave the order to resume work. Not a man moved.

"It's Mr. Aston's wish," he shouted, "if you've got any heart in you to show him what you feel, you'll attend to it."

The crowd swayed and broke up, melted once more into units, who disappeared their several ways. The head foreman wiped his forehead and went into the office.

Outside the ante-room to Christopher's private office the glass was strewn on the pathway, and that was the only sign in the mill yard of what had occurred.

Christopher found a group already assembled round

Ann Barty's cottage. They drew back from him with curious eyes.

"Is anyone with her?" he asked, his hand on the latch.

"Mrs. Toils and Jane Munden, what's her sister," said a woman, eagerly seizing a chance of a speaking part in this drama of life and death.

Christopher went in. The mother was sitting dry-eyed and staring, her hands twisted in her coarse apron. She swayed to and fro with mechanical rhythm, and paid no heed at all to the two weeping women who kept up a flow of low-uttered sentences of well-meant but inadequate comfort. Christopher bent over her and took both her hands, neither remembering the other nor seeing aught but the mother with a burden of grief slowly dropping on her.

"Ann," he whispered, "Ann, there was no choice for me. Forgive me if you can, for being alive."

The strained, ghastly face twitched and she stopped swaying and looked at him uncomprehendingly as he knelt before her.

"They say he's dead, he's dead. My boy Dick," she moaned.

Christopher put his arm round her. "God help mothers," he gasped, under his breath, as the poor, shaking woman dropped her head on his shoulder with an outbreak of fierce weeping.

CHAPTER XXXV

The Roadmaker lay at the edge of the cliff and looked out on a green sea flecked with white, whose restless soul, holding to some eternal purpose, forever attains and relinquishes in peace and storm, in laughter or tears.

A week had passed since the attempt on Christopher's life for which Ann Barty had paid so high a price. Happily for Christopher, it had been a week so full of affairs that although they were mostly in connection with the one thing, yet they claimed his outward active attention to the exclusion of the inner point of view. The unhappy man from Birmingham was found, when he recovered from the seizure, to be in a semi-imbecile state with no knowledge of his deed and was accordingly handed over to the authorities proper to his condition. He was easily traced to the works from which he had been harshly enough discharged, as it turned out on investigation, and Christopher came into active opposition with the directors of the Steel Axle Company over the question of providing for his wife and children. It had been impossible to keep the affair quiet and there had been innumerable reporters to circumvent, and more innumerable friends from far and near, eager to express their interest in his providential escape. Little Dick Barty received more honour in death than in life and the bereaved mother drew more consolation from the impressive funeral than poor Christopher.

Mr. Saunderson bustled down in well-meant concern for Christopher's well-being, and received certain emphatic instructions, which he took with shrewd docility, and a wink of his eye to the world.

All the while, as he went through the day's particular and general business, the wild words in the rasping, incoherent voice haunted Christopher so persistently that he heard them through the enthusiastic platitudes of congratulations, the calm official statements of plain facts, behind even Patricia's healing voice of love. It was not till the following Sunday he awoke to find a stillness instead of clamour, calm instead of turmoil. He rose early while the day was still holding the hand of dawn and went out to the cliff edge, as if there in the heaving waters he might read the Eternal Meaning and Purpose of it all. He thought how every individual man is one with the great tide of humanity, advancing with it, receding with it, subject to one eternal law he could not read. How the suffering and sin of one was the burden of all: the heroic endeavours and victories of one the gain of all. The little isolated aim of the individual must subject itself to the wider meaning or be swept back to nothingness, just as the stranded pools among the rocks that for a few hours caught the sunshine and reflected the heavenly lamp, but were overswept each tide and their being mingled again with the great sea.

Christopher knew the work he had done had been good, that hundreds were the happier for his direct concern with their lives, that he indeed had made the Road of Life more possible for those who would set out thereon for far or nearer goals. It was all he aspired to do. He knew it was not his to show them the goal, or to direct them thereto; that was for themselves and others; but it was his to make the way possible, that they need not stumble on unbroken ground, or toil in blinding dust of ages, or wade in clogging mud of tradition, these children of the world who tramped with patient feet to a vague end.

What was wrong was that he had chosen his own ground, that when he had stood at the cross roads of life he held himself qualified as a god to say "that road is evil and this good," taking council only of what was most in accord with his own will, forgetting that the Great Power embraces all within itself, knowing no good or evil, but seeing only a means to fulfil the eternal purpose of creation. It is we who must be the alchemists to transmute what we term evil into good, we, who are the servants and instruments by which that purpose must be achieved. If, seeing evil, we pass by on the other side, how shall the waste places of the earth be cleansed or the wilderness break forth into song?

The message so roughly delivered had sunk into Christopher's heart at last. Looking back at his life he saw how everything had fitted him for the task he had refused. How he was born to it, trained to its needs unconsciously by his mother and Cæsar, shaped by his own experience, armed by the completion of his inner life in his marriage. He had refused it with blindness, had closed his ears to the voice of thousands who had called to him in the unattractive voice of a conventional law. It had taken the deafening report of a madman's pistol and the sight of a dead child to teach him the lesson.

At that thought he hid his face in his arm on the short turf and lay very still.

The sea sung its endless Te Deum below him, a lark soared high to heaven with its morning hymn, and the wind, rustling along the cliff edge, breathed strength to the land. Day stood free and open upon earth and called for service from those to whom the Dominion of the earth is promised. Only by service comes lordship, only by obedience can be found command.

At the moment of renunciation, Christopher realised for the first time the greatness of the cost and knew how dear his life and surroundings were to him. The Roadmaker had been his own master; the successor of Peter Masters must be the servant of thousands. The work here would go on, there were men ready to take his place, but he found no salve in the thought. Deep in his heart he knew he feared the grim struggle that lay before him, the uprooting of the old "system," the antagonism, the necessary compromises, the slow result. His age, or rather his youth, would be a heavy weapon against him. How could he hope to make his voice heard above the dictates of a dozen committees of men intent on their personal interests? He told himself passionately the thing was Impossible, and as quickly came the remembrance of the hoarse cry for help that had made itself heard above the report of Plent's pistol.

Step by step through the door of humility he reached the hall of Audience and in silence surrendered himself to the eternal Purpose.

At length he again stood on the edge and looked out to sea and for the moment the simplicity instead of the complexity of life visible and invisible, was written on the face of the deep. He stood bareheaded and read the message thankfully and went back to the house with peace in his heart.

He found a new beauty in the house he had made for himself, and as Patricia came down the garden path to meet him, he was glad for the real worth of the outward things he must surrender.

She met him with a question on her lips which was not uttered in face of what she saw in his eyes. They stood for a moment with clasped hands and he looked at her smiling, and she at him gravely, and presently they walked to a corner of the garden overlooking the sea, from where each dear beauty of the place was visible.

"Will it hurt you greatly to leave it, dear?" he asked, prefacing the inevitable with question of her will to do so.

"Just as much as it will hurt you. No more or less," she answered, her head against his arm. "But I am glad it is so good to leave."

"That's my mind, too. How do you know what I mean, though?"

"I've always known it must come, Christopher."

She spoke low and looked away, weakly hoping for the moment he would leave it at that, but Christopher never left uncertain points behind him.

"You knew I should come to take this other work—this inheritance?"

She nodded. He put his hands on her shoulders and turned her to him.

"Why didn't you tell me so, Patricia?"

"I was so sure you would know yourself. I hated to be the one to speak," her voice shook a little. "Oh, forgive me, Christopher, dearest," she cried suddenly, "it was weak of me, for I did know always, only I wanted all this for a little time so badly. Just a taste of the beautiful good life you had planned. I thought it would not matter, just two years."

He put his arms round her and drew her close.

"We have had it, beloved. It has been beyond anything I ever dreamt. Only—" his voice broke a little, "we must remember it had to be paid for—No, no," he cried, seeing the wave of sorrow sweep over her face, "not you. It is I who should have known and listened. My fault!"

"It is I who should have spoken," she said steadily, "we can't divide ourselves even in this, dear, but we can bear it together."

"And pay the debt together," he added and raised her face to his and kissed her. And they crossed the Threshold of the New with this understanding between them.

CHAPTER XXXVI

In the great buildings in Princes Street, Birmingham, the days continued as of old, with the ebb and flow of business. On each floor clerks bent over their high desks and the workers of each concern sat behind their mahogany defences and toiled early and late for the treasure they desired. At stated times rows of grave gentlemen, who carried due notice of their own importance on their countenances, met in the respective committee rooms, and discussed wide interests with closed doors and a note of anxious irritation that was new since the demise of Peter Masters.

He who had concentrated the whole of the executive business of these many affairs under one roof had done so of definite purpose and with no eye to merely his own convenience. His presence there was a tangible power offering a final court of appeal that, whether they knew it or not, had as great an effect on the various committees as it had on the managers of each business themselves.

So perfect was the organisation and adjustment of the machinery of routine that after the dominant visible power had gone down to the land of shadows, the vague note of personal anxiety that lurked on each floor was the only perceptible change apparent in the great body.

But the wives of the working heads could have told of more enduring change in men who have suddenly become responsible for great issues, for laws, for a system they had had no voice in founding. Men who found themselves limited masters where unconsciously they had been tools and were selected as such—there men sooner or later bend before the strain put on them and for the most part seek salvation in blind obedience to the rules they dare not criticise. In the daily compromise between the individual character and the system which he must serve, many an excellent man was ground down in nerve and heart and health to a strange shadow of his former self, and many a woman shed secret tears over half-understood changes in one near and dear to her.

Mr. Saunderson by right of informal instructions, which no one troubled to dispute, acted as steward over the late Peter Masters' private affairs during those two years of waiting, and his stewardship was prosperous and able, but beyond that he neither would nor could move. To the appeals of distracted secretaries he only replied, "My dear sir, act to the best of your ability. I can only assure you your responsibilities are limited to two years."

He never allowed to anyone the possibility that Peter Masters' son might even then fail to accept his place, but alone to himself he faced it often and felt his scanty hair whiten beneath the impending wreckage, if the misguided young man continued his foolish course.

"He will probably wreck the whole thing if he accepts it," sighed Mr. Saunderson, "but at least it will be done legally, and in the regular course of things. If he'll only be sensible and see he's wanted just as a figurehead, everyone will be comfortable and prosperous."

But he sighed again as he thought it, for Christopher did not at all strike him as a man likely to make a good figurehead, or to be the mouthpiece of a system he evidently disliked. He was even more confirmed in this opinion a fortnight after the unhappy affair at the Patrimondi works, when Christopher walked into his London office and without any explanation announced himself ready to take his place as Peter Masters' son. He was sufficiently wise to conceal his own triumph and accepted the intimation without question. As they sat there in the dull London office hour after hour, Mr. Saunderson realised that the mantle of Peter Masters, millionaire, had fallen on shoulders that would wear it maybe in a very different fashion, but none the less royally.

"I am to understand then," said Christopher after long hours of instruction, "I can go there when I like, see what I like, decide what I like, at all events with regard to these mines and works which are almost private property."

"You can go to-morrow if you like," answered his Mentor, rising. "I advise you to let things run for some time as they are, till you know the ropes."

He went to a safe and unlocking it produced a key.

"That is the key of your father's room at Princes Buildings," he said, putting it on the table. "There are two locks. Clisson, the head clerk, has the key of one and this is the other. You are free to walk straight in when you like, but it would be best to send Clisson a wire you are coming and he would bring you the day's business, your private affairs that is, precisely as he used to bring it to your father."

This time, because he was looking intently at the young man, he saw his mouth tighten at that term and felt a resigned wonder thereat.

Christopher took up the key and looked at it, thinking of all the doors in the world it would unlock for him, thinking of the powers of which it was a symbol, of how it fastened the door of his freedom and opened for him the door of a great servitude of which he was already proud.

Mr. Saunderson also was silent a moment listening to his own thoughts and looking at Christopher with misgivings.

"Will you live at Stormly Park?" he asked airily.

"I expect so. It is not let, is it?"

Mr. Saunderson permitted himself a little smile of superiority as he answered.

"Everything has been kept just ready for you these two years. But it will hardly be to your taste. Perhaps you will like it done up—altered?"

Christopher shook his head. "Not yet."

"You can afford it, you know."

At that the young man suddenly faced him, as if he meant to say something of importance, and stopped.

"Yes, I suppose I can afford it," he returned, and added with apparent irrelevance, "Do you happen to know Stormly village, Mr. Saunderson?"

"I've driven through it."

Christopher nodded. "So have I. I'll not detain you any longer. Will you let Clisson know I shall be there on Thursday?"

"Certainly. Will you like me to accompany you?"

Christopher shook his head. "Not this time, I think. I would rather be alone."

"And one thing," Mr. Saunderson coughed a little nervously, "the name? We can arrange the legal identification this afternoon, but what name will you ultimately take?"

Christopher came to a standstill at the door. Here was a decision thrust on him for which he was oddly unprepared. He recognised at once it meant setting the seal to his own committal if he answered as the lawyer evidently expected and hoped he would do. He paused just long enough to remember how hardly he had taken Mr. Aston's insistence he should sign his marriage register as Aston Masters.

"I must take the name since I take its belongings," he said ruefully, and Mr. Saunderson felt his victory was complete.

On the following Thursday morning there was nothing in the aspect of earth or sky to indicate to the workers in Princes Buildings the importance of that day to their respective fortunes. On the top floor only a sense of gentle expectancy was present, and a complacent faith in their own readiness to receive and set at ease the young man who was to be the outward visible sign of all that for which they toiled so unceasingly.

As an individual, the younger men bestowed a certain curiosity not unmixed with envy on him; as the successor of Peter Masters, they entertained no doubt whatever he would obediently adhere to the prescribed system as they themselves did. Christopher had arrived in Birmingham the night before and put up at an hotel. Early the next morning he went up the steps into the central corridor of the great buildings that were to all intents and purposes his. There was no one about but a lift boy who did not recognise him, but seeing him look round with deliberate curiosity, asked him civilly what floor he wanted.

"Mr. Masters' private offices," Christopher explained. "Top floor, aren't they?"

The boy nodded. Christopher studied him gravely as they went up in the lift as one of the smallest and probably least important items into whose service he had entered.

The porter at the door of the offices asked Christopher his name, and he hesitated a moment.

"You need not announce me," he said quietly, at last. "I am Mr. Masters."

The man gave a guttural gasp of amazement. A rumour of the possible arrival of the young millionaire had percolated despite Mr. Clisson's care, through the range of desks to the doorkeeper, who without discernible reasons had expected some time in the day a procession of black coats and grave men to appear from the doors of the lift and with formal solemnity to proceed to the closely locked door of that remote silent office. He opened the door for this calm, quiet young man in flurried trepidation, half expecting that Mr. Clisson would dismiss him on the spot for transgressing such a fundamental rule as admitting a stranger without announcing his name, but as totally unable to disobey the stranger as if it were Peter Masters himself.

Christopher walked quickly down the line of clerks, who looked up one after the other, and did not look back at their work again. At last a senior man advanced and accosted him.

"Do you want Mr. Clisson, sir?" he asked, in a tone verging between deference and curiosity.

Christopher said he did, and added abruptly, "I remember you, you are Mr. Hunter. I saw you four years ago when I came here with my father."

He caught his breath when he had said it. It was purely involuntary. Some unaccountable association of ideas was bridging the distance between him and the dead man minute by minute. But Mr. Hunter transferred his allegiance from the dead to the living in that moment of recognition, and led him away to Mr. Clisson's hitherto all-important presence with mechanical alacrity rather than personal desire to relinquish the honours of escort.

Mr. Clisson was a keen, sharp-featured man of narrow outlook, the best of servants, the worst of masters. A genius for detail and a miraculous memory had carried him from the position of junior clerk to his present prominence when the death of the Principal left him with his minute knowledge of routine and detail practically master of the situation as far as Mr. Saunderson was concerned. But his inability to bend with the need of the day, or to cope with wider issues than those concerned with office work had had far-reaching results, not even wholly unconnected with the tragedy in the mill yard at the Patrimondi works.

He apologised to Christopher for the lack of a better reception, as if he, and not Christopher, were responsible for the informality of it.

"We imagined from Mr. Saunderson's letter you would arrive by the 12.30 from town. I had ventured to order lunch for you here on that understanding," the head clerk explained deferentially. "What will you like to do first, sir?"

"I wish to go into the inner office and for you to carry on the usual routine precisely as in my father's time."

There was no hesitation over the term now.

"Bring me such letters and reports as you would bring him. I must find out for myself how much or how little of it I am capable of understanding."

"It will be a question of practice rather than of understanding with you, sir, I am confident," returned Mr. Clisson politely, turning over in his mind what business it would be least embarrassing to submit to this decided young man.

"It will be your business to see I get the practice," Christopher answered.

Together they unlocked the door of Peter Masters' sanctum and the head clerk flung it open.

"It is precisely as he left it that day. Nothing has been done excepting the sorting of the papers, which Mr. Saunderson and myself did between us. The last time Mr. Saunderson was here we had it cleaned out. You will find the bells and telephones all labelled. If you will wait a few minutes I will send a man in with ink and writing material, and the keys, and I will bring you this morning's letters myself."

Christopher thanked him mechanically and entered the room. He stood in the window silently waiting, while a young clerk trembling with excitement performed the small services necessary, and asked nervously if he could do more.

"Nothing else now. What is your name?"

He gave it with faltering tongue. In the old days such an inquiry was a distinction hardly earned.

Christopher was alone at last. He walked slowly across the room and sat down in his father's chair and touched the big bunch of keys laid there on the table before him.

An overwhelming desire for some direct message from the dead man, some defined recognition of his right to be there at all, pressed on him. He opened the drawers and pigeon-holes of the great table with a faint hope he might light on some overlooked note, or uncomplete memorandum addressed to him. Mr. Saunderson had assured him no such thing existed beyond the curt exact clue he had put in his hand four years ago when the old will had been destroyed.

He glanced at the neat documents, the piles of labelled papers; there was nothing personal here, nothing that conveyed any sense to him but that of a vast machine of which he had become a part.

In the pen tray lay a collection of pen-holders and pencils, a knife he had seen his father use, and a smaller knife. He picked this up and looked at it.

It was rather a unique little knife, with a green jade handle, and the initials A. A. were plainly engraved on the label. He had recognised it at once and he stared at it as it lay in his hand, trying to comprehend what its presence there might mean. He had lent it one day to Peter Masters, who had asked him where he had got it. And he had answered it had belonged to Aymer Aston, but he had found it as a boy and Aymer had given it to him. Peter had given it back without the further explanation that he had originally given it to Aymer. A day or so later Christopher had missed it, and he told his host regretfully it was lost. Again Peter failed to explain he was the finder. Yet here was the knife on the desk where he had sat day after day.

Perhaps it had not seemed worth returning. Yet Christopher was curiously loath to accept that simple answer. It seemed to him as he fingered the smooth green sides, as if other fingers had done this in this precise spot before, a strange aching familiarity attached itself to the simple action. For someone's sake Peter Masters *had* so touched and handled this cool green thing, he was sure of it, and suddenly he was conscious here was the message he sought. Here in the mere sensation of touch lay the thread of recognition that linked him with the dead man, so slight and intangible that it would bear no expression in heavy words.

There was a knock at the door. Christopher laid the little green knife back in its place before he answered it. Mr. Clisson entered with a handful of letters.

"This is a very good sample, sir. As many as you will get through at first, I expect," he said apologetically.

He sat down opposite Christopher and handed him letter after letter, giving such explanations as were necessary. Christopher made few comments. He put the letters into two separate piles. Presently there was one concerning the sale of some land in the neighbourhood of the Stormly Foundry.

"It is only just started, sir. I think we shall get a good price if we hold out."

"I am not going to sell any land at all. You will write and say I have altered my mind."

He spoke with the keen decision of his father. Mr. Clisson gazed at him with pained amazement.

"It is only the leasehold we sell, sir, not the actual land."

"I do not sell land," repeated Christopher sharply.

"Of course, it shall be as you wish, sir."

"Of course. Do you know if Mr. Fegan is still at Stormly Foundry?"

"I can ascertain."

"Do so. If he is, tell him to come and see me here to-morrow. And who is the best builder you employ?"

"Builder? What kind of builder, sir?"

"Bricks and mortar. Cottages. I don't want an architect. I'll employ the man we used in Hampshire."

"You mean to build?"

"I mean to build."

Mr. Clisson coughed. "The late Mr. Masters found it did not pay—"

"Mr. Clisson," said Christopher firmly, "let us understand one another from the beginning. I do not intend to work on the same lines as my father worked. I intend to do many things which he would not have done, but I am inclined to think he knew it would be so. I believe I am a very rich man. At all events I mean to spend a lot of money. You would have no objection to my spending it on yachts and motors and grouse moors, I suppose? These things do not, however, interest me. You probably won't approve of my hobbies, and I've no doubt I shall make heaps of mistakes, but I've got to find them out myself. You can help me make them, but once for all, never try to prevent me. Those are all the letters I can manage to-day. You can take the others. I'll answer these myself."

The flabbergasted Mr. Clisson rose, trembling a little in his agitation.

"I hope, Mr. Masters, I should know better than ever attempt to dictate to you on any matter."

Christopher gave him one of his rare half-shy, half-boyish smiles and leant forward over the big desk.

"Mr. Clisson, I shall need your help and advice every hour of the day. I haven't the slightest doubt you could dictate to me to my great material advantage on every point, only I don't care for this material advantage and I don't want us to misunderstand each other, that is all."

Mr. Clisson thawed, but his soul was troubled. He looked at the letters as he gathered them up. It was a goodly pile yet left to his decision, but he missed one that Christopher had passed over without comment.

"The application for the post of gardener at Stormly Park, sir. Did you wish to attend to that yourself?"

"What has happened to Timmins? Wasn't that his name? Is he dead?"

"Oh, no."

"He wishes to go?"

Mr. Clisson shook his head. "It is simply a matter of routine, sir. Timmins is a very excellent man, but the invariable rule is that no one remains after they are fifty-five."

"After they are fifty-five?" repeated Christopher slowly.

"Not those employed in manual labour: with very few exceptions that is. Timmins will be fifty-five next month. He suffers from rheumatism already, I find."

Christopher never took his eyes from the other's face.

"He would be pensioned, I suppose."

"Oh, dear me, no. We have no pension list. Timmins has received very high wages. He has no doubt put by a nice little sum."

"How long has he worked for—for us?"

"I cannot tell without reference. I believe for twenty years or so. I can easily ascertain."

Christopher stared out of the window for so long that the head clerk thought he had forgotten the matter and was disagreeably surprised when he spoke again.

"I shall be at Stormly this week and will see if Timmins wishes to retire or not. You have no fault to find with him as a gardener, I suppose?"

Mr. Clisson smiled. "A man who has served for twenty years will not be an indifferent workman sir. Timmins' accounts are exemplary."

"The matter will stand over. Please see no one is dismissed under this age regulation without my knowledge. That is all now." His manner was as curt again as his father's. Mr. Clisson closed the door behind him with a vague feeling that the two years of his authority were but a dream and that the thin, square figure behind the office table had unaccountably widened out to the portly proportions of his old master.

Christopher drew to him the pile of letters he had reserved and fell to work. He dared not allow himself to think yet, but now and again when his heart and soul ran counter to the tenor of what he read he put out his hand and touched the little green knife his father had handled for some unknown person's sake.

CHAPTER XXXVII

"I understand the fortune well enough now," said Christopher bitterly; "anyone can do it if they take one aspect of things and subordinate everybody and everything to it."

He was at Marden again. It was a glorious spring evening and Cæsar's couch was drawn up to the open window. Mr. Aston sat on the far side of it and Christopher leant against the window-frame smoking moodily.

"You will dissipate it fast enough at the rate you are going," remarked Cæsar. His eyes followed every movement of the young man with a jealous hunger.

Christopher shook his head resignedly. "It can't be done. It goes on making itself. We are going to allow ourselves ten thousand a year. It's a fearful lot for two people"—his eyes wandered across the lawn to Patricia, where she sat with Renata—"or even three, but that's what it costs to live properly at Stormly, and the rest has to be used somehow."

"How about Stormly Park? Do you and Patricia like the place?"

He shook his head again. "I'm afraid we don't. We both feel we are living in an hotel. But I must be there on the spot, and she too. As it is, we have only had time to do so little."

"Cottages, schools, hospitals," murmured Mr. Aston, softly.

"They are only means to an end," returned Christopher quickly, "only what they are entitled to as human beings in a civilised world. Think of having to begin at that. We've got to make restitution before we can make progress. They mistrust all one does, of course. They use the bathrooms as coal stores, their coppers for potatoes, their allotments as rubbish ground, but it's better than the front yard, and, anyhow, the children will know a bit more about it."

"You have laid down Patrimondi roads for them," Cæsar put in.

"Of course," Christopher answered, accepting it literally, "they appreciate *that* at least. The roads were beastly."

Mr. Aston looked at Cæsar and they both smiled.

"I've persuaded Sam to open a shop in Stormly and put Jim into it. He *says* you can't make a living honestly in grocery, but I'd take himself in preference to his word."

"You've beaten him after all, old chap."

It was Cæsar who spoke, and he held out his thin hand towards his big boy, who came and sat by him in silence a while. The twilight crept up over the earth and freed the soul of things as it stole their material forms. The two men looking out and watching the gentle robber, wasted no regrets on the day, no fears on the approaching night. Behind them, where Mr. Aston sat, it was dark already, and as his son watched Christopher, so he watched Aymer.

"We have made our roads," he thought, "Aymer and I, and thank God we leave behind us a better Roadmaker still, who will make smooth paths for the children's feet."

Outside two white figures came slowly towards the house and were joined by a third, Nevil, to judge by his height.

"Cæsar," said Christopher, "have you forgiven me taking my own way and giving up what you gave me?"

"Do you think I see anything to forgive in it?"

"You gave me my choice, and you gave me my chance. It looked on the surface so ungrateful," persisted Christopher.

"You question the quality of my eyesight?"

"I doubt your forgiveness when you are so flippant, my best of fathers."

"For what do you want forgiveness specifically?"

"For giving up my work as a Roadmaker."

"I did not know you had given it up."

In the quiet hours of the night Aymer Aston paced those even roads his feet had never trodden, saw them spreading far and wide across the earth, heard the echo of countless footsteps stepping down the ages, knew that life itself was made an easier road for thousands of little feet that would take their first steps on better ground than their parents had done, knew that there were less crippled, less maimed, less halt in the sum total of the world's suffering by reason of one Roadmaker's career.

But it was Aymer Aston with the crippled form and maimed life who had put the spade first into the Roadmaker's hand.

Meanwhile the Roadmaker slept the sleep of the just and forgot all these things.